THE SAVVY COOK.

@IzyHossack

An Hachette UK Company
www.hachette.co.uk

First published in Great Britain in 2017
by Mitchell Beazley, a division of
Octopus Publishing Group Ltd
Carmelite House
50 Victoria Embankment
London EC4Y 0DZ
www.octopusbooks.co.uk

ISBN 978-1-78472-263-0

A CIP catalogue record for this book is available
from the British Library.

Printed and bound in China

10 9 8 7 6 5 4 3 2 1

Publisher: Alison Starling
Art Director: Juliette Norsworthy
Design: Isabel de Cordova
Assistant Editor: Ella Parsons
Senior Production Controller: Allison Gonsalves

Author portrait on page 7 by Portia Hunt

RECIPE NOTES

Standard level spoon measurements are used in all recipes.
1 tablespoon = one 15ml spoon
1 teaspoon = one 5ml spoon

Read recipes all the way through first before attempting
to make them. It sometimes helps to measure out the
ingredients before starting the recipe. This can help you
stay organized while cooking.

When reading a recipe's ingredients list, if an action comes
after the ingredient, do that action after measuring the
ingredient. If the action is before the ingredient, do the
action and then measure.
For example:
100g dates, pitted – weigh out 100g of dates with
their stones inside and THEN remove the stones
100g pitted dates – remove and discard the stones
from the dates first and THEN weigh out 100g of dates.

When storing dishes in the freezer, it's best to put
on a label saying what's in it and when you made it.

When a recipe states: 'bring to the boil, then reduce the
heat to a simmer', place a pan of liquid over a high heat
until large bubbles appear in that liquid (this is usually done
for water in which you are cooking grains). Once those
large bubbles appear you can reduce the heat to low or
medium-low so that the liquid is only gently bubbling.

Eggs should be medium unless otherwise stated. The
Department of Health advises that eggs should not be
consumed raw. This book contains dishes made with raw
or lightly cooked eggs. It is prudent for more vulnerable
people such as pregnant and nursing mothers, invalids, the
elderly, babies and young children to avoid uncooked or
lightly cooked dishes made with eggs. Once prepared these
dishes should be kept refrigerated and used promptly.

THE SAVVY COOK.

@IzyHossack

MITCHELL BEAZLEY

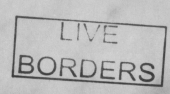

CONTENTS

Key:

V Vegetarian

VG Vegan

DF Dairy Free

GF Gluten Free

EF Egg Free

LS Low Added Sugar

NS No Added Sugar

'You stand in the kitchen at 7pm peering into the fridge wondering what to make...'

Lots of my friends find the idea of cooking a bit daunting. It's not that they don't have the ability to make themselves a meal, but they are lacking in the confidence that they can make something delicious and inexpensive. As someone starting university this year, I wasn't sure how to tackle the new challenges I'd face. Cooking in a small, basic kitchen is a challenge in itself – many of us don't have a lot of equipment, fridge/freezer or general storage space. Along with that, budgeting a pay cheque or weekly stipend of loan money, which barely covers your rent, is a scary prospect. On top of all that, you'd like to be healthy! But you don't have the cash to splash on daily avocado toast and the idea of having to cook kale freaks you out. You stand in the kitchen at 7pm peering into the fridge wondering what to make with the random head of cauliflower you bought on a whim because it was on offer. Another challenge: you have no bloody idea what to cook.

That's where this book comes in – helping overcome the idea that healthy, cheap cooking is arduous and tasteless, for a new cook operating on a tight budget and a busy schedule. With things like menu plans, clever alternatives to meat (although I include omnivore options, all my recipes are vegetarian), dishes that can be prepped ahead of time and ideas for giving last-night's leftovers a makeover, these recipes will be kind to your body, wallet and free time. They'll also give a little help to the earth. Consuming fewer animal products, and more local, seasonal food in general is a simple way to reduce one's environmental impact, boost your health and leave you with some extra moolah. It's not about health fads, 'antioxidants' or obscure ingredients. Just honest, nourishing and delicious cooking that will make you glow inside and out!

THE BASICS

Must-have Kitchen Tools

Essential

CHEF'S KNIFE – a good chef's knife saves time and is also safer to use. Get one about 20cm long from the tip of the blade to the end of the handle. I like Sabatier knives as they are good-quality and not too expensive. Remember, a blunt knife is more likely to slip on food, leading to accidents.

PARING KNIFE – a smaller knife, for small, precise slicing jobs like removing the tops from strawberries.

WOODEN CHOPPING BOARD – wood is better than plastic for hygiene, your knives and the environment.

BAKING TRAY – use a flat one with a slight rim.

WOODEN SPOON – use for baking, sautéeing, stirring sauces and grains.

SILICONE SPATULA – flexible and good for scraping sauces out of pans, stirring porridge, risotto or bread dough, sautéeing and scraping cake batter from bowls.

METAL SPATULA (FISH SLICE OR PANCAKE TURNER) – use for flipping pancakes or flatbreads, roasted vegetables and removing food from frying pans.

MEASURING SPOONS – essential for baking! You can use a non-measuring teaspoon for spices when you are cooking but when baking you do need a set of measuring spoons.

DIGITAL KITCHEN SCALES – use for weighing out everything, including liquids such as water and oil (1 millilitre oil or water = 1 gram). Obviously very important in baking.

VEGETABLE PEELER – use for peeling butternut squash, or sweet/white potatoes and peeling vegetables into ribbons. Create shavings of cheese (especially Parmesan) or chocolate for decorating cakes.

HAND-HELD BLENDER – these often come with attachments to turn it into a mini food processor – good for making pesto, pastes, purées, soups and flours.

BOX GRATER – this is indispensable for grating cheese, apples, carrots and courgettes.

CASSEROLE DISH OR DEEP ROASTING TRAY – needed for any casserole-type dish, such as pasta bakes, pies or bread pudding. At a pinch, it can be used for baking simple cakes or roasting vegetables.

GOOD-QUALITY NONSTICK FRYING PAN – you need a medium or large frying pan depending on the number of people you are cooking for. Check that the handle is heat-resistant (Bakelite handles can be placed under high heat) if you are making frying pan pizzas (see page 158).

LARGE, MEDIUM AND SMALL PANS – always useful to have a range of sizes! Especially good if they all have lids, but sometimes you can just use a plate or baking tray as a makeshift lid anyway.

MIXING BOWL – These are super-useful for baking, but even if you don't like to bake, mixing bowls are always good to have. Toss together a salad in one or mix ingredients for making fritters, frittatas and quiches.

Useful equipment

GARLIC PRESS (GARLIC CRUSHER) – I love these because I hate having garlicky hands. And you don't even have to peel the cloves before putting them into a garlic press.

MICROPLANE GRATER – for grating the zest of citrus fruits, chocolate, cheese or even garlic (instead of using a garlic press or very finely chopping garlic by hand).

BAMBOO GINGER GRATER – amazing! You can grate fresh root ginger without peeling it first. Find them online.

FREESTANDING MIXER OR FOOD PROCESSOR – this can take on more heavy-duty kitchen tasks than a hand-held blender, such as making cake batter, blending soup and making breadcrumbs (which you can only do with a hand-held blender if you have the attachment to make it into a mini food processor).

BAKING TINS – I like to have a standard 900g loaf tin, a 20cm round cake tin and a 20cm square brownie tin. You can also include a 450g or mini loaf tin, 20cm bundt tin and a 12-hole muffin tin if you like baking.

MEASURING JUG – useful for crude measurements of liquid, such as how much vegetable stock or milk to use in a sauce. However, they are prone to inaccuracy so I weigh all my liquids on digital kitchen scales.

Ingredients

Eggs
I use medium, free-range eggs. When baking, always allow the eggs to come to room temperature first – place in a bowl of warm (not hot) water and leave for 5–10 minutes.

Butter
You can freeze butter for up to 3 months and use frozen butter straightaway by grating it. Buy unsalted for baking.

Oils
Buy light, refined olive oil, as it has very little flavour and is perfect for cooking and baking.

RAPESEED OIL – another favourite of mine. It is neutral in flavour and has a vibrant yellow colour. I buy cold pressed.

COCONUT OIL – makes a good substitute for butter in vegan baking as it is a saturated fat so is solid at room temperature. 'Virgin' coconut oil has a coconut flavour and 'refined' coconut oil (which is cheaper) has no flavour.

EXTRA VIRGIN OLIVE OIL – keep this for salad dressings and other uses (such as for pesto, drizzling over soup or dipping bread into).

Seeds
Seeds are packed with healthy mono – and polyunsaturated fats, fibre and protein.

GROUND FLAXSEED (AKA LINSEED) – in many of my baking recipes, eggs are either not used or can be substituted with ground flaxseed mixed with water, a vegan egg replacement suitable for baking.

CHIA SEEDS – I use these occasionally and sometimes slip them into overnight oats for a fibre boost or use them as a vegan egg substitute in baking.

SUNFLOWER AND PUMPKIN SEEDS – these are cheap and cheerful! I especially like pumpkin seeds in salads because of their colour. Sunflower seeds are delicious raw but are even tastier when toasted in a frying pan until crisp.

SESAME SEEDS – these are packed with flavour. They can be used for both sweet and savoury recipes.

Oats
I love oats as they are high in fibre and protein. Some 'gluten free' or 'gluten-free option' recipes may contain oats. I have suggested using oats that are certified gluten free, but some coeliacs are not able to eat oats due to cross contamination. If you aren't able to tolerate oats I have given suitable alternatives, wherever possible.

QUICK-COOKING OATS – also called porridge oats, these are milled quite finely

OLD-FASHIONED ROLLED OATS – sometimes called jumbo oats, these are chunkier and take longer to cook.

Nuts

I keep a range of nuts in the cupboard for baking and store them in the refrigerator or freezer to stop them from going rancid. I use almonds or ground almonds, almond butter or, occasionally, almond milk.

Milk and non-dairy milk

I generally use non-dairy milk. For savoury recipes, make sure it doesn't contain any added sugar. If you're relying on non-dairy milk for your calcium intake check the label to ensure it does have added calcium, as the 'organic' varieties usually don't. Cow's milk with 1% fat, semi-skimmed and full-fat milk will also work in my recipes.

Yogurt and cheese

I often use Parmesan for topping my pasta dishes – although technically it isn't vegetarian as the rennet (an enzyme) used in it is extracted from cow's stomachs. One of the many vegetarian cheeses available will be fine – just check the label to make sure it's suitable.

I love using full-fat yogurt for both savoury and sweet dishes. If using soya yogurt for savoury dishes, make sure it's unsweetened and unflavoured.

Coconut products

CREAMED COCONUT – to use, microwave the packet on high in short bursts, kneading until liquid. Alternatively, place the packet in a bowl and cover it with hot water, leave for 20 minutes to soften, then knead. Once liquid, open the packet and pour it into a clean, lidded glass jar, which can be kept in the cupboard at room temperature for a few months. In warmer weather, store in the refrigerator. When ready to use, microwave the jar of creamed coconut (without the lid on) until liquid OR place it in a bowl of just-boiled water and leave it to soften.

A 200g packet (when mixed with hot water) will be equal to 2 x 400ml cans of coconut milk.

COCONUT CREAM – can be bought in small cartons, but it's usually more expensive than simply buying a can of coconut milk, chilling the can overnight, then scooping off the soft, creamy stuff that accumulates on the top.

COCONUT MILK – if you have excess canned coconut milk freeze it in ice-cubes, then pop each cube into a little plastic bag and freeze for use another day.

DESICCATED COCONUT – dry-toast unsweetened desiccated coconut in a frying pan over a medium heat, stirring constantly. Watch it carefully (it burns very easily) and as soon as it turns golden, immediately tip it out.

Aromatics and herbs

RED ONIONS – to prepare, remove the pointy tip and root base of the onion. Cut straight down the middle, from top to base, then peel off the papery skin and discard it. If you only need half, wrap the other half in clingfilm or place in a lidded container and chill for up to 2 weeks.

GARLIC – a 'clove' is the little segment that you separate out from the head of garlic. One clove of finely chopped garlic is about a scant teaspoon. Always peel garlic before using unless you have a garlic press. Store in a cool place.

GINGER – keep ginger in a small pot of soil with the cut/broken edge just nestling slightly in the soil. Water it when the soil feels dry. This will keep the ginger fresh for months! Rinse it before cutting off a chunk to use.

CHILLIES – finely chop and freeze in a plastic bag.

CORIANDER – store by placing in a jar with just enough water to cover the end of the stems by 2cm. Cover with a plastic bag and chill for 1–2 weeks (you may need to change the water after 1 week).

BASIL – never refrigerate the leaves as they will turn into a dark mush. Buy a plant to use for garnishes and to make pesto, or blend a large bunch of basil and freeze in ice-cube trays.

THYME – good as a potted plant. If you buy loose thyme, roll it up in a few layers of slightly damp kitchen paper and slot it into a little plastic bag to keep in the refrigerator.

SAGE – good as a potted plant. It's pretty hardy!

DRIED HERBS – in my view the only ones worth buying are thyme, oregano (or marjoram) and rosemary. I buy a dried herb mix called 'herbes de Provence' but mixed dried herbs will work just as well.

Food	Weight at start	Weight when cooked	Cook Method	Storage
Green lentils	100g	120g	Rinse. Cover with water, add a pinch of salt and 1 teaspoon vinegar, bring to the boil. Turn down to simmer for 20–30 minutes. Drain.	Keep in a container in the refrigerator for 5 days.
Short-grain brown rice	100g	200g	Rinse, cover with water in a pan and bring to the boil. Turn down to simmer for 30 minutes. Drain, return to the pan and cover with a lid or large plate for 5 minutes.	COOL QUICKLY (rinse with cold water or spread out on plate). Refrigerate for 1 day or flat-pack and freeze for 2 months.
Long-grain brown rice	100g	200g	Rinse, cover with water and bring to the boil. Turn down to simmer for 20 minutes. Drain, return to the pan and cover for 5 minutes.	COOL QUICKLY (see above). Refrigerate for 1 day or flat-pack and freeze for 2 months.
Quinoa	100g	330g	Rinse. Cover with water and bring to the boil. Turn down to simmer for 10 minutes. Drain, return to the pan and cover for 5 minutes.	Keep in a container in the refrigerator for 5 days.
Pearl barley	100g	300g	Rinse, cover with water and bring to the boil. Turn down to simmer for 25–30 minutes. Drain and rinse, return to pan and cover for 5 minutes.	Keep in a container in the refrigerator for 5 days.
Pasta	100g	200g	Cover with boiling, salted water. Bring to the boil and simmer for directed time on packet. Drain.	Keep in a container in the refrigerator for 5 days.
Chickpeas	100g	240g	Soak overnight. Drain. Cover with water, bring to the boil. Turn down to simmer for 1–1½ hours.	Cover with cooking liquid ideally or water. Keep in the refrigerator for 3 days or freeze for 2 months.
Cannellini beans	100g	220g	Soak overnight. Drain. Cover with water, bring to the boil. Turn down to simmer for 30–45 minutes.	Cover with cooking liquid ideally or water. Keep in the refrigerator for 3 days or freeze for 2 months.
Black beans	100g	180g	Soak overnight. Drain. Cover with water, bring to the boil. Turn down to simmer for 45–60 minutes.	Cover with cooking liquid ideally or water. Keep in the refrigerator for 3 days or freeze for 2 months.
Kidney beans	100g	230g	Soak overnight. Drain. Cover with water, bring to the boil. Turn down to simmer for 1–1¼ hours.	Cover with cooking liquid ideally or water. Keep in the refrigerator for 3 days or freeze for 2 months.
Puy lentils	100g	120g	Rinse. Cover with water, add a pinch of salt and 1 teaspoon vinegar, bring to the boil. Turn down to simmer for 30–45 minutes. Drain.	Keep in a container in the refrigerator for 5 days.
Sweet potato	100g	70g	Peel or leave skin on, cut into 3cm cubes. Toss with enough olive oil to coat and sprinkle with salt. Roast in the oven at 180°C for 30 minutes.	Keep in a container in the refrigerator for 3 days.
White potato	100g	70g	Peel or leave skin on. Cut into 3cm cubes. Cook in very salty boiling water for 5 minutes. Toss with olive oil to coat and sprinkle with salt. Roast in an oven preheated to 180°C for 40–50 minutes.	Keep in a container in the refrigerator for 3 days.

Spices

BASICS – ground cumin, coriander (seed), cinnamon, (sweet) smoked paprika, cayenne pepper or chilli flakes.

EXTRAS – garam masala, Chinese five spice, turmeric, star anise, cardamom, fennel seeds. Buy packets of spices in supermarket world foods sections, online or in Middle Eastern and Indian grocers.

Miso

Miso is a paste made from fermented soya beans and salt (similar to soy sauce). It has a rich, salty, umami (savoury) taste, which adds a unique depth of flavour to dishes. I buy miso from Chinese, Thai or Japanese supermarkets or on online through speciality retailers. Always check the label on the pack – you don't want 'miso soup paste' or 'miso glaze', which will contain other ingredients. The ingredients of miso should be soya beans, salt, water, rice (and possibly 'koji' which is used to ferment the soya beans). It keeps well in the refrigerator for a few months.

There are a few types of Miso – white (shiro), yellow (shinshu) or red (aka). The darker the colour, the stronger the flavour. I suggest trying white miso first, then when you are used to the flavour, move on to a darker miso. You can find miso made from other ingredients such as barley or chickpeas, but they are usually more expensive.

Vegetables

TOMATOES – store tomatoes at room temperature. If they are starting to go wrinkly, roast them, whole or cut up, with a drizzle of olive oil in an oven preheated to 180°C fan, 200°C, Gas Mark 6 for 30 minutes. Use in a salad or sandwich, or freeze for later.

BAGGED LEAVES – rocket, spinach, pea shoots and mixed salad leaves. If the bag doesn't say that they're ready to eat, always rinse, drain and dry the salad leaves before eating. To dry leaves without a salad spinner, twist the washed leaves up in a tea towel, then swing the bundle around outside to remove excess water.

BUTTERNUT SQUASH – this can be stored, uncut, at room temperature for a month or two.

FROZEN PEAS, SHELLED EDAMAME AND SWEETCORN – so useful and they make a store cupboard meal less sad!

CANNED SWEETCORN – check there's no added sugar or salt.

WHITE AND SWEET POTATOES – keep in a cool, dark place. You shouldn't refrigerate white potatoes, but you can refrigerate sweet potatoes. If green patches appear on white potatoes, throw them away as the green parts are poisonous. You can simply snap off any 'eyes' and still use the potato. I usually leave the skins for the enhanced nutrition and texture – just give them a good scrub.

Flours

When mixing a gluten-containing flour (such as wheat/rye/spelt flour) into wet ingredients, DO NOT overmix if you are baking muffins, cakes or scones – you will end up with tough, dense results due to an overdeveloped gluten network. This matters less for brownies and cookies, but you should still avoid overmixing the batter. For recipes that contain yeast, you usually mix and knead the dough as much as possible to develop the gluten network.

WHOLEMEAL – strong wholemeal flour (or wholemeal bread flour) contains more gluten and is useful for baking bread; otherwise use plain wholemeal flour, which has less gluten and is better for baking cakes and cookies.

PLAIN WHITE – even when I use wholemeal flour, I often mix it with some plain flour for a better texture.

WHITE BREAD FLOUR – this contains more gluten than plain white flour so use for bread baking.

GRAM FLOUR – a.k.a. chickpea flour. Find it in the world foods section of the supermarket or Indian or Middle Eastern food shops. It is gluten free and high in protein.

BUCKWHEAT FLOUR – a gluten-free flour that is sometimes used in baking recipes.

OAT FLOUR – this is wheat free, but is only gluten free if you use certified gluten-free oats. Even if certified gluten free, coeliacs may still not be able it consume it safely.

Grains

QUINOA – try to find British-grown quinoa and rinse it before use.

PEARL BARLEY – a chewy, nubbly little grain, pearl barley is good in stews and salads. It contains gluten.

COUSCOUS – this is quick to cook so it's perfect for lunch. It contains gluten.

PASTA – there are many different shapes of pasta and pastas made with different flours. You can also get brown rice pasta for gluten-free dishes.

BROWN RICE – I like short-grain brown rice for its incredible flavour and texture. You need to be very careful when cooking and cooling rice as the bacteria that live in rice can produce toxic, heat-resistant spores that can give you food poisoning or, scarily, even kill you. If you are planning on keeping rice in the refrigerator, it's vitally important to cool it down as quickly as possible after cooking it. Either rinse it under cold running water or spread it out on a plate or baking tray. Once cooled, place in a lidded container in the refrigerator or flat-pack it in individual portions in re-sealable sandwich bags then freeze. Store in the refrigerator for 1 day or in the freezer for 2 months – label and date the bag. When reheating, make sure the rice is piping hot.

Sweeteners

All sugars are sugar and in my opinion, there's nothing special about the unrefined sugars that you can buy nowadays, except for their flavour. Just use granulated sugar when appropriate. Some granulated sugars may not be considered vegan, so just check the brand you're using is vegan-friendly, if needed.

Liquid sweeteners can be useful for salad dressings or drizzling on pancakes, so I tend to keep runny honey and real maple syrup (without any added flavourings) in the refrigerator. Some brands of maple syrup may not be considered vegan, so check the syrup before using, if needed.

LEFTOVERS

Refer to pages 228–233 to help you plan meals and use up leftovers. The most efficient way to spend your time in the kitchen is to batch prep individual ingredients for the week – boiling grains to keep in the refrigerator or freezer, roasting or steaming different vegetables, blending a pesto and making salad dressings.

Below each recipe you'll find a box of 'leftover' ingredients (see example box below). These are perishable (cheeses, vegetables, open cans of beans) or niche ingredients (miso, creamed coconut). Referring to the 'leftovers table' on pages 228–233, use these boxes to find out how to use any leftover ingredients.

Whenever I cook grains, beans, legumes or roast vegetables for a recipe, I double or triple the batch, then store them in the refrigerator or freezer to use through the week. It's a good habit to get into and will save you money and time, plus it's a more eco-friendly way to cook (especially the roasted veggies).

LEFTOVERS: see pp228–233

- Butternut squash
- Creamed coconut
- White potatoes
- Spring onions

FOOD WASTE

Food waste is a big issue for first-world countries. We all get outraged when we see supermarkets dumping out-of-date food (due to legal obligations) but it's the food waste in our homes that we can most easily tackle. Food gets lost at the back of the refrigerator and forgotten about until it's gone mouldy. Here are some pointers on how to tackle your cooking and shopping habits:

● Start food planning so you don't stray from your shopping list.

● Stop falling for the '3 for the price of 2' offers if you know you will never eat it all.

● Start cooking grains and beans from scratch and freezing them rather than relying on cans or sachets of ready-cooked food.

● Use food more efficiently, such as trying to buy local and seasonal food as much as possible.

● Try to look at where your food is coming from the next time you go food shopping; it can make a difference to the environment if it has flown in from a country far away.

● Go to farmers' markets as the produce is more likely to be local and you can ask about their farming practices.

● Buying produce at farmers' markets also helps the environment as it's not usually covered in plastic packaging.

ORGANIC FOOD

If you live in the UK don't feel obligated to buy organic food. Here is why I don't always buy organic produce:

● Organic fruit and vegetables are not pesticide free so they still require rinsing before eating and, as farmers use manure to fertilize organic crops, you should wash the produce before using.

● Organic fruit and vegetables are not always more environmentally friendly as they still rely on pesticides.

● More water is often used in growing the crops.

● Organic produce is often smaller than non-organic.

● Certification of a product being organic doesn't have a uniform definition.

● Under EU law in the UK no animals are given growth hormones, whether they are 'organically' reared or not.

WHAT IS GLUTEN?

Gluten is a protein found in certain grains, including wheat, spelt, rye and barley. It is made up of two sub-units called 'glutenin' and 'gliadin'. Glutenin molecules look like little strands and gliadin molecules look like small spheres. When gluten comes into contact with water; for example, when wheat flour is added to water, the water starts to form links ('bonds') between the glutenin and gliadin molecules inside. By mixing or kneading the mixture, those bonds are repeatedly formed and broken, which starts to build up a strong network of linked glutenin strands and gliadin molecules. This strong network is the reason why we knead bread – it allows CO_2 produced by yeast in the bread dough to become trapped, which causes the bread to rise and create a light, airy texture.

● About 3 per cent of the UK population suffers from coeliac disease, a condition in which gluten causes an immune response in a person's body and their digestive systems become damaged, leading to malnutrition.

● Some people have a type of wheat-intolerance.

● FODMAPs (fermentable oligosaccharides, disaccharides, monosaccharides and polyols) are short-chain carbohydrates found in certain foods and are digested by the bacteria living in our guts, which make by-products, such as gases. FODMAPS may make you feel bloated and unwell.

● If you suspect that wheat makes you feel bloated it's possible that you need to decrease your intake of certain FODMAP-containing foods in your diet (see final bullet point).

● Oats do not contain gluten, but as they are often grown or processed near gluten-containing crops, they can become contaminated.

● Some of the recipes in this book use oats or oat flour and have been labelled 'gluten free', but if you are cooking for a coeliac check that they can consume (gluten-free) oats as they may be sensitive to them.

● Always consult your doctor or nutritionist or dietician before making a drastic change to your diet.

Breakfast & Grab-and-go Snacks

Breakfast really is the most important meal of my day. It sets me up to be alert and able to pay attention in lectures without being distracted by a grumbling stomach. I always have a sweet tooth but especially in the morning, when I crave soul-warming bowls of porridge or stacks of fluffy pancakes. I always find it important to strike the right balance though, so I incorporate wholegrains, healthy fats and some portion of fruit or vegetable into my breakfast to keep me full and happy. I do occasionally foray into savoury breakfasts but, really, I think the best savoury breakfast of all is poached eggs with spinach and toast — which I wouldn't bother writing a recipe for, anyway!

For those rushed breaks between lectures or those times when you get back from work/uni/school and you're desperate for some food, turn to these snack recipes. Dips, crackers, roasted chickpeas and small, sweet bites for satisfying yet light meals to fill that gap.

OVERNIGHT OATS

When hot weather finally rolls around, overnight oats become my calling card breakfast. Make a large batch and divide it into jars, and it will last a few days. It travels extremely well and is a super-healthy, but still delicious, breakfast on the go (just don't forget to pack a spoon!).

PEACH & RASPBERRY CRUNCH

Serves 2

1 peach, pitted and cut into small cubes
handful of fresh or frozen raspberries
1 apple, grated
80g rolled oats
250ml milk or non-dairy milk
2 tablespoons dried cranberries or raisins
1 tablespoon chia seeds or flaxseeds mixed with
   3 tablespoons water (optional)
2 tablespoons pumpkin seeds
1 teaspoon sugar, any kind
1 teaspoon water
¼ teaspoon ground cinnamon

1 Mix the peach, raspberries, apple, oats, milk and dried cranberries or raisins in a medium bowl, then mix in the chia seeds or flaxseeds, if using. Divide between 2 x 250ml jars and chill in the refrigerator overnight.

2 Toast the pumpkin seeds, sugar and water in a small frying pan over a medium heat until the sugar starts to melt and the seeds clump together. Stir in the cinnamon, then remove from the heat and set aside.

3 In the morning, sprinkle the crispy pumpkin seeds over the muesli and eat immediately or pop a lid on the jar and you are good to go! The other jar can be left in the refrigerator for up to 3 days.

Vegan Use non-dairy milk.

Gluten Free If you can tolerate oats, use gluten-free certified oats.

CARROT CAKE

Serves 2

2 tablespoons desiccated coconut
80g rolled oats
300ml milk or non-dairy milk
1 medium carrot, grated
½ teaspoon ground cinnamon
1 teaspoon finely grated orange zest
1 apple, grated
2 tablespoons raisins
4 tablespoons natural yogurt
  or soya yogurt (optional)

1 Toast the coconut in a frying pan over a medium heat, stirring constantly. Watch carefully and once it starts to turn golden, immediately pour it into a bowl. Set aside for the morning.

2 Mix the oats, milk, grated carrot, cinnamon, orange zest, grated apple and raisins together in a medium bowl. Divide the mixture between 2 x 250ml jars and leave overnight in the refrigerator.

3 In the morning, top the oat mixture with the coconut and yogurt (if using) and eat immediately or pop a lid on the jar and you are good to go! The other jar can be kept in the refrigerator for up to 3 days.

Vegan Use non-dairy milk and soya yogurt.

Gluten Free If you can tolerate oats, use gluten-free certified oats.

CARROT CAKE

PEACH & RASPBERRY CRUNCH

LEFTOVERS: see pp228–233

- Apple
- Raspberries (fresh or frozen)
- Peach

- Carrots
- Yogurt, if using
- Apple

TIPS & SWAPS

Buy strawberries or other fruit in
season and freeze it to enjoy all year round.
Or use frozen fruits, such as blueberries
and raspberries.

If you have extra fruit, double up on the compote
and keep in a lidded jar in the refrigerator to swirl
into yogurt or drizzle over pancakes.

Use chopped pecans or hazelnuts instead of the coconut.

Substitute muesli for the same weight of oats
for a different flavour and texture.

Instead of creamed coconut, try stirring
peanut butter into hot water.

V GF

VG option

OAT SQUARES WITH STRAWBERRY COMPOTE & COCONUT

This is a cross between a muffin and a thick, cooked porridge. If you enjoy eating the same breakfast for a week, then try this recipe. Just leave a square in a warm oven for 10 minutes while you make your coffee in the morning, then douse it in fridge-cold milk and top with fresh fruit, and some honey if you're feeling it. The compote, which is swirled into the oats before baking, can be changed up as you wish or you can just top the oats with a handful of blueberries or sliced apple.

Makes 9 squares

COMPOTE
150g fresh or frozen strawberries
1 tablespoon water
1 tablespoon sugar, honey
    or Date Paste (see page 221)

OATS
oil, for greasing
20g desiccated coconut
200ml water
300ml milk or non-dairy milk
1 egg
100ml coconut milk or 2 tablespoons
    creamed coconut mixed with
    100ml hot water
200g rolled oats
1 teaspoon baking powder
¼ teaspoon salt
1 tablespoon granulated sugar
    or honey or 2 tablespoons
    Date Paste (see page 221)

TO SERVE (OPTIONAL)
milk
natural yogurt
fresh fruit
honey

1 Preheat the oven to 180°C fan, 200°C, Gas Mark 6. Grease a 20cm square brownie tin or deep cake tin with a little oil.

2 Toast the desiccated coconut in a frying pan over a medium heat, stirring constantly. Watch carefully and once it starts to turn golden, immediately transfer to a bowl and set aside.

3 Return the pan to the heat and add all the compote ingredients. Bring to the boil, then reduce the heat to a simmer and cook for 10 minutes until the strawberries soften and the juice thickens.

4 Meanwhile, mix the water, milk, egg and coconut milk or creamed coconut for the oats together in a large bowl. Add the oats, baking powder, salt and sugar and stir together until combined. Pour into the prepared tin. Once the compote is ready, spoon it over the surface of the oatmeal, then sprinkle over the toasted coconut.

5 Bake in the oven for 20–25 minutes until it looks dry on top. Remove from the oven, then cut into 9 squares and eat warm. Keep any leftovers wrapped in clingfilm in the refrigerator. Reheat a square by placing it in a heatproof bowl or on a baking tray and warming in an oven preheated to 180°C fan, 200°C, Gas Mark 6 for 10 minutes.

6 Serve with milk, yogurt, fresh fruit and honey, if you like.

Vegan Use 1 tablespoon ground flaxseed mixed with 3 tablespoons water instead of the egg. Use non-dairy milk and sugar or Date Paste, and use sugar or Date Paste in the compote.

Gluten Free If you can tolerate oats, use gluten-free certified oats.

LEFTOVERS: see pp228–233

● Strawberries (fresh or frozen)
● Coconut milk or creamed coconut

TIPS & SWAPS

*The water should be just slightly warm to the touch. Too hot, and it will kill the yeast and the bread won't rise!

**In the winter, set the oven to the lowest heat for 5 minutes, then switch it off and leave the dough in there with the door closed.

CARROT BREAKFAST BREAD

Makes 1 loaf

7g sachet (2¼ teaspoons)
   fast-action dried yeast
200ml lukewarm water*
3 tablespoons honey or granulated sugar
2 tablespoons olive oil,
   plus extra for greasing
finely grated zest of 1 orange
2 teaspoons ground cinnamon
1 teaspoon ground ginger
200g coarsely grated carrot
400g strong wholemeal bread
   flour, plus extra for dusting
½ teaspoon salt
80g raisins

Baking bread can seem daunting if you have never done it before, but once you have made it a few times, you will get the hang of it! If you don't know how to knead bread dough, a quick Internet search for a video will help you out. Essentially, kneading is just the process of stretching and folding the dough with your hands until it is smooth and stretchy. This helps develop the gluten network (gluten is a protein found in certain grains such as wheat), which makes the dough elastic. One golden rule: never let the yeast come into contact with a super-high temperature until you are ready to bake. So be sure to use lukewarm liquids in the dough and let the dough rise in a warm, not hot, place. As yeasts are living organisms they like warmth but will die in high heat conditions!

1 Stir the yeast, lukewarm water and honey or sugar together in a large bowl until combined. Set aside for 5 minutes. Stir in the olive oil, orange zest, cinnamon, ginger and carrot. Add the flour and salt and stir until it forms a rough dough. Tip the dough out on to a lightly floured work surface and knead for 10 minutes, dusting lightly with more flour as needed to stop the dough sticking to the surface.

2 Pour a little extra olive oil into the bowl you were mixing the dough in, place the dough into it and turn it over until the dough and bowl are coated in oil. Cover loosely with clingfilm or kitchen paper and leave in a warm place** to rise for 1 hour, or until doubled in size.

3 Using kitchen paper, your hands or a pastry brush, grease a 900g loaf tin with a little olive oil. Tip the risen dough out on to a clean work surface and pat it out into a rectangle as long as the loaf tin and about 2cm thick. Scatter the raisins over the surface of the dough, press them down and roll the dough up, then place the dough into the prepared loaf tin, seam-side down. Cover loosely with oiled clingfilm and leave to rise in a warm place for 30 minutes.

4 Meanwhile, preheat the oven to 180°C fan, 200°C, Gas Mark 6.

5 Once the dough has risen for 30 minutes, remove the clingfilm and bake the bread in the oven for 40–50 minutes, or until golden on top. Remove from the oven and leave to cool for 10 minutes before tipping out of the tin on to a wire rack. Leave to cool completely before slicing.

Vegan Use sugar instead of honey.

LEFTOVERS: see pp228–233

● Carrots

NO-KNEAD LOAF

Makes 1 loaf

¼ teaspoon fast-action dried yeast
350ml lukewarm water*
300g strong wholemeal
    bread flour
200g strong white bread flour,
    plus extra for dusting
1 teaspoon salt
handful of mixed seeds, such as
    pumpkin, sunflower, sesame,
    flax, poppy, etc. (optional)

This internet-famous bread baking technique is known as Jim Lahey's no-knead bread and it is very simple. I have changed the method slightly and have used a slightly lower percentage of water, but one thing stays the same and that is baking the bread in a heavy, cast-iron casserole dish with a lid. The pan holds the heat in and traps steam around the loaf while it bakes, leading to a better rise and crust. You can bake it on a tray, but you won't get the same gorgeous, crispy crust.

1   Mix the yeast and lukewarm water together in a large bowl, then set aside for 5 minutes. Add the flours, salt and seeds, if using, and stir together until all the flour is incorporated. Cover the bowl with clingfilm and set aside for 8–12 hours at room temperature.

2   Cut a strip of nonstick baking paper about 15cm wide and dust it lightly with flour. Punch the dough down in the bowl and tip it out on to a lightly floured work surface. Dust your hands with flour and shape the dough into a ball by gently passing it back and forth around in circles with slightly cupped hands. You want the dough to be as tight and as taut as possible. Lift the dough up and place it in the centre of the floured baking paper. Dust with flour, then turn the bowl you were using upside down and place it over the dough. Leave to rise for 30 minutes.

3   Meanwhile, preheat the oven to 220°C fan, 240°C, Gas Mark 9. If you have a large, lidded, cast-iron casserole dish place it in the oven for 30 minutes while the dough is rising.

4   Uncover the dough and slash a cross in the top of the bread with the tip of a sharp knife.

5   If you are using a cast-iron casserole dish, remove it from the oven and place on a heatproof surface. Lift the lid of the dish. Take hold of the edges of the baking paper on which the dough is sitting and carefully lift it into the hot dish. Replace the lid and bake in the oven for 30 minutes, then remove the lid and bake for a further 15 minutes until the loaf is dark brown. Alternatively, if you are using a baking tray, grab the edges of the baking paper on which the dough is sitting and carefully lift the dough on to the tray. Bake for 40–45 minutes until dark brown.

6   Leave the bread to cool uncovered in the casserole dish or on a wire rack before slicing. I usually slice the whole loaf and freeze half of it.

TIPS & SWAPS
*See Tip, p22

The dough will keep in the refrigerator for up to 3 days so you could just bake half of it (takes 30 minutes) and store half. Let the dough come to room temperature for about an hour before using.

For bread rolls, divide the dough into 16 pieces after it has been left for 8–12 hours, then roll into balls and leave to rise in a warm place for 30 minutes. Bake in the oven for 18–20 minutes, or until golden.

MICROWAVE BLUEBERRY OAT 'MUFFIN'

Serves 1

30g (5 tablespoons) porridge oats
⅛ teaspoon baking powder
¼ teaspoon ground cinnamon
1 egg
(4 tablespoons) milk or non-dairy milk
1 heaped tablespoon fresh or frozen
   blueberries
1–2 teaspoons preferred sweetener
   such as honey, maple syrup or
   Date Paste (see page 221)

EXTRA TOPPINGS

natural yogurt
nut butter
fresh fruit
chopped nuts

This is my go-to winter breakfast on mornings when I only have 15 minutes to get dressed and eat before heading to uni (hello, 9am lectures). If you know you'll be really pressed for time, mix the oats, baking powder and cinnamon in the mug the night before, and in the morning just mix in the wet ingredients and microwave away! Please note that these oats seem to absorb the taste of sugar when you mix it in – it's far better to drizzle most of the sweetener over the cooked oats and/or top with a handful of ripe, fresh fruit.

1 Mix the oats, baking powder, cinnamon, egg and milk together in a tall mug until well combined. Briefly stir in the blueberries.

2 Microwave for 2 minutes on high. It will rise to the top of the mug and sink back a little once it is removed from the microwave. I like to tip the muffin out into a bowl (more room for toppings!) but you can eat it straight out of the mug. Just let the muffin cool briefly before drizzling with your preferred sweetener and adding on extra toppings of choice.

3 Eat while still warm as this gets weirdly rubbery when cold.

Gluten Free If you can tolerate oats, use gluten-free certified oats.

Dairy Free Use non-dairy milk.

LEFTOVERS: see pp228–233

● Blueberries (fresh or frozen)
● Yogurt (if using)
● Nut butter (if using)

TIPS & SWAPS

Use fresh or frozen raspberries or strawberries instead of the blueberries.

For a chocolatey treat add 20g chopped plain dark chocolate to the mixture before microwaving.

A TRIO OF PORRIDGES

TIPS & SWAPS

Try the Banana Bread Porridge as a dessert: omit the dates and sprinkle a handful of chopped plain dark chocolate over your porridge!

Porridge is my go-to breakfast and snack during the winter. I used to think that whenever you mix something into it, such as sugar, jam or nut butter, the flavour just disappears, but I have now perfected my formula for the best porridge. Pick mix-ins that provide flavour, salt or sweetness but which won't dissolve into the oats. Dried fruits are always good for a sweet hit and if you gently swirl in nut butter you get some in each bite. Toasting sunflower seeds in soy sauce makes them salty and crunchy, which is a great topping for sweet porridges. I also like savoury porridge for a quick and easy lunch – cook it the night before and just microwave until hot.

(V) (VG) (GF)

Serves 1

1 banana or ½ frozen sliced banana
150ml just-boiled water
40g rolled oats
pinch of salt
¼ teaspoon ground cinnamon
1 heaped teaspoon peanut
  or cashew butter
milk or non-dairy milk, for thinning
2–3 dried dates, pitted and roughly
  chopped

LEFTOVERS: see pp228–233

- Bananas
- Dates
- Nut butter

- Raspberries (fresh or frozen)
- Miso

- Miso
- Mushrooms

BANANA BREAD PORRIDGE

1 If using a fresh banana, mash half of it and slice the other half (for the topping). If using a frozen, sliced banana set it aside for now.

2 Pour the water into a small pan and bring to the boil. Add the oats, salt, cinnamon and all the mashed fresh banana or all the frozen sliced banana. Bring to the boil, then reduce the heat to low and simmer gently for 5 minutes. Turn the heat off, cover with a lid or plate and leave to stand for a further 5 minutes.

3 Meanwhile scoop up the heaped teaspoon of nut butter on the spoon you want to eat with and place the spoon into a cereal bowl.

4 Uncover the oats and check the texture, adding milk as desired, then stir in the chopped dates. Pour the porridge over the spoonful of nut butter in the bowl and leave for 30 seconds, allowing the heat of the porridge to melt the nut butter, then gently swirl the spoon through the porridge. The idea is that you are not mixing the nut butter in but rippling it through, so you get a bite of pure flavour in each mouthful.

5 Top with the remaining sliced, fresh banana (if you weren't using frozen) and enjoy!

Vegan Use non-dairy milk.

Gluten Free If you can tolerate oats, use gluten-free certified oats.

DOUGHNUT PORRIDGE

Serves 1

150ml just-boiled water
40g rolled oats
pinch of salt
milk or non-dairy milk, for thinning
1 teaspoon vanilla extract
handful of fresh or frozen raspberries
2 teaspoons soft light brown sugar
½ teaspoon ground cinnamon

1 Pour the water into a small pan and bring to the boil. Pour in the oats and salt, then bring to the boil. Reduce the heat to low and simmer gently for 5 minutes. Turn the heat off, cover with a lid or plate and leave to stand for a further 5 minutes.

2 Once the oats have sat for 5 minutes, uncover and check the texture, adding milk to thin it out as desired, then stir in the vanilla extract and gently fold in the raspberries. Pour the porridge into a cereal bowl.

3 Mix the sugar and cinnamon together and sprinkle in an even layer over the surface of the porridge. DON'T mix it in! You want each scoop of porridge to have a nice layer of cinnamon-sugar on it. Enjoy!

Vegan Use non-dairy milk.

Gluten Free If you can tolerate oats, use gluten-free certified oats.

TIPS & SWAPS

Make the Rocket, Mushroom & Fried Egg Porridge lunchbox friendly by using a peeled soft-boiled egg.

Add leftover roasted veg such as roasted squash with sautéed leeks.

Try using miso, peas, thyme and Parmesan.

ROCKET, MUSHROOM & FRIED EGG PORRIDGE

Serves 1

2 teaspoons olive oil or rapeseed oil
60g mushrooms, sliced
1 teaspoon miso, any kind (optional)
150ml just-boiled water or hot vegetable stock
40g rolled oats
milk or non-dairy milk, for thinning
1 egg
handful of rocket leaves
salt and freshly ground pepper

1 Heat half the oil in a small, nonstick frying pan over a medium heat. Add the mushrooms and cook, stirring frequently, until darkened and soft. Stir in the miso with a little water and cook until the water has evaporated. Remove the pan from the heat and set aside.

2 Pour the water or stock into a small pan and bring to the boil. Add the oats and a pinch of salt and bring to the boil. Reduce the heat to low and simmer gently for 5 minutes. Turn the heat off, cover with a lid or plate and leave to stand for a further 5 minutes.

3 Once the oats have sat for 5 minutes, uncover and check the texture, adding milk to thin it out as desired. Pour the mushrooms from the frying pan into the porridge, then return the empty frying pan to a medium-low heat and pour in the remaining oil. Crack in the egg and cook until the white is set.

4 Pour the porridge and mushrooms into a serving bowl, top with the rocket and the fried egg, then season with salt and pepper and serve.

Gluten Free If you can tolerate oats, use gluten-free certified oats.

Dairy Free Use non-dairy milk.

SCRAMBLED CHICKPEA TACOS WITH PEACH SALSA

Serves 2–3
(makes extra salsa)

SALSA
1 peach, pitted and roughly chopped
5–6 cherry tomatoes, finely chopped
juice of ½ lime
handful of coriander, roughly
    chopped (leaves and stalks)
½ large red onion, finely chopped
pinch of salt

CHICKPEA SCRAMBLE
2 tablespoons olive oil
½ large red onion, roughly chopped
2 teaspoons smoked paprika
1 teaspoon ground cumin
¼ teaspoon ground cinnamon
¼ teaspoon ground coriander
pinch of chilli flakes
240g (1 can, drained weight) cooked
    chickpeas, drained and rinsed
1 teaspoon miso, any kind
4 tablespoons milk or non-dairy milk
4–6 tortillas, (see page 214)
    or shop-bought, warmed
2 tablespoons natural yogurt or
    non-dairy yogurt or Avocado Cream
    (see page 219)

Most of the time I try to eat plant-based meals for breakfast and lunch, but the one thing I find difficult to try and replace is scrambled eggs. They are such a quick, savoury meal and always taste good. However, I have found that these scrambled chickpeas fill that gap. If you get into having these for breakfast, brunch or lunch, just multiply the quantities of spices by eight, mix in a jar and use about 3½ teaspoons of the mixture when needed.

1   Prepare all the ingredients for the salsa then stir them together in a bowl and set aside. You can do this the night before and leave the salsa in the refrigerator overnight, if you like.

2   Heat the olive oil in a medium frying pan over a medium heat. Add the onion and cook, stirring frequently, until translucent. Add the spices and chilli flakes and cook for 1 minute, then tip in the drained chickpeas and stir to coat. Reduce the heat to medium-low and mash the chickpeas with the wooden spoon or the back of a fork in the pan. You want some chickpeas to remain a little chunky.

3   Mix the miso and milk together in a small bowl and tip into the pan, stirring until it has mostly evaporated.

4   Divide the chickpea scramble among the tortillas and top with some salsa and yogurt, if you like. Serve immediately! Store any excess salsa in a bowl covered in clingfilm in the refrigerator.

Vegan Use non-dairy milk and non-dairy yogurt or Avocado Cream.

Gluten Free Use gluten-free corn tortillas.

LEFTOVERS: see pp228–233

● Peach
● Cherry tomatoes
● Red onion
● Fresh coriander
● Lime juice
● Cooked chickpeas
● Avocado Cream or yogurt
● Miso

MULTI-GRAIN PANCAKES

Makes 6–8 (serves 2)

DRY MIX (ENOUGH FOR 3 BATCHES)
150g Oat Flour (see page 216)
90g rolled oats
240g plain white
  or wholemeal flour
3 teaspoons baking powder
¾ teaspoon bicarbonate of soda
¾ teaspoon salt
3 tablespoons granulated sugar
3 tablespoons ground flaxseed
  (for the vegan version only)

FOR VEGAN VERSION
190g dry mix
200ml non-dairy milk
1 teaspoon apple cider vinegar
  or lemon juice
2 tablespoons olive oil or rapeseed oil,
  plus extra for frying

FOR NON-VEGAN VERSION
185g dry mix
1 egg
160ml dairy or non-dairy milk
1 teaspoon apple cider vinegar
  or lemon juice
2 tablespoons olive oil or rapeseed oil,
  plus extra for frying

TO SERVE (OPTIONAL)
maple syrup
natural yogurt
fruit
chopped nuts

If you find yourself lying in bed on a Saturday morning, wishing someone else would get up and make pancakes, but knowing that won't happen, this pancake mix could help you out. When it's not a weekend morning, mix up the 'dry mix' to keep in a jar in the cupboard. That way, when your brunch longings hit, you know you are just a scoop of pancake mix plus a few ingredients away from tasty homemade pancakes.

1 Combine all the dry mix ingredients in a medium bowl. Stir to mix everything well then transfer to a labelled airtight container or a large, labelled sandwich bag. Store in the cupboard until needed. (It will last for up to 3 months.)

2 When ready to make pancakes, weigh your dry mix into a medium bowl or jug according to the version you're making. Add the wet ingredients to the bowl or jug and stir with a fork or small whisk until just combined.

3 Heat a large, nonstick frying pan with just enough oil to coat the base of the pan. Once the oil is hot, turn the heat down to medium-low and pour a few tablespoons of batter into the pan to form a pancake, about 8cm in diameter. Repeat this so you have 3 or 4 pancakes cooking in the frying pan. Cook the pancakes until the edges change colour and the underside is golden, then flip over and cook on the other side until golden. Transfer to a plate and cook the remaining batter as before.

4 Serve hot with maple syrup, yogurt, fruit and chopped nuts, if you like.

TIPS & SWAPS

As you cook, put the pancakes on a baking tray in a warm oven.

To make pancakes in bulk, triple the wet ingredients and mix into all the dry mix. Cook and keep pancakes in the refrigerator in a sandwich bag for up to 3 days or in the freezer for up to 1 month. Pop in the toaster to defrost and warm up.

For blueberry pancakes, pour the batter into the pan, then drop in a few blueberries.

MULTI-GRAIN
PANCAKES

FRENCH TOAST
WITH MISO-DATE
BUTTER

VG option

FRENCH TOAST WITH MISO-DATE BUTTER

Serves 2–3

MISO DATE BUTTER
5 soft Medjool dates*
  or 6 Deglet Noor dates, pitted
75g unsalted butter, softened
2 teaspoons miso, any kind

FRENCH TOAST
3 tablespoons plain flour
  or gram (chickpea) flour
pinch of salt
½ teaspoon ground cinnamon
3 green cardamom pods,
  seeds removed and ground
  in a pestle and mortar (optional)
200ml milk or non-dairy milk
2 teaspoons granulated sugar
  or maple syrup
1 teaspoon vanilla extract
olive oil or rapeseed oil, for frying
4–6 slices of wholemeal bread,
  stale is best

TO SERVE (OPTIONAL)
maple syrup
fruit

I have this pet peeve about that little tail of egg white which attaches the yolk to the albumen – it never mixes into French toast batter properly. But then I discovered how to make this dish without using eggs! Serve the French toast with a little salty, sweet miso-date butter for a great way to jazz it up.

1 Make the butter first. Place the dates in a medium bowl and mash into a rough paste with the back of a fork. Add the butter and miso to the bowl and mix together until the dates are marbled through the butter. Dollop on to a piece of nonstick baking paper in a line, then roll up into a log and twist the ends of the paper. Place in the refrigerator for at least 30 minutes or the freezer for at least 10 minutes to set.

2 For the French toast, mix the flour, salt, cinnamon and cardamom pods (if using) together in a shallow bowl. While whisking, gradually pour in the milk until fully combined, then stir in the sugar and vanilla extract.

3 Heat a large, nonstick frying pan with just enough oil to lightly coat the base. Take 1 or 2 pieces of bread (depending on how large your bowl is) and submerge it into the milk mixture, flipping it to coat. Leave for 2 minutes or so then lift up the piece of bread, letting the excess batter drip off. Place the battered bread into the frying pan and leave to cook. Meanwhile, dunk another piece of bread into the batter and leave it in there for 2 minutes or so. Check on the piece of bread in the pan – when it's golden underneath flip it over and cook on the other side. Once it's golden, remove to a plate. Repeat the dunking and cooking with the rest of the bread as before until all the batter has been used up.

4 Serve the French toast hot with slices of the miso-date butter and maple syrup and fruit, if you like.

Vegan Use vegan spread or even cashew, almond or peanut butter in the miso-date butter and non-dairy milk in the batter.

TIPS & SWAPS

*To soften dates, soak them in boiling water for 15 minutes, then drain and allow to cool before mixing into the butter.

To reheat cold French toast, pop it in the toaster for a minute until hot.

Store any extra French toast in the refrigerator or freezer in a sandwich bag for a weekday breakfast. Pop the slices in the toaster to defrost.

LEFTOVERS: see pp228–233

● Dates
● Miso
● Bread

SALTY OR SWEET CRACKERS

Makes 8 large crackers (to be broken into smaller crackers)

7g sachet (2¼ teaspoons)
   fast-action dried yeast
150ml water
250g plain or strong wholemeal
   bread flour, plus extra for dusting
½ teaspoon salt
4 tablespoons olive oil

SWEET FLAVOUR MIX

2 tablespoons sesame seeds
1 tablespoon granulated sugar
1 teaspoon ground cinnamon

SAVOURY FLAVOUR MIX

3 teaspoons mixed dried herbs
1 teaspoon sea salt flakes
1 teaspoon smoked paprika

I always forget how moreish crackers are until I make them. They are a great snack eaten on their own, but they are also good served with dips and are a much healthier alternative to tortilla chips or crisps. They keep well in a sealed container and if they start getting a little bendy, just place them on a baking tray and put in an oven preheated to 160°C fan, 180°C, Gas Mark 4 for a few minutes to crisp them up again.

1 Mix the yeast and measured water together in a medium bowl. Add the flour, salt and oil, then mix with a spoon to form a rough dough. Use your hands to knead the dough in the bowl until just smooth, then cover with a clean tea towel or clingfilm and leave to rest at room temperature for 30 minutes.

2 Preheat the oven to 180°C fan, 200°C, Gas Mark 6.

3 Divide the dough into 8 equal pieces. Roll each piece into a ball, then roll each ball out into long ovals as thin as possible on individual strips of nonstick baking paper, dusting the dough with a little flour as needed to stop it sticking to the rolling pin. Sprinkle on your choice of flavour mix, then lift the baking paper and place on a baking sheet so the cracker is still on top (I can usually fit 2 large crackers on a tray).

4 Bake in the oven for 8–12 minutes until golden. Remove from the oven and leave to cool on a wire rack. Bake the rest of the crackers.

SMOOTHIE BOX TRIO

Pre-made smoothie mixes are great to have on hand for rushed mornings – they'll keep in the freezer for a couple of months or in the refrigerator for a few days. Pop a few ingredients into a freezer bag or plastic box and store until needed. Tip the contents into a blender with a little bit of liquid to get it going and you'll have a meal or snack in no time. Once blended, I pour my smoothie into a thermos to take with me on particularly busy days.

I like to make sure there's a source of fibre (aside from the fruit), fat and protein in my smoothies, so I have added veggies, yogurt and nut butter to the recipes below. They'll make you feel fuller for longer and prevent that dreaded mid-morning sugar crash.

FOR ANY OF THE BELOW RECIPES:

Assemble the smoothie mix ingredients and place into a freezer bag or small, lidded plastic box. Place in the freezer for up to 2 months.

For a thin smoothie (with a freestanding or hand blender): The night before, take the smoothie bag out of the freezer and place in the refrigerator. In the morning, tip the contents of the bag into the blender or a jug, if using a hand-held blender. Add the 'to blend' ingredients and blend until smooth.

For a thick smoothie (with a freestanding blender only): No need to defrost the smoothie bag. When you are ready to make your smoothie, tip the frozen contents of the bag into the blender. Add the 'to blend' ingredients and blend until smooth, adding some extra liquid to get the blending going.

TOP LEFT: MANGO, BANANA & SPINACH
BOTTOM LEFT: CHOCOLATE
BELOW: CARROT & BERRY

(V) (VG) (GF)

CHOCOLATE

Serves 1

1 small sweet potato, or ½ large one* (about 200g)
1 tablespoon cocoa powder
1 teaspoon sugar, any kind, or 1 pitted date
1 tablespoon almond or cashew or peanut butter,
  tahini or creamed coconut
pinch of salt
pinch of ground cinnamon (optional)

TO BLEND
a glug (4–6 tablespoons) of milk or non-dairy milk

1 Preheat the oven to 160°C fan, 180°C, Gas Mark 4.
   Prick the sweet potato all over with a fork, wrap in foil
   and throw into the oven for 1 hour.

2 Unwrap the baked sweet potato and leave to cool for
   a few minutes, then cut it in half lengthways. Scoop
   out the flesh and discard the skin, then chop the sweet
   potato flesh into chunks and mix with the cocoa, sugar,
   salt and cinnamon in a resealable sandwich bag or
   plastic container. Stash in the freezer.

3 Follow the blending instructions opposite.

Vegan Use non-dairy milk to blend.

TIPS & SWAPS

*If you only have large sweet
potatoes, roast the whole potato but
only use half and store the other half.

Roast 2 sweet potatoes to double
up this recipe and keep the extra
potato in a sealed container in the
refrigerator until ready to use.

MANGO, BANANA & SPINACH

Serves 1

1 small, overripe banana, peeled and sliced into coins
75g fresh or frozen mango, cubed
20g baby spinach, washed
2 tablespoons rolled oats
2 teaspoons almond or cashew butter,
    tahini or creamed coconut

TO BLEND
A glug (4–6 tablespoons) of milk or non-dairy milk
2 tablespoons natural yogurt or unsweetened soya yogurt
squeeze of lemon, lime or orange juice

1 Place the banana, mango, spinach, oats and nut butter, tahini or creamed coconut in a resealable sandwich bag or plastic container and stash in the freezer.

2 Follow the blending instructions on page 36.

Vegan Use non-dairy milk and soya yogurt.

Gluten free If you can tolerate oats, make sure they are certified gluten free.

CARROT & BERRY

Serves 1

1 medium carrot, washed
50g mixed berries (I prefer strawberries and raspberries here)
1 small, overripe banana, sliced into coins

TO BLEND
4 tablespoons full-fat Greek-style yogurt
    or unsweetened soya yogurt
milk or non-dairy milk

1 Cut the carrot into coins about 2mm thick or grate them on the coarse side of a box grater (if using a hand-held blender to make the smoothie you will have to grate the carrot). Place the carrot, berries and banana into a resealable sandwich bag or plastic container and stash in the freezer.

2 Follow the blending instructions on page 36.

Vegan Use non-dairy milk and soya yogurt.

LEFTOVERS: see pp228–233

- Sweet potato (roasted or raw)
- Nut butter or creamed coconut or tahini
- Dates

- Banana
- Mango (fresh or frozen)
- Spinach
- Yogurt

- Carrots
- Mixed berries (fresh or frozen)

TIPS & SWAPS

If you have a freestanding (NOT a hand-held blender), add a few handfuls of ice as you blend. It will make the smoothie thicker and colder – more like a milkshake!

Use fresh or frozen cubed pineapple instead of mango.

APPLE CINNAMON SCUFFINS

Makes 12

60g red lentils, rinsed

2 eggs

6 tablespoons milk or non-dairy milk

80ml olive oil or rapeseed oil

60g granulated or demerara
   sugar, plus a little extra for sprinkling

¼ teaspoon salt

1 teaspoon ground cinnamon

160g plain wholemeal flour

60g rolled oats

1 teaspoon baking powder

½ teaspoon bicarbonate of soda

300g (about 2–3) apples,
   peeled, cored and roughly
   chopped into cubes

12 walnuts

TIPS & SWAPS

Replace the apple with 300g
frozen blueberries, raspberries
or chopped pear.

Change the cinnamon for ground
ginger, vanilla extract or ½ teaspoon
almond extract.

Swap the walnuts for pecans,
pumpkin seeds or chopped
hazelnuts.

LEFTOVERS: see pp228–233

● Apples

Scuffins are the shape and size of a scone but the texture of a muffin. They are ideal when you don't have a muffin tin to hand but still want a cake breakfast bake. Don't stop at the flavour combo I've used here; try other flavours, such as blueberry and pecan, ground ginger and pear or raspberry and almond extract.

1 Preheat the oven to 180°C fan, 200°C, Gas Mark 6 and line a baking tray with nonstick baking paper.

2 Place the lentils into a medium pan and cover well with water. Bring to the boil, then reduce the heat and simmer for 10 minutes.

3 Drain the lentils and return them to the pan off the heat, then stir in the eggs, milk, oil, sugar, salt and cinnamon until well combined. Add the flour, oats, baking powder, bicarbonate of soda and apple cubes and stir in until just combined.

4 Scoop mounds of the batter on to the prepared baking tray. Each mound should be about 3 heaped tablespoons of batter spaced about 3cm apart. I can usually fit all 12 on to a single baking tray but you may need to bake these in 2 batches of 6 if your baking tray is small.

5 Top each one with a light sprinkle of the remaining sugar and a walnut, then bake in the oven for 17–20 minutes until they spring back when poked in the middle. Leave to cool on a wire rack.

Vegan Replace the eggs with 2 tablespoons ground flaxseed mixed with 6 tablespoons water. Use non-dairy milk.

(V) (VG) (GF) (NS)   BANOFFEE PEANUT BITES

Makes 20–30 bites

2 ripe bananas, peeled
3 tablespoons peanut, cashew
   or almond butter
75g dried dates, pitted*
1 teaspoon vanilla extract
pinch of salt
4 tablespoons milk or non-dairy milk
handful of peanuts, almonds
   or cashews, roughly chopped
50–100g plain dark chocolate
   (at least 70% cocoa solids)

When bananas are sliced and frozen they transform into creamy, slightly chewy nuggets of sweetness, which are perfect on a hot summery day. I have jazzed them up with peanut butter, date 'caramel' and a drizzle of plain dark chocolate – delicious and, oh, also adorable.

1 Line a plate or baking tray with nonstick baking paper. Cut the bananas into 1cm thick coins, then place on the prepared plate or baking tray.

2 Spread a layer of nut butter on top of each piece of banana and freeze for 30 minutes.

3 Using a hand-held blender or a freestanding blender, blend the dates, vanilla extract, salt and milk until smooth. Alternatively, cover the dates with 4 tablespoons water and cook over a low heat for 4–5 minutes until the water has mostly evaporated. Mash with a fork until it is as smooth as possible then stir in the vanilla extract, salt and milk.

4 Spread the caramel over the frozen sections of banana, then sprinkle with the nuts and freeze again for 30 minutes.

5 Break the chocolate into small chunks and place in a bowl in a small pan of simmering water, over a low heat. Stir constantly until just melted, then remove from the heat. Alternatively, melt the chocolate in a low heat in a bowl in the microwave.

6 Transfer the melted chocolate to a sandwich bag; cut the tip off one corner and use it like a piping bag to drizzle the chocolate over the frozen banana pieces. Freeze again for at least 1 hour before eating. Store them in an airtight container in the freezer for up to 2 weeks.

Vegan Use non-dairy milk. Ensure your chocolate is suitable for vegans.

LEFTOVERS: see pp228–233

● Bananas
● Dates
● Nut butter

TIPS & SWAPS
Use 120g Date
Paste (see page 221) instead
of the dates.

*If the dates aren't soft and sticky,
soak them in boiling water for
15 minutes before removing
the stones.

COCONUT & COCOA BITES

Makes 14–16

100g dried dates
(weighed with the stones)
or 5 tablespoons Date Paste
(see page 221)
3 tablespoons cocoa powder
140g desiccated or shredded
coconut (unsweetened)

These are a breeze to make and considering they only have three ingredients, are pretty damn tasty! The raw mixture is nice on its own, but I like to bake it briefly to create a kind of shell on the outside so they aren't so sticky.

1 If using the Date Paste, skip this step. Place the dates in a pan and pour in enough water to cover. Bring to the boil, cover with a lid, reduce the heat and simmer for 10 minutes. Drain the dates and cool for 5 minutes, then remove the stones and mash the dates with a fork in a bowl.

2 Add the cocoa powder and coconut and stir to combine into a dough.

3 Scoop tablespoons of the date mixture and roll into balls. Either leave as they are for a sticky treat OR arrange the balls on a nonstick baking paper-lined baking tray and bake in an oven preheated to 180°C fan, 200°C, Gas Mark 6 for 4 minutes. Store in an airtight container for up to 5 days.

LEFTOVERS: see pp228–233

● Dates

(V)

TORTILLA OR PITTA CHIPS 4 WAYS

Serves 2–4

2 wholemeal pitta breads
   OR 2 large wholemeal tortillas
   (see page 214) or shop-bought
   OR 3 small corn or wholemeal tortillas
2 teaspoons olive oil or rapeseed oil

SWEET & SMOKY FLAVOUR MIX
½ teaspoon sweet smoked paprika
½ teaspoon ground coriander seeds
pinch of granulated sugar
pinch of salt
½ teaspoon ground sumac (optional)

HERBS & SALT FLAVOUR MIX
2 teaspoons mixed dried herbs
pinch of salt (sea salt flakes are
   especially good here)

**GARLIC & PARMESAN FLAVOUR MIX
(NOT VEGAN)**
1 large garlic clove, halved
2 tablespoons finely grated Parmesan*
½ teaspoon mixed dried herbs

CINNAMON-SUGAR FLAVOUR MIX
1 teaspoon granulated sugar
1 teaspoon ground cinnamon
pinch of salt

I am so obsessed with making my own chips for serving with dips. It's incredibly easy to do because they are baked (no messing around with a couple of litres of hot oil, thanks) and it's up to you to choose the flavours. I have included a few savoury flavour mixes for serving with guacamole or the Fattoush Dip on page 51, but there is also a cinnamon-sugar mix, which is definitely A+ snacking material on its own.

1 Preheat the oven to 200°C fan, 220°C, Gas Mark 7.

2 For pitta breads, cut around the edge of each pitta bread with a pair of scissors and separate them each into 2 thin halves. Cut each half into roughly 10 even pieces and toss with the oil on a baking tray, then lay them out in a single layer on the tray.

3 For tortillas, use a pair of scissors to cut the tortillas in half. Stack the halves together and cut into quarters. Stack the quarters together and cut into eighths. Toss the triangles with the oil on a baking tray and spread them out in a single layer on the tray.

4 Sprinkle on your choice of flavour mix and bake in the oven for 5–10 minutes, keeping a close watch, until they are just starting to go golden. Remove from the oven and leave to cool and crisp up.

5 Store in an airtight container for up to 5 days. If they soften, just place them on a baking tray and warm in an oven preheated to 180°C fan, 200°C, Gas Mark 6 for 2–3 minutes.

Note For the Garlic & Parmesan flavour mix you will need to rub the outside of the pitta or the surface of the tortilla with the cut side of the garlic clove before cutting into smaller pieces and sprinkling with the Parmesan and herbs.

TIPS & SWAPS
*Parmesan is not technically vegetarian – choose an alternative vegetarian hard cheese.

SWEET & SMOKY

GARLIC &
PARMESAN

HERBS & SALT

CINNAMON–SUGAR

ROASTED CHICKPEAS

If you're looking for a relatively healthy snack that will fill you up then go for these roasted chickpeas. You can flavour them in myriad ways and munch on them knowing that they are giving you lots of protein and fibre. Toss them into salad or sprinkle on soup for a healthier alternative to croutons.

Serves 2

oil, for greasing
400g can chickpeas

CINNAMON-SUGAR FLAVOUR MIX
2 teaspoons olive oil or rapeseed oil
pinch of salt
1 tablespoon ground cinnamon
2 tablespoons soft brown sugar

CURRY FLAVOUR MIX
2 teaspoons garam masala
1 teaspoon ground cumin
1 teaspoon ground turmeric
¼ teaspoon salt
2 teaspoons olive oil

'BACON' FLAVOUR MIX
1 tablespoon soft brown sugar
4 teaspoons smoked paprika
2 teaspoons olive oil
1 teaspoon soy sauce or tamari

1 Preheat the oven to 180°C fan, 200°C, Gas Mark 6 and lightly grease a baking tray.

2 Drain the chickpeas but don't rinse. Toss with the flavour mix of choice (see note below). Tip on to the baking tray and roast in the oven for 25–35 minutes, tossing every 10 minutes or so until crisp. Leave to cool, then eat!

Gluten Free Ensure that your tamari or soy sauce is certified gluten free.

Note If using the cinnamon-sugar flavour mix, toss the drained chickpeas with the oil and salt. Roast for 15 minutes. Mix the cinnamon-sugar in a bowl then sprinkle over the chickpeas. Toss, then return to the oven for 10 minutes.

TOP LEFT: CINNAMON-SUGAR
BOTTOM LEFT: 'BACON'
BELOW: CURRY

LEFTOVERS: see pp228–233
● Cooked chickpeas

COCONUT-BANANA GRANOLA BARS

Makes 16

4 tablespoons olive oil or rapeseed oil
2 tablespoons creamed coconut
1 tablespoon water
1 tablespoon honey or maple syrup
85g soft brown sugar
1 small, ripe banana, mashed
  (70–80g peeled weight)
160g rolled oats
30g plain wholemeal flour
½ teaspoon baking powder
pinch of salt
20g sunflower seeds or pumpkin seeds
20g desiccated coconut

With a slight banana flavour and a tropical aroma, these bars are a great, oaty snack for when you're on the go. You can make endless variations by mixing in your choice of nuts, dried fruit, chocolate and nut butters. Try adding seeds and dessicated coconut for something cheap and cheerful.

1 Preheat the oven to 180°C fan, 200°C, Gas Mark 6 and line a 20cm square tin with nonstick baking paper – no need to grease or flour it.

2 Heat the oil, creamed coconut, water, honey or maple syrup and sugar together in a medium pan over a medium heat for 2 minutes, stirring constantly. Remove from the heat and stir in the mashed banana. Add the oats, flour, baking powder, salt, seeds and desiccated coconut and stir together until combined.

3 Press the mixture into the prepared tin and bake in the oven for 15 minutes.

4 Remove from the oven and cut into 16 bars or squares, then leave to cool in the tin. Store in an airtight container at room temperature for up to 5 days.

Vegan Use maple syrup instead of honey.

TIPS & SWAPS

Replace the creamed coconut with a different nut butter and use finely chopped peanuts instead of the desiccated coconut.

Try using roasted puréed butternut squash instead of the banana.

Stir 3 tablespoons cocoa powder into the mix.

Mix in dried fruit, such as chopped dates or raisins or chopped plain dark chocolate.

LEFTOVERS: see pp228–233

● Bananas
● Creamed coconut

A TRIO OF PUREES

These three purées are all extremely different in flavour and use but are all creamy dip-like things which I use to jazz up other recipes. They can also be used simply as a dip for fruit, vegetables or crackers.

PEA HUMMUS

Serves 4–6

150g frozen petits pois or peas
1 tablespoon tahini
good pinch of salt
juice of ½ lemon
1 garlic clove, crushed or finely chopped

1 Put the peas in a bowl, cover with just-boiled water and leave to stand for 2 minutes. Drain, return to the bowl, cover with cold water and leave for 5 minutes to cool. Drain again and return to the bowl if using a hand-held blender or into a food processor or freestanding blender. Blitz with the remaining ingredients until smooth.

2 Store the dip in a lidded container in the refrigerator for up to 3 days.

WAYS TO USE
- With floured and pan-fried fish and roasted potatoes.
- On crostini (toasted baguette slices) with fried halloumi, thyme and pea shoots.
- Use lime juice instead of lemon juice or add finely chopped red onion, coriander, cherry tomatoes and some hot sauce to make a fake guacamole (you can also add mashed avocado to make it go further).
- Use in tacos as you would salsa or guacamole.
- As a dip for quesadillas (see Spanakopita Quesadillas on page 78).

SQUASH & CINNAMON DIP

PEA HUMMUS

'CHORIZO' DIP

LEFTOVERS: see pp228-233

- Tahini
- Lemon juice

- Sun-dried tomatoes
- Miso
- Cooked kidney beans

- Butternut squash
- Dates

(V) (VG) (GF) (LS)

'CHORIZO' DIP

Serves 4–5

1 teaspoon fennel seeds
75g (about ½ jar) sun-dried tomatoes, packed in oil
3 tablespoons sun-dried tomato oil from the jar
240g (1 can drained weight) cooked kidney beans,
    drained and rinsed
2 teaspoons sweet smoked paprika
¼–½ teaspoon chilli flakes or a ¼ teaspoon cayenne
    pepper
grinding of fresh black pepper
2 tablespoons miso paste, soy sauce or tamari
2 teaspoons apple cider vinegar
2 garlic cloves, crushed
½ teaspoon granulated sugar or 1 dried date, pitted
4 tablespoons water

1   Toast the fennel seeds in a dry frying pan over a high
    heat, stirring frequently until they begin to colour and
    smell fragrant. Transfer them to a mortar and crush
    them with a pestle. Alternatively, pour them on to a
    chopping board and crush with the back of a spoon.

2   Using a hand-held blender, food processor or
    freestanding blender, blitz the fennel seeds with
    the remaining ingredients until smooth.

3   Store in a lidded container in the refrigerator for up to
    3 days or, using a tablespoon, scoop blobs of the dip on
    to a baking tray lined with nonstick baking paper and
    freeze. Keep the blobs in a labelled and dated sandwich
    bag for up to 2 months, defrosting as needed.

Gluten Free   Make sure your soy sauce or tamari are
certified gluten free.

WAYS TO USE
● On toast, with an egg.
● With crunchy raw vegetables, crackers (see page 35)
  or pitta chips (see page 42) for dipping.
● In a sandwich or on a flatbread with leftover roasted veg.
● Dollop into a frittata, on to pizza or spread into tacos.
● In a savoury galette (use instead of the pesto in the recipe
  on page 101).

(V) (VG) (GF) (NS)

SQUASH & CINNAMON DIP

Serves 4–6

½ small squash or ¼ large squash (about 250g), deseeded
    and cut into 3 or 4 large chunks
2 dried dates, pitted or 1 tablespoon Date Paste (see page 221)
½ teaspoon ground cinnamon
1 teaspoon vanilla extract

1   Preheat the oven to 180°C fan, 200°C, Gas Mark 6.

2   Put the squash in a baking tray and roast in the oven for
    45 minutes until soft. Remove from the oven and leave
    to cool for 15 minutes, then scoop the flesh from the
    skin, discarding the skin.

3   Cover the dates with boiling water if they aren't already
    soft and set aside for 15 minutes, then drain.

4   Using a hand-held blender, freestanding blender or food
    processor, blend the roasted squash, dates, cinnamon
    and vanilla extract together until smooth.

5   Store in a lidded container in the refrigerator for up to
    3 days or, using a tablespoon, scoop blobs of the dip on
    to a baking tray lined with nonstick baking paper and
    freeze. Keep the blobs in a labelled and dated sandwich
    bag for up to 2 months, defrosting as needed.

WAYS TO USE
● Serve with yogurt and granola.
● Use a dollop in your porridge with raisins, chopped apple
  and pecans.
● Spoon on to Overnight Oats (see page 18).
● Spread on toast, after your butter or spread.
● Serve with sliced apple or pear, for dipping.
● Smear on to warm scones (see page 187), Scuffins
  (see page 39) or sliced banana bread (see page 194).
● Stir in 2 tablespoons cocoa powder.
● If you have already roasted butternut squash to hand, use
  about 130g instead. Just skip the first and second steps.

Light Bites

I always find it difficult to define the difference between lunch and dinner meals. I mean most of the time I eat the same stuff but for lunch I'd just have a smaller portion or eat it cold. These light bites fall somewhere in between lunch and dinner – they're light mains or hearty sides. Usually if you pair them with some bread, dressed leaves or a poached egg they'll do well as a meal. You can also combine two or three of them to make a mezze meal for dinner – whatever works for you!

V VG NS

GF option

FATTOUSH DIP

Serves 3–4

DIP
240g (1 can, drained weight) cooked
  kidney beans, drained (except for
  3 tablespoons water from kidney bean
  can) and rinsed
2 tablespoons extra virgin olive oil
2 garlic cloves, roughly chopped or crushed
salt
juice of ½ lemon

SALAD
handful of cherry tomatoes,
  halved or quartered
2 radishes, thinly sliced
handful of rocket or pea shoots
handful of fresh coriander, roughly
  chopped (leaves and stalks)
handful of mint leaves, roughly chopped
1 spring onion, finely sliced
handful of pomegranate seeds (optional)

DRESSING
2 tablespoons olive oil
½ teaspoon ground cinnamon
juice of ½ lemon
pinch of salt

TO SERVE
1 batch of pitta chips (see page 42),
  a few pitta breads (see page 215)
  or crackers (see page 35)

I prefer this purple dip made with kidney beans to its more common chickpea-based cousin hummus as it's easier to make it smooth, light and creamy. (Seriously, I'm never going to hand peel a bowl of cooked chickpeas just to get smooth hummus.) I swirl the resulting pastel purée on to a platter and top it with a mixture of herbs, tomatoes, leaves and pomegranate seeds with a cinnamon-lemon dressing inspired by the Middle Eastern salad called 'fattoush'. Serve with homemade pitta chips (see page 42) and you have one impressive and beautiful sharing plate of food.

1 Using a hand-held blender or a freestanding blender, blend all the dip ingredients together until smooth. Tip the dip out on to a serving plate, spread it out slightly, then top with the salad ingredients.

2 Combine all the dressing ingredients in a screw-top jar, put on the lid and shake to mix.

3 Pour the dressing over the salad and dip, then serve with pitta chips, pitta bread or crackers for dipping.

Gluten Free Serve with certified gluten-free crackers or corn tortilla chips.

TIPS & SWAPS
Use mixed salad leaves or
chopped gem lettuce instead
of pea shoots or rocket.

LEFTOVERS: see pp228–233

● Rocket or pea shoots
● Cherry tomatoes
● Fresh coriander
● Mint
● Pomegranate
● Spring onions
● Cooked kidney beans

SPICED SWEET POTATO FRIES WITH SMOKY DIP

I've gotta say that when it comes down to a toss up between regular and sweet potato fries, the latter always wins for me. There's no parboiling needed for these sunny wedges to caramelize and crisp up in the oven. It seems a shame to make some special homemade chips then drown them in overly sweet ketchup, but this smoky dip is a nicer alternative with a kick from the paprika and a creamy tang from the yogurt.

Serves 1–2

1 large or 2 small sweet potatoes
1 tablespoon cornflour (optional)*
½ teaspoon ground cinnamon
¼ teaspoon ground cayenne pepper
   or ½ teaspoon chilli flakes
2 teaspoons olive oil
generous pinch of salt

SMOKY DIP
3 tablespoons natural yogurt
   or crème fraîche
1 tablespoon tahini
juice of ½ lemon
1 garlic clove, crushed
   or very finely chopped
½ teaspoon sweet smoked paprika
½ teaspoon honey or maple syrup or 1
   teaspoon Date Paste (see page 221)

1 Preheat the oven to 180°C fan, 200°C, Gas Mark 6.

2 Peel the sweet potato and cut into chip-shaped wedges. Place on a baking tray, add the cornflour, if using, cinnamon and cayenne pepper or chilli flakes and toss until the sweet potato is coated. Drizzle with the oil, sprinkle with salt and toss again to coat.

3 Bake the wedges in the oven for 30 minutes, flipping them halfway through cooking with a metal spatula.

4 Stir the smoky dip ingredients together in a bowl and serve with the warm sweet potato wedges.

Vegan Use Chickpea Mayonnaise (see page 222), puréed silken tofu or unsweetened soya yogurt instead of the yogurt. Use date paste or maple syrup instead of the honey.

TIPS & SWAPS

*Adding the cornflour will make the sweet potato fries extra crispy.

Make some extra sweet potato wedges, tossed in oil and salt (but no spices or cornflour); roast on a separate tray.

LEFTOVERS: see pp228–233

● Sweet potato
● Tahini
● Yogurt or crème fraîche
● Lemon juice

SPICED SWEET POTATOES WITH RAW BEETROOT & MISO DRESSING

(V) (VG) (GF) (LS)

Serves 2

2 small sweet potatoes (about
   400g total), peeled and cut
   into about 3cm cubes
1 tablespoon olive oil
½ teaspoon ground coriander
½ teaspoon garam masala
¼ teaspoon ground cumin
pinch of salt
2 small or 1 large beetroot, rinsed
handful of mixed salad leaves
handful of walnuts, roughly chopped

MISO DRESSING
2 tablespoons miso, any kind
4 tablespoons olive oil
1 garlic clove, crushed
   or very finely chopped
1 shallot or ¼ red onion, finely diced
2 teaspoons granulated sugar or honey
1 tablespoon lemon juice or
   apple cider vinegar or rice vinegar

Here, squidgy, stubby pieces of sweet potato are tossed together with wispy shreds of beetroot in a salty, addictive miso dressing. It's a satisfying warm salad, which is best eaten from a bowl while you snuggle under a blanket, cross-legged on the sofa.

1 Preheat the oven to 180°C fan, 200°C, Gas Mark 6.

2 Spread the sweet potato cubes out on a baking tray, drizzle with the oil and sprinkle on the spices and a pinch of salt. Toss until the sweet potato is coated, then roast in the oven for 30 minutes, flipping halfway through cooking with a metal spatula.

3 Slice the beetroot as thinly as possible. Stack up a few slices at a time and cut into small matchsticks. Toss with the salad leaves and chopped nuts.

4 Combine all the dressing ingredients in a screw-top jar, put on the lid and shake to mix.

5 Drizzle some of the dressing over the salad leaves and toss to coat, then divide between 2 bowls or plates and top with the warm roasted sweet potato and extra dressing, if you like.

Vegan Use sugar in the dressing.

TIPS & SWAPS

Use pumpkin or sunflower
seeds instead of walnuts.

Use rocket, baby spinach, pea
shoots, chopped chicory or chopped
gem lettuce instead of mixed
salad leaves.

LEFTOVERS: see pp228–233

● Sweet potatoes
● Miso
● Red onion

A TRIO OF SLAWS

Slaw is a bit of a weird concept. It's like an overdressed mayo salad without any actual salad leaves. For a while this put me off, but when I discovered it can be made without the mayo and with loads of different vegetables I was sold. These are lovely as a side dish, spooned on a (veggie) burger, topped on a bowl of grains with dressing and a poached egg or tossed with some baby spinach for a ready-dressed salad – BOOM.

Serves 4–6

3 tablespoons sesame seeds
2 tablespoons tahini
juice of 1 lemon
1 garlic clove, crushed
½ teaspoon ground cumin
pinch of salt
25g raisins or chopped dried
    apricots
2 large carrots, shredded or grated
handful of fresh coriander
    (leaves and stems), finely chopped

TAHINI CARROT SLAW

1 Toast the sesame seeds in a small, dry frying pan over a high heat, stirring frequently, until browned.

2 Pour them into a medium bowl together with the tahini, lemon juice, garlic, cumin and salt and add enough water to thin the mixture to a pourable consistency.

3 Add the raisins or apricots, carrots and coriander and stir to combine, then serve. Cover and store in the refrigerator for up to 3 days.

LEFTOVERS: see pp228–233

● Fresh coriander
● Tahini
● Carrots
● Lemon

MISO MANGO SLAW

Serves 4–6

1 tablespoon miso, any kind
juice of ½ lime
2 tablespoons olive oil or extra virgin olive oil
½ large mango, flesh scooped from the skin and thinly sliced
¼ head of red or white cabbage, shredded
handful (about 10g) of fresh coriander
    (leaves and stems), roughly chopped
1 spring onion, finely sliced

1 Mix the miso, lime juice and oil together in a medium bowl.

2 Add the mango, cabbage, coriander and spring onion and stir to combine, then serve. Cover and store in the refrigerator for up to 3 days.

V GF EF LS

VG option

BROCCOLI APPLE YOGURT SLAW

Serves 4–6

4 tablespoons natural yogurt
½ teaspoon granulated sugar or honey
    or 1 teaspoon Date Paste (see page 221)
pinch of salt
2 teaspoons apple cider vinegar or lemon juice
½ head (about 80g) of broccoli
1 dessert apple, grated
1 small red onion, finely diced
25g walnuts, roughly chopped

1 Mix the yogurt, sugar, salt and vinegar or lemon juice in a medium bowl.

2 Thinly slice the broccoli, then cut the slices into thin matchsticks. It doesn't matter if the flowery part of the broccoli is crumbling everywhere. Sweep all of the broccoli into the bowl and add the grated apple, red onion and walnuts. Stir until everything is coated with the dressing, then serve. Cover and store in the refrigerator for up to 3 days.

Vegan Use Chickpea Mayonnaise (see page 222) or unsweetened soya yogurt instead of the yogurt. Use sugar or Date Paste.

LEFTOVERS: see pp228–233

- Mango
- Spring onions
- Fresh coriander
- Miso
- Lime juice
- Red or white cabbage

LEFTOVERS: see pp228–233

- Yogurt
- Apples

VG option

FALAFEL SMASH

This falafel smash comes together quickly using mainly cupboard-friendly ingredients and makes a super satisfying lunch or, when served with a fried egg and salad, a perfect dinner. I like to make my own bread so if you fancy doing the same, make your own pitta breads or flatbreads using the recipes towards the back of this book.

Serves 3–4

240g (½ can, drained weight) cooked
   chickpeas, drained and rinsed
¼ teaspoon salt
1 teaspoon ground cumin
1 teaspoon ground coriander
¼ teaspoon chilli flakes
juice of ½ lemon
1 tablespoon olive oil
4 tablespoons natural yogurt or
   unsweetened soya yogurt
a few handfuls of pea shoots or rocket
a few slices of Quick Pickled Red Onion
   (see page 223) or thinly sliced
   raw red onion
½ recipe for pitta breads or flatbreads
   (see page 215) or 4–6 shop-bought
   pitta breads

CORIANDER SAUCE
1 garlic clove, crushed or finely chopped
2 large handfuls (about 30g)
   of fresh coriander, finely chopped
   (including stems)
4 tablespoons olive oil
   (I like to use extra virgin, here)
2 tablespoons sesame seeds, toasted*
generous pinch of salt

1 Slightly mash the chickpeas in a bowl with the back of a fork or pulse them briefly in a food processor or blender, if you have one. Stir in the salt, cumin, coriander, chilli flakes, lemon juice and oil.

2 Stir all the ingredients for the coriander sauce together in a small bowl.

3 Layer up the yogurt, the pea shoots or rocket, chickpea mixture, coriander sauce and pickled or raw red onion on to the breads and serve.

Vegan Use non-dairy yogurt or Avocado Cream (see page 219) instead of the yogurt.

TIPS & SWAPS
*To toast sesame seeds place them in a dry frying pan and stir over a high heat until they smell toasty and turn golden.

If you're cooking for only 1–2 people, keep leftovers in the refrigerator. It will make an easy lunch in the next couple of days, served with bread or a tortilla.

LEFTOVERS: see pp228–233

- Cooked chickpeas
- Fresh coriander
- Red onion
- Yogurt
- Lemon juice
- Pea shoots or rocket

VG option

BEETROOT FLATBREAD

Serves 4–6

1 tablespoon olive oil, plus extra
    for greasing
4 small or 2 large beetroot
½ recipe for pizza dough (see page 220)
    or 1 recipe for unbaked pitta bread
    dough (see page 215)
4 tablespoons balsamic vinegar
1 tablespoon granulated sugar
50g feta, crumbled
5 sprigs of thyme
salt

This pretty little dish has a great combo of flavours – there is sweetness from the beetroot, salt from the feta and the sugary balsamic vinegar mix gives the dish a lovely tart taste. I usually make this recipe when I've got some pizza or flatbread dough sitting in the refrigerator from a previous day so I have less prep to do.

1 Preheat the oven to 180°C fan, 200°C, Gas Mark 6.

2 Wrap the beetroot in foil and bake in the oven for 45–60 minutes, depending on size, until fork-tender. Unwrap and leave them to cool slightly.

3 Rub the beetroot skins under cool running water to remove them, then slice the beetroot into 2mm thick coins.

4 Meanwhile, prepare the dough according to the recipe on page 220 or page 215.

5 Preheat the oven to 200°C fan, 220°C, Gas Mark 7 and grease a baking tray with a little oil.

6 Press the dough out on the prepared baking tray into a rough 24 x 20cm oval shape. Arrange slices of the beetroot on top, sprinkle with salt and drizzle with the olive oil. Bake in the oven for 20–25 minutes until the edges are golden.

7 Heat the balsamic vinegar and sugar in a small pan over a medium heat for 1 minute until it is reduced and thick. Drizzle over the flatbread then sprinkle on the feta and thyme to serve.

Vegan Use Sun Feta (see page 219) instead of the feta or chop a handful of pitted black olives and sprinkle those over instead.

TIPS & SWAPS

Use 2 tablespoons 'balsamic glaze' instead of the combo of the balsamic vinegar and sugar.

Roll out 250g vegetarian shop-bought puff pastry on a lightly floured work surface to about 5mm thick. Prick all over with a fork, then top with the cooked beetroot slices and bake as in the recipe.

Roast extra beetroot and store in the the refrigerator for up to 3 days.

LEFTOVERS: see pp228–233

- Beetroot
- Feta
- Thyme

V **VG** **GF** **LS**

CHILLI-ROASTED POTATOES WITH GRANOLA & LIME-SOY DRESSING

Serves 3–4

2 medium white potatoes
(e.g. Maris Piper, King Edward),
cut into about 3cm cubes
2 medium sweet potatoes, peeled and
cut into about 3cm cubes
1 tablespoon olive oil or rapeseed oil
½ teaspoon chilli flakes
a few handfuls of rocket
2 spring onions, finely sliced
½ red chilli, deseeded and thinly sliced
salt

GRANOLA

4 tablespoons rolled oats
3 tablespoons pumpkin seeds
small handful (about 20g) cashews or
peanuts, roughly chopped
1 tablespoon olive oil or rapeseed oil
1 teaspoon soy sauce or tamari
1 teaspoon honey or maple syrup
or golden syrup

LIME-SOY DRESSING

1 tablespoon soy sauce or tamari
2 teaspoons honey or maple syrup
or golden syrup
juice of 1 lime
1 tablespoon toasted sesame oil

If stovetop granola is a new concept to you, get ready for a revelation. It's super-quick to toast up oats with crunchy nuts and seeds and coat them in a delicious mix of honey and soy sauce. It's then sprinkled on a mix of roasted sweet and white potatoes with a dressing kissed with toasted sesame oil and lime. It's gorgeous warm or cold.

1 Preheat the oven to 180°C fan, 200°C, Gas Mark 6.

2 Place the white potatoes in a large pan of boiling water. Salt well then bring to the boil over a high heat. Reduce the heat to a simmer and cook for 5 minutes. Drain the potatoes then return them to the pan and cover with a lid. Set aside for 5 minutes so the potatoes absorb excess moisture.

3 Toss the cooked potatoes and raw sweet potato with the oil, a generous pinch of salt and the chilli flakes on a baking tray. Roast in the oven for 50–60 minutes until golden, flipping them halfway through.

4 To make the granola, toast the oats, pumpkin seeds and cashews or peanuts in a frying pan over a medium-high heat, stirring frequently, until it all smells nutty and is beginning to brown. Reduce the heat to low then pour in the oil and stir to coat the oats. Make a well in the centre of the mixture, add the soy sauce or tamari and honey or syrup and stir into the oats until coated. Tip out on to a plate and leave to cool and crisp up.

5 Mix all the dressing ingredients together in a small bowl. Pour the mixture over the roasted potatoes and stir to coat with the dressing. Divide the rocket between serving plates, top with the dressed potatoes, then sprinkle with the granola, spring onions and sliced chilli to serve.

Vegan Use golden syrup or maple syrup in the granola and dressing.

Gluten Free Make sure your oats and tamari or soy sauce are certified gluten free.

TIPS & SWAPS

If you have roasted sweet potatoes and white potatoes to hand use them instead of the raw potatoes. Skip steps 2 and 3 and spread the potatoes on a baking tray, then place in an oven preheated to 180°C fan, 200°C, Gas Mark 6 for 10 minutes until warmed through. Continue with the recipe.

LEFTOVERS: see pp228–233

- White potatoes
  (raw or roasted)
- Sweet potatoes
  (raw or roasted)
- Spring onions
- Red chilli

SWEET MISO AUBERGINE & WALNUT SALAD

Serves 3–4

2 large aubergines, sliced into
   5mm-thick coins
2–3 tablespoons toasted sesame oil
1 tablespoon sesame seeds, toasted*
handful of pea shoots
2 large handfuls of salad leaves
   or baby spinach
small handful (30g) of walnuts,
   roughly chopped

GLAZE

2 tablespoons miso, any kind
juice of ½ lime or lemon
1 garlic clove
1 tablespoon granulated sugar or
   honey or 2 tablespoons Date Paste
   (see page 221)
4 tablespoons water

DRESSING

2 teaspoons finely chopped or grated
   fresh root ginger
juice of ½ lemon or lime
1 teaspoon honey or maple syrup
2 tablespoons soy sauce or tamari
1 spring onion, finely sliced
2 tablespoons olive oil or rapeseed oil

You may have noticed that I love miso. I use it in so many dishes instead of salt to punch up the umami flavours. This salad is based on one of my favourite miso dishes, a Japanese recipe called 'Nasu Dengaku'. Instead of halving the aubergines and brushing them with glaze, I slice them into coins to create more area for that salty-sweet miso mixture to cling to.

1 Preheat the oven to 180°C fan, 200°C, Gas Mark 6.

2 Lay the aubergine slices on a baking tray (you may need to do this in batches) and score a shallow crosshatch pattern into the slices with the tip of a knife. Drizzle with sesame oil and bake in the oven for 10 minutes to soften.

3 Meanwhile, mix all the glaze ingredients in a small pan, stirring frequently over a medium heat, for 1 minute. Remove from the heat and brush or spoon the glaze over the aubergine slices. Return to the oven for a further 20 minutes, then sprinkle with toasted sesame seeds and leave to cool.

4 Mix all the dressing ingredients together in a screw-top jar, put on the lid and shake to combine.

5 Arrange the pea shoots and salad leaves or spinach on a plate and pour over the dressing. Toss the salad, then adorn with the cooled aubergine and walnuts.

Vegan Use sugar or Date Paste in the glaze. Use maple syrup in the dressing.

Gluten Free Ensure your tamari or soy sauce is certified gluten-free.

LEFTOVERS: see pp228–233

- Aubergines
- Miso
- Baby spinach
- Pea shoots

TIPS & SWAPS

*Toast the sesame seeds in a dry frying pan over a high heat.

Can't find pea shoots? Use extra salad leaves instead.

LIME-CHILLI CORN & CRISPY ONIONS

Serves 2

3 tablespoons rapeseed oil or olive oil
½ red onion, thinly sliced
1 tablespoon plain flour
2 ears of fresh corn, kernels
   cut off with a knife
1½ teaspoons honey
juice of ½ lime
½–1 jalapeño chilli, finely chopped
30g feta, crumbled
salt

Sautéed fresh corn is the ultimate way to eat corn in my opinion. It has that crisp bite which I want to describe as al dente but in a non-pasta way. Coupled with a bit of balance from the lime juice and some addictively crispy slices of fried onion, this takes fresh corn to the next level. Sprinkle over crumbled feta for that salty, creamy something, but finely grated Parmesan or Cheddar are also banging substitutions.

1 Line a plate with kitchen paper. Heat the oil in a small frying pan over a high heat. Reduce the heat to medium-low, then toss the onion with the flour and fry in the oil until golden. Remove the onion from the pan with a spoon or tongs, leaving behind some of the oil and place them on to the prepared plate. Sprinkle with salt and set aside.

2 Place the pan back on the heat. Add the corn kernels and turn the heat up to high. Cook, stirring occasionally, until the corn is nice and hot. Add the honey, lime juice and jalapeño chilli and stir to combine. Season with salt to taste.

3 Remove the pan from the heat and transfer to a serving platter. Adorn with some crumbled feta and the crispy onions and serve.

Vegan Use Sun Feta (see page 219) or ½ cubed avocado instead of the feta. Use maple syrup instead of honey.

Gluten Free Use cornflour, rice flour or gram flour to coat the red onion before frying.

TIPS & SWAPS

No fresh corn? Use 200g drained, canned sweetcorn or defrosted frozen corn instead.

Use an equal weight of finely grated Parmesan or Gruyère instead of the feta.

LEFTOVERS: see pp228–233

- Chilli
- Feta
- Red onion
- Lime juice

ROASTED BEETROOT, CUMIN & CRISPY CHICKPEAS

Serves 2–3

2 small or 1 large beetroot
3 tablespoons olive oil
120g (½ can, drained weight)
   cooked chickpeas, drained and rinsed
juice of ½ lemon
5 tablespoons Greek yogurt
1 teaspoon cumin seeds
½ teaspoon ground coriander
¼ teaspoon smoked paprika
small handful of mint leaves,
   roughly chopped
salt

The fuchsia-pink vibrancy that you get from puréed beetroot always gives me heart-eye-emoji feelings when I see it. The addition of yogurt adds a slight piquancy and creaminess. The scattering of chickpeas on top is needed to mop up that sexy sauce while the tempered spices and a sprinkle of mint bring the whole dish together. Serve with flatbread (see page 215) or tortillas (see page 214) for a lunch to make you smile.

1 Preheat the oven to 180°C fan, 200°C, Gas Mark 6. Wrap the beetroot in foil and roast in the oven for 1 hour, or until tender.

2 Heat 1 tablespoon of the oil in a frying pan over a high heat. Add the chickpeas and season with a pinch of salt. Cook, stirring frequently, until the chickpeas are just starting to brown.

3 Remove the beetroot from the oven. Leave to cool for at least 15 minutes, then rub the beetroot under cool running water to remove the skins. Chop half of the beetroot into small cubes and toss with the lemon juice

4 Blend the other half of the cooked beetroot with a hand-held blender or freestanding blender or mash with a potato masher until smooth. Mix the yogurt and a generous pinch of salt into the beetroot, pour on to a serving plate and top with the cubed beetroot and chickpeas.

5 Heat the cumin seeds in a dry frying pan over a high heat for 1 minute. Add the remaining oil, ground coriander and smoked paprika, stir to mix, then remove from the heat. Pour over the beetroot and chickpeas, then top with the mint and serve.

Vegan Use unsweetened soya yogurt or puréed silken tofu and 1 tablespoon lemon juice instead of the yogurt.

TIPS & SWAPS

If you have some whole, roasted beetroot to hand use it. Skip step 1 and continue with the recipe.

This makes a great lunchbox dish as it's delicious served cold with a tortilla.

Use cooked green or Puy lentils instead of chickpeas.

LEFTOVERS: see pp228–233

● Beetroot, raw or roasted
● Cooked chickpeas
● Yogurt
● Lemon juice
● Mint

GINGER-PICKLED MUSHROOMS WITH DATE RICE

Serves 2

100g mushrooms, cleaned
100ml rice vinegar
  or apple cider vinegar
100ml water
½ teaspoon salt
20g piece of fresh root ginger,
  peeled and cut into matchsticks
  (about 3 tablespoons matchsticks)
75g uncooked brown rice, rinsed
  or 140g cooked brown rice
½ tablespoon olive oil
50g frozen, shelled edamame beans
3 dried dates, pitted
  and roughly chopped
1 garlic clove, very finely chopped
1 teaspoon dark soy sauce
  or tamari
handful of baby spinach
1 spring onion, finely sliced

Pickling mushrooms seems a bit weird, I know. However, with the clean flavour from the rice vinegar and the spicy spears of ginger you may just fall in love with them. A few pickled mushrooms will go a long way to bring a lift to whatever dish you add them to. Use them in noodle salads or miso-based soups, or here with some date-speckled brown rice.

1 If you have some larger mushrooms (chestnut, button, shiitake), cut them into slices. Smaller mushrooms like enoki or shimeji mushrooms are fine to leave whole. Place the mushrooms in a small bowl or clean jar.

2 Heat the vinegar, water, salt and ginger together in a small pan until it is simmering. Pour the mixture over the mushrooms and set aside for at least 30 minutes.

3 If starting with uncooked brown rice, place the rice in a medium pan and pour in enough water until well covered. Season with salt and bring to the boil. Reduce the heat and simmer for 20 minutes for long-grain brown rice or 30 minutes for short-grain brown rice, adding more water if needed. Once cooked, drain the rice and return it to the pan. Cover with a lid and leave for 5 minutes to absorb the excess moisture.

4 Heat the oil in a frying pan over a medium heat. Add the frozen edamame beans and sauté for 2 minutes until hot. Add the dates, cooked rice and garlic and sauté for a further minute, then add the soy sauce or tamari and stir until coated.

5 Place the spinach in a serving bowl and pour the rice over the top. Garnish with 3 tablespoons of the mushrooms, and some of the ginger from the pickle too, if you like. Finally, add the spring onion. Eat warm.

Gluten Free Ensure that you are using a certified gluten-free tamari or soy sauce.

LEFTOVERS: see pp228–233

● Mushrooms
● Brown rice, uncooked or cooked
● Dates
● Spring onions
● Baby spinach

TIPS & SWAPS
Top with a halved, soft-boiled egg. Simmer the egg in its shell in boiling water for 5–6 minutes, then place it in a bowl of cold water before peeling.

Keep any excess mushrooms in a sterilized, sealed jar for up to 1 week in the refrigerator.

GF option

ROASTED CARROTS WITH COUSCOUS & PICKLED ONION

Serves 2–3

200g carrots
2 tablespoons olive oil
150g couscous
200ml boiling water
5 tablespoons pesto, homemade
    (see pages 224–225) or
    shop-bought
juice of ½ lemon
handful of Quick Pickled Red Onion
    (see page 223)
50g pitted black olives, roughly chopped
salt

Sweet and soft coins of roasted carrot meet herby pesto and toasty couscous, while the salty, tangy nuggets of olives and Quick Pickled Red Onion ping some extra life into this dish. It's a great side salad at dinner or casual lunch (especially with a fried egg on top).

1 Preheat the oven to 200°C fan, 220°C, Gas Mark 7.

2 If you have baby carrots (the small ones with the greens still attached), cut off the carrot tops. For standard carrots, cut into coins about 3mm thick. Toss the baby carrots or carrot coins with 1 tablespoon of the oil and a pinch of salt on a baking tray, then roast in the oven for 20–25 minutes, flipping halfway through cooking. They should be soft and sweet.

3 Meanwhile, place the couscous in a large bowl and pour over the measured boiling water. Cover with a plate and set aside for about 5–10 minutes, or until all the water has been absorbed, then transfer to a plate and fluff the couscous with a fork. Stir in the remaining oil, the pesto and lemon juice. Season with salt to taste, then tip out on to a plate. Top with the roasted carrots, pickled onion and black olives. Serve warm or cold.

Vegan If using shop-bought pesto, make sure it is certified vegan.

Gluten Free Instead of couscous, cook 150g quinoa or brown rice according to the table on page 11.

TIPS & SWAPS

Try cooked green or Puy lentils, orzo or Israeli couscous (sometimes called pearl couscous or fregola) instead of regular couscous.

Use 150g of ready-roasted carrots, butternut squash or sweet potato instead of the raw carrots. Skip steps 1 and 2 and continue with the recipe.

Sprinkle some crumbled feta or dry-fried pieces of halloumi over the top.

LEFTOVERS: see pp228–233

● Lemon juice
● Carrots, raw or roasted
● Pesto

AUBERGINE, POMEGRANATE & CHICKPEA SALAD

(V) (VG) (GF) (LS)

Serves 2–3

2 medium aubergines, cut into about
   3mm coins
2 tablespoons olive oil or rapeseed oil
2 tablespoons lemon juice
2 teaspoons granulated sugar or honey
pinch of salt
handful of mint, finely chopped
½–1 red chilli, finely chopped
   (depending on taste)
2 large handfuls of baby spinach,
   rinsed if needed
120g (½ can, drained weight) cooked
   chickpeas, drained and rinsed
seeds from ½ pomegranate
2 tablespoons tahini

TO SERVE
pitta bread or crusty bread (optional)

Aubergines are definitely best a little burnt. Thinly slicing them means that you increase the surface area of their spongy inner flesh so they are the perfect receptacle for soaking up a tangy, sweet dressing.

1 Lay the sliced aubergine out on a baking tray or chopping board in a single layer. Use a spoon to drizzle half the oil over the top of the aubergine layers, then use your hands to spread it around to coat the top of the slices. Flip the slices over and repeat on the other side with the remaining oil.

2 Mix the lemon juice, sugar or honey, salt, mint and chilli together in a medium bowl to make a dressing.

3 Heat a stovetop grill pan or large, nonstick pan over a high heat. Once the pan is hot add a few aubergine coins and cook for 3–4 minutes, or until they are dark underneath (we are talking verging on burnt here), then flip them over and cook until the other side is golden. Transfer the cooked aubergine to the bowl with the dressing and toss until the aubergine is coated all over. Continue until all the aubergine slices are cooked. Leave to cool for at least 30 minutes or up to 12 hours in the refrigerator.

4 Arrange the spinach on a serving platter and top with the marinated aubergine, drained chickpeas and pomegranate seeds. Drizzle with the tahini and serve. I like it with pitta bread or crusty bread for lunch or as a side with dinner.

Vegan Use granulated sugar.

LEFTOVERS: see pp228–233

- Red chilli
- Mint
- Cooked chickpeas
- Pomegranate
- Baby spinach
- Tahini
- Aubergine
- Lemon juice

TIPS & SWAPS

Replace the pomegranate seeds with a handful of fresh raspberries.

Use courgettes instead of the aubergines. Trim 2 medium courgettes then cut them into long slices about 3mm thick.

To make the tahini easy to drizzle, give the jar a good stir or combine 2 tablespoons tahini with 1 tablespoon extra virgin olive oil.

Use cooked green or Puy lentils instead of chickpeas.

GF & VG options

CHICKPEA 'TUNA' SALAD

Serves 2–3

120g (½ can, drained weight) cooked
   chickpeas, drained* and rinsed
1 dessert apple, core removed and
   flesh roughly chopped
1 celery stick, finely chopped
½ small red onion, finely chopped
1 medium carrot, grated
4–5 tablespoons natural yogurt,
   mayonnaise or Chickpea Mayonnaise
   (see page 222)
pinch of granulated sugar
juice of ½ lemon
2 tablespoons olive oil
handful of fresh coriander, roughly
   chopped
salt and freshly ground pepper

TO SERVE
crusty wholemeal bread or tortillas

The idea of using canned chickpeas instead of tuna is an idea I picked up from a few vegan blogs. It's just as convenient to mash up this mixture as it is to make a usual tuna salad, which I know many people rely on for quick lunches. The combo of flavours may sound weird but my mum has been making this for years with canned albacore tuna instead of the chickpeas.

1 Place the chickpeas in a bowl and lightly mash with a fork until they are still slightly chunky. Add the apple, celery, onion and carrot and stir together. Mix in the yogurt or mayonnaise, the sugar, lemon juice and oil and stir to combine, then season with salt and pepper to taste.

2 Top the salad with the chopped coriander and serve with crusty bread or tortillas.

Vegan Use Chickpea Mayonnaise (see page 222).

Gluten Free Serve with warmed gluten-free corn tortillas instead of bread.

TIPS & SWAPS

*If making the vegan Chickpea Mayonnaise, reserve the liquid from the canned chickpeas (or the cooking liquid, if you have cooked them yourself) to use in the recipe.

Replace the chickpeas with cannellini or haricot beans.

LEFTOVERS: see pp228–233

● Cooked chickpeas
● Apples
● Celery
● Carrots
● Lemon juice
● Yogurt
● Fresh coriander
● Red onion

CANNELLINI BEANS
WITH BALSAMIC ONIONS

Serves 2 as a side

75g runner or string beans, trimmed
   and cut into about 3cm lengths
1 tablespoon olive oil or rapeseed oil
1 red onion, cut into 2mm-thick slices
pinch of salt
2 tablespoons balsamic vinegar
200g cherry tomatoes, quartered
120g (½ can, drained weight) cannellini
   beans, drained and rinsed
pinch of granulated sugar
handful of basil leaves, torn

This light summer stew of sorts makes the most of seasonal produce. The cherry tomatoes break down slightly into a barely cooked sauce to keep the dish fresh and quick. In the winter use green or red cabbage in place of the beans and half a can of chopped tomatoes in place of the cherry tomatoes.

1 Cover the green beans with just-boiled water in a small pan. Bring to the boil, then reduce the heat and simmer for 3 minutes. Drain and set aside.

2 Heat the oil in a frying pan over a medium heat. Add the onion and salt and cook, stirring frequently, until it begins to darken in colour. Splash in a few tablespoons water and continue to stir until the water has mostly evaporated. Add the balsamic vinegar and stir again.

3 Add the cherry tomatoes and a few more tablespoons water and cook until the water has evaporated and the tomatoes have softened, about 7–10 minutes. Stir in the cooked green beans and the cannellini beans and cook for about 1 minute, just to heat them through. Stir in the sugar and serve warm with the torn basil.

TIPS & SWAPS

For a main-sized salad for 2, double the recipe and serve with steamed spinach or kale and wholemeal bread.

For a simple lunch, double everything except the green beans and cannellini beans. Cook 100g dried wholemeal pasta until al dente, reserving some of the pasta water. Follow the recipe as above, then stir in the cooked pasta and loosen it with some of the reserved pasta water.

Use cooked green or Puy lentils instead of canellini beans.

LEFTOVERS: see pp228–233

- Green beans
- Cherry tomatoes
- Cannellini beans
- Basil

V **VG** **GF** **LS**

BEETROOT, HAZELNUT & CRISPY SAGE SALAD

Serves 2–3

2 medium or 3 small beetroot, thinly sliced
3 tablespoons olive oil or rapeseed oil
6–10 sage leaves, depending on size
120g (½ can, drained weight) cooked cannellini or haricot beans, drained and rinsed
30g hazelnuts
generous pinch of granulated sugar
3 tablespoons balsamic vinegar
2 tablespoons extra virgin olive oil
juice of ½ lemon
salt

This is a salad with which to embrace autumn. The ingredients in this salad seem to be made for each other with their earthy flavours. I love to combine raw and cooked sliced beetroot because the textures are so different but complement each other so well. If you manage to find some pretty Chioggia beetroot (those 'candy stripe' ones) it's a great way to display their stunning interiors.

1 Preheat the oven to 180°C fan, 200°C, Gas Mark 6.

2 Toss half of the sliced beetroot in 1 teaspoon of the olive oil and a pinch of salt. Spread in a single layer over a baking tray and bake in the oven for 10 minutes until softened.

3 Heat the remaining oil in a small frying pan over a medium heat. Add the sage leaves and cook until crispy, then remove with a slotted spoon and drain on kitchen paper.

4 Keeping the pan of oil on the heat, pour in the beans and a pinch of salt and cook until the beans are slightly crisp and beginning to colour. Place the beans in a bowl.

5 Return the pan to a medium heat and add the hazelnuts. Toast for 1 minute, then add the sugar, balsamic vinegar and a pinch of salt and then stir for 2 minutes until thickened and sticky. Turn off the heat and leave to cool.

6 Add the baked beetroot and raw beetroot to the bowl with the beans. Pour in the extra virgin olive oil, lemon juice and candied hazelnuts and toss together. Tip out on to a serving plate and top with the crispy sage.

LEFTOVERS: see pp230–233

- Beetroot
- Sage leaves
- Lemon juice
- Cannellini beans

TIPS & SWAPS

Replace the hazelnuts with walnuts or pumpkin seeds.

Use an equal weight of lentils instead of the cannellini beans. Refer to the cooking table on page 11 if you need guidance.

If you can't find sage, use (unfried) basil or thyme instead.

CHARRED LETTUCE WITH BAKED TOFU & PEANUT DRESSING

Serves 2

200g firm tofu
1 tablespoon olive oil or rapeseed oil
1 tablespoon soy sauce or tamari
2 teaspoons sesame seeds
2 heads of gem lettuce
4 teaspoons olive oil or rapeseed oil
1 radish, thinly sliced
1 spring onion, finely chopped
1 red chilli, finely chopped (optional)

PEANUT GINGER DRESSING
2 tablespoons peanut butter, almond
    butter, cashew butter or tahini
1 teaspoon granulated sugar
    or honey or 1 tablespoon
    Date Paste (see page 221)
juice of ½ lime
1 tablespoon soy sauce or tamari
1 teaspoon grated fresh root ginger

If you're not convinced by tofu, try it baked. It's less fuss and healthier than fried tofu and produces the cutest crisp, golden cubes. I like to double the recipe and keep the extra tofu in the fridge for a few days – it provides a great protein boost for salads, stir fries or tacos. Grilling the lettuce might seem weird but I love it – you end up with half the lettuce charred, warm and wilted and the rest still crisp and cooling.

1 To press the tofu, wrap it in a clean tea towel and place on a flat surface. Cover with a chopping board, then weigh the chopping board down with something heavy, such as a stack of cookbooks or a pan full of water. Leave for 30 minutes to drain.

2 Preheat the oven to 180°C fan, 200°C, Gas Mark 6 and line a baking tray with nonstick baking paper.

3 Unwrap the tofu, cut it into 1cm cubes and place in a bowl. Add the oil and soy sauce or tamari and toss until the tofu is coated all over. Sprinkle over the sesame seeds and toss again. Spread out on the prepared baking tray and bake in the oven for 30 minutes until golden.

4 Cut the lettuce heads in half and drizzle the cut sides with oil. Place them cut-side down in a frying pan or griddle pan, if you have one, over the highest heat. I can fit 2 halves at a time into my pan. Cook for about 4 minutes, or until the underside is blackened. Place on a plate.

5 Mix all the dressing ingredients together in a bowl until smooth. Add a little water to thin the dressing into a drizzle-able sauce.

6 Drizzle the sauce over the charred lettuce and top with the baked tofu, thinly sliced radish, chopped spring onion and chilli to serve.

Vegan Use sugar or Date Paste.

Gluten Free Make sure that you are using a certified gluten-free tamari or soy sauce.

TIPS & SWAPS
If you drain and bake double the tofu, double up on the olive oil, soy and sesame seeds. Use the extra tofu as snacks or with steamed veg for a quick dinner.

Asian supermarkets will usually have tofu in their chiller cabinets. Drain before using.

Serve with brown rice for a more filling dish.

LEFTOVERS: see pp228–233

- Red chilli
- Nut butter or tahini
- Spring onions
- Lime juice
- Firm tofu

GF option

SQUASH, POTATO & CHILLI CAKES

Makes 6–8

200g butternut squash, peeled
   (about ⅙ large or ⅓ small)
200g white potatoes
   (about 2 medium)
3 tablespoons plain flour
2 spring onions, very finely chopped
½ red chilli, very finely chopped
   or ¼ teaspoon dried chilli flakes
generous pinch of salt
olive oil or rapeseed oil, for cooking

Both butternut squash and potatoes can keep at room temperature for quite a while. I always feel happy knowing I have a stock of squash, which I buy in the autumn, sitting on my windowsill to use for a few months. These fritters are very basic but I love the bite of the chilli and the fresh flavour of the spring onions. They are great with a fried egg and some greens for lunch or with rice, Tahini Dressing (see page 226), chopped coriander and steamed greens for dinner.

1 Line a plate with kitchen paper.

2 Coarsely grate the butternut squash and potato and place on a square of muslin or a clean tea towel. Gather up the edges at the top to make a little bundle, then squeeze over the sink to remove as much liquid as possible. Dump the squeezed squash and potato into a medium bowl, add the flour, spring onions, chilli and the salt and use your hands to combine it all together.

3 Heat just enough oil to coat the base of a nonstick pan over a medium heat. Once the oil is hot place heaped tablespoons of the mixture into the pan. I can fit 3–5 in my frying pan depending on how strategically I place them. Flatten each mound down with the back of the spoon so you have little fritters, then cook until dark golden and crispy underneath. Flip them over and cook until the other side is golden too. Transfer to the prepared plate and cook the remaining mixture as before, adding more oil to the pan as needed.

Gluten Free Use gram (chickpea) flour instead of the plain flour.

TIPS & SWAPS
Use grated raw
sweet potato instead of the
butternut squash.

LEFTOVERS: see pp228–233

● Butternut squash (raw)
● White potatoes
● Spring onions
● Red chilli

SPANAKOPITA QUESADILLAS

Makes 3

200g baby spinach
200g cavolo nero
  (weighed with the stems)
50g Cheddar cheese, grated
50g feta cheese, crumbled
1 teaspoon mixed dried herbs or 3 sprigs
  of fresh thyme, stems removed
1 egg
generous pinch of salt
3 teaspoons olive oil or rapeseed oil
3 large wholemeal tortillas
  or 6 small wholemeal tortillas

TO SERVE
Pea Hummus (see page 46)

This stroke of genius happened when my friend Sam couldn't find filo pastry to make me a birthday spanakopita. He turned to tortillas instead and I'm glad he did — they were so good!

1   Place the spinach and cavolo nero in a large pan with a little water over a medium heat. Cover with a lid, reduce the heat to low and leave for a few minutes to wilt.

2   Once wilted, rinse the greens under cold running water, then squeeze as much water out as possible. Roughly chop the greens and add to a medium bowl with the cheeses, herbs, egg and salt and stir until evenly mixed.

3   Heat 1 teaspoon of the oil in a large frying pan over a medium heat. Tilt the pan so the oil spreads to cover the base of the pan. Place 1 tortilla into the pan and cover half of it with one-third of the spinach mixture. Fold the tortilla in half up and over the filling and press down to seal. Cook over a medium-low heat until the underside is golden, then flip over and cook the other side until golden. Transfer to a plate and repeat with the rest of the filling and tortillas.

4   Cut the tortillas into wedges and eat hot with Pea Hummus!

COURGETTE & GARLIC QUESADILLA

Serves 2

1 tablespoon olive oil
1 medium courgette, coarsely grated
1 garlic clove, crushed
  or very finely chopped
2 large wholemeal tortillas
handful of grated Cheddar cheese
a few basil leaves, torn
salt

TO SERVE
natural yogurt (optional)

Simple, quick and tasty, this is my go-to lunch when I need something hot and carby to fill me up. By grating the courgette you'll go from zero to food in about 10 minutes.

1   Heat the oil in a medium frying pan over a medium heat. Add the courgette and garlic and sauté for 1–2 minutes until softened. Season with salt to taste and transfer to a plate. Wipe out the pan and place it back on the heat.

2   Place a tortilla in the frying pan, then sprinkle half the cheese over the surface of the tortilla. Sprinkle the basil over the cheese, then spread half the cooked courgette over half the tortilla. Fold the tortilla in half to cover the filling and cook until golden underneath. Flip over and cook until the other side is golden. Remove from the pan and cut into 2 wedges. Repeat with the last tortilla and remaining filling. Eat warm with yogurt for dipping!

TIPS & SWAPS

Spanakopita Quesadillas can be kept
in the refrigerator in clingfilm for up to
3 days. Reheat in a dry frying pan over
a medium heat to serve.

Use 50g grated or chopped mozzarella
cheese instead of the Cheddar in the
Spanakopita Quesadillas for a more
gooey quesadilla.

LEFTOVERS: see pp228-233

- Feta
- Baby spinach
- Cavolo nero
- Thyme

- Courgettes
- Basil
- Yogurt

VG option

ROASTED TOMATOES & CARROTS WITH BLACK BEANS & TAHINI

Serves 2–3

200g carrots
200g cherry tomatoes, halved
1 tablespoon olive oil or rapeseed oil
120g (½ can, drained weight) cooked
   black beans, drained and rinsed
handful of fresh coriander,
   roughly chopped
handful of mint, roughly chopped
5–6 dried dates, pitted and
   roughly chopped
1 tablespoon pomegranate molasses

SAUCE
2 tablespoons tahini
½ teaspoon ground turmeric
3 tablespoons natural yogurt
juice of ½ lemon
pinch of salt

Roasting carrots is something I never used to do, but then I realized they are the quicker, cheaper cousin to sweet potatoes or butternut squash. When I find them, I like to use baby carrots that come tied in a bunch with a head of luscious carrot tops – I wash the tops, cut them off and use them instead of rocket in my Basil & Rocket Pesto (see page 224).

1 Preheat the oven to 200°C fan, 220°C, Gas Mark 7 and line a baking tray with nonstick baking paper.

2 If you have baby carrots, just wash them and remove the tops. If you have regular carrots, cut them into about 4mm-thick coins.

3 Toss the tomatoes and carrots in the oil and place on the baking tray. Roast in the oven for 30 minutes, tossing them with a spatula halfway through.

4 Mix all the ingredients for the sauce in a small bowl. Spread the mixture on to a serving plate. Top with the black beans, the roasted tomatoes and carrots, the herbs and the dates and drizzle with pomegranate molasses.

Vegan Use Chickpea Mayonnaise (see page 222) or unsweetened soya yogurt in the sauce.

LEFTOVERS: see pp228–233

● Tahini
● Lemon juice
● Yogurt
● Carrots (raw or roasted)
● Cherry tomatoes (raw or roasted)
● Fresh coriander
● Mint
● Dates
● Cooked black beans

TIPS & SWAPS

Omit the pomegranate molasses and cook 4 tablespoons balsamic vinegar with 2 teaspoons granulated sugar in a small pan over a low heat for 1–2 minutes until reduced and syrupy.

Use any beans. I like chickpeas or kidney beans.

Instead of fresh tomatoes, use 120g oil-packed, sun-dried tomatoes and toss them into the dish at the end.

A sprinkle of pomegranate seeds is a colourful, crunchy addition.

V VG

GF option

CORN, PEACH & PEARL BARLEY SALAD

Serves 2–3

60g pearl barley
  or 180g cooked pearl barley
2 ears fresh corn*, corn kernels
  cut off with a knife
1 peach, pitted and cut into eighths
½ red onion, thinly sliced
handful of sorrel leaves or baby spinach
3 tablespoons pumpkin seeds
juice of ½ lime
¼ teaspoon smoked paprika
salt

BASIL AVOCADO DRESSING
½ an avocado, pitted and peeled
10g (a large handful) basil leaves
pinch of salt
3 tablespoons water
juice of ½ lime

If you have half an avocado slowly turning brown in the refrigerator and you know you're not going to smash it on to some toast, why not turn it into dressing? It's a great way to use it up. Having that creamy, light dressing on chewy pearl barley with fresh peaches and corn is a summer salad delight.

1   Place the pearl barley in a small pan and cover with cold water. Bring to the boil, reduce the heat and simmer for 30–40 minutes or until cooked. Drain, rinse, drain again well and spread out on a serving plate to cool.

2   Meanwhile, blend all the ingredients for the dressing together by mashing the avocado with a fork until smooth, then finely chopping the basil and stirring it in to the avocado with the salt, water and lime juice. It will be quite a thick consistency. Alternatively, use a hand-held blender in a jug or a freestanding blender.

3   Scatter the corn kernels over the pearl barley along with the peach and onion, then toss with the sorrel or spinach and a pinch of salt until combined.

4   Toast the pumpkin seeds in a small dry frying pan over a high heat, stirring frequently, until they start to pop. Remove from the heat and pour into a bowl. Squeeze over the lime juice, then add the paprika and a pinch of salt and stir until the seeds are coated in the mixture. Sprinkle over the salad and drizzle with the avocado dressing to serve.

Gluten Free Swap the pearl barley for cooked quinoa, brown rice or millet.

TIPS & SWAPS

*No fresh corn? Use 200g drained, canned corn or defrosted frozen corn.

A firmer peach works best in this salad.

Instead of raw red onion, use Quick Pickled Red Onion (see page 223).

LEFTOVERS: see pp228–233

- Avocado
- Basil
- Red onion
- Baby spinach
- Peaches
- Lime juice

LIGHT BITES | **81**

CARROT RIBBON, CINNAMON & HALLOUMI SALAD

Serves 2

3 large carrots
¼ red onion, thinly sliced
handful of fresh coriander,
    finely chopped
2 tablespoons sesame seeds
½ x 225g block of halloumi,
    cut into 5mm-thick slices
2 handfuls of baby spinach

DRESSING
juice of ½ lime or lemon
½ teaspoon honey or granulated sugar
¼ teaspoon ground cinnamon
½ teaspoon ground cumin
1 teaspoon olive oil
pinch of salt

The lip-smacking salinity of the halloumi is tempered here by the sweet carrot ribbons and lime-pepped dressing. This salad is quick to assemble and looks super-impressive thanks to the undulating ribbons of carrot. Don't forget to add the sesame seeds, which bring toasty pops of flavour to each bite!

1 Mix all the dressing ingredients together in a medium bowl until smooth. Set aside.

2 Using a vegetable peeler, peel the carrots into lots of lovely ribbons and put them into the bowl together with the sliced onion and chopped coriander. Toss the mixture together with your hands until everything is well coated in the dressing and set aside.

3 Place the sesame seeds in a dry frying pan over a medium-high heat and toast them, stirring frequently, until golden. Transfer to a bowl and set aside.

4 Set the frying pan back on the heat and add the sliced halloumi. Fry for 2–4 minutes until it is light golden, then flip over and fry on the other side. Remove from the pan, let them cool a little, then tear into rough chunks.

5 Place a handful of spinach leaves into the base of each serving bowl and top with the carrot mixture, a sprinkle of sesame seeds and the torn halloumi chunks.

TIPS & SWAPS

Replace the baby spinach with rocket, mixed salad leaves or sliced gem lettuce.

Use 50g feta instead of halloumi. Don't fry it – just crumble over the salad.

LEFTOVERS: see pp228–233

● Lime or lemon juice
● Halloumi
● Red onion
● Fresh coriander
● Carrots
● Baby spinach

WARM ROASTED CAULIFLOWER & CHICKPEA SALAD

V **VG** **GF** **LS**

Serves 2–3

1 large head of cauliflower, outer leaves removed, head cut into medium florets (about 500g once leaves are removed)
1 tablespoon olive oil
240g (1 can, drained weight) cooked chickpeas, drained and rinsed
2 heads of chicory, separated into leaves
salt

DRESSING

2 tablespoons miso, any kind
4 tablespoons olive oil
1 garlic clove, crushed or very finely chopped
1 shallot or ¼ red onion, finely diced
2 teaspoons granulated sugar or honey
1 tablespoon lemon juice or apple cider vinegar or rice vinegar

I can (and have) happily eaten this dish for dinner on a dark, wintery evening. It's a homely combination of slightly chewy chickpeas, crisp-yet-soft cauliflower and hardy spears of crisp chicory. I have found that I prefer chicory when it's subjected briefly to heat as it loses its bitter edge but stays crisp and juicy. If you are a fan of the bitterness that chicory brings, by all means skip the frying and toss them in raw.

1 Preheat the oven to 180°C fan, 200°C, Gas Mark 6.

2 Place the cauliflower on a baking tray or in a roasting pan, drizzle with the oil and sprinkle with salt. Toss until the cauliflower is coated in the oil, then roast in the oven for 45 minutes.

3 Twenty minutes into roasting the cauliflower, add the chickpeas to the tray and toss using a metal spatula to coat them in the oil. Return the tray to the oven for the remaining 25 minutes.

4 Combine all the dressing ingredients in a screw-top jar, put on the lid and shake to mix.

5 Working in batches, place the chicory leaves in a dry frying pan or stovetop grill pan over the highest heat. Let the heat slightly wilt the leaves, which will remove their bitterness, then transfer them to a large bowl.

6 Tip the warm cauliflower and chickpeas into the bowl with the chicory together with the dressing. Toss to coat, then serve warm.

Vegan Use granulated sugar in the dressing.

LEFTOVERS: see pp228–233

- Cauliflower, raw or roasted
- Miso
- Cooked chickpeas
- Lemon (if you used lemon juice in the dressing)
- Red onion

TIPS & SWAPS

If you have roasted cauliflower florets to hand use about 300g instead of the raw cauliflower. Skip step 1 and just roast the chickpeas for 20 minutes, tossing the cauliflower on to the tray in the final 5 minutes.

CANNELLINI BEAN & APPLE SALAD WITH APPLE YOGURT DRESSING

Serves 3–4

2 carrots
1 dessert apple, thinly sliced
juice of 1 lemon
1 head of gem lettuce, rinsed
120g (½ can, drained weight) cooked
   cannellini beans, drained and rinsed
handful of sunflower seeds
2 spring onions, finely sliced

APPLE YOGURT DRESSING
1 dessert apple, grated
1 tablespoon honey
generous pinch of salt
80g extra virgin olive
   oil or olive oil
6 tablespoons natural yogurt
   or crème fraîche
2 tablespoons apple cider vinegar

This salad is nothing fancy in itself – just a crunchy, bright thing to eat in the autumn. The real star is the dressing made with cooked, blended apple and creamy yogurt.

1   First, make the dressing. Cook the apple and honey in a small frying pan over a low heat until softened. Remove from the heat and leave to cool. Pour the apple and honey mixture into a jug with the salt, olive oil and yogurt or crème fraîche and blend using a hand-held blender until smooth. Alternatively, chuck it all into a freestanding blender and blend until smooth. Stir in the vinegar and add enough water as needed to make a pourable dressing.

2   Using a vegetable peeler, peel the carrots into ribbons and place in a bowl. Add the thinly sliced apple and lemon juice and toss until coated.

3   Shred the lettuce into bite-sized chunks and toss with the apple, carrots and cannellini beans in a salad bowl. Add half of the dressing and toss until everything is coated, then top with the sunflower seeds and spring onions. Serve with more dressing as needed.

TIPS & SWAPS

Store extra dressing in the refrigerator in a sealed jar for up to 1 week – handy for quick lunches or salads.

Use pears instead of the apples in both the salad and dressing.

Replace the gem lettuce with 100g baby spinach, mixed salad leaves or rocket.

LEFTOVERS: see pp228–233

● Cannellini beans
● Yogurt or crème fraîche
● Apples
● Carrots
● Spring onions

V **GF** **EF** **LS**

PEAR, RICOTTA & CHICORY SALAD WITH THYME DRESSING

Serves 2–3

1 pear, thinly sliced
2 large handfuls of mixed salad leaves
2 heads of chicory, separated into leaves
30g sunflower seeds
4 tablespoons ricotta
Parmesan*, shaved with
  a vegetable peeler

HONEY-THYME DRESSING
2 teaspoons honey
3 tablespoons olive oil
juice of 1 lemon
pinch of salt
¼ red onion, finely chopped
4 sprigs of thyme, leaves picked

Creamy ricotta dolloped into the gentle curves of chicory leaves and that always satisfying sweet and salty combo coming from pears, honey and wisps of Parmesan is just delicious. If you're unconvinced by salad, try this one out – it might just make you reconsider.

1 Combine all the dressing ingredients in a screw-top jar, put on the lid and shake to emulsify.

2 Place the sliced pear and mixed salad leaves on a large serving plate. Drizzle some of the dressing over and toss gently until coated (the lemon juice in the dressing will help prevent the pear browning).

3 Working in batches, place the chicory leaves in a dry frying pan or stovetop grill pan over the highest heat. Let the heat slightly wilt the leaves, which will remove their bitterness, then transfer them to the serving plate. Return the empty pan to the heat and add the sunflower seeds. Toast over a high heat, stirring frequently, until slightly golden and smelling toasty. Scatter them over the chicory.

4 Dot the salad with spoonfuls of ricotta and a few big flakes of shaved Parmesan. Drizzle over some more dressing, if you like, and serve.

TIPS & SWAPS

*Parmesan is not technically vegetarian – choose an alternative vegetarian hard cheese.

Replace the pear with apple, peach or grapes.

Chopped walnuts or almonds are fab instead of the sunflower seeds.

Omit the chicory and replace it with a few more handfuls of mixed salad leaves.

LEFTOVERS: see pp228-233

● Red onion
● Ricotta
● Thyme

Bigger Meals

These heartier dishes are definitely what you would want at the end of a long day. There are rib-sticking stews, thick soups, all sorts of pasta dishes and some lighter more salad-like meals. I think the key to not getting exhausted from cooking every night is to batch cook certain ingredients at the weekends, such as chickpeas or roasted vegetables and salad dressings. It makes stepping into the kitchen in the evening seem like less of a monotonous task as you get most of the hard work out of the way on a single evening. I've left gentle reminders in the 'Tips' sections at the bottom of each recipe to get you to start cooking extra food while you are making a recipe so you can make your future life a little easier. Once you get into the habit, it'll become second nature and trust me, you'll be happier for it.

V GF NS

VG option

ROASTED SQUASH WITH BROWN RICE & HALLOUMI

Serves 2

400g butternut squash (roughly ½ small squash or ¼ large one), peeled and cut into about 3cm chunks
½ tablespoon olive oil or rapeseed oil
150g uncooked brown rice, rinsed or 300g cooked
125g halloumi, cut into 3mm slices
a few handfuls of pomegranate seeds or raisins
2 handfuls of baby spinach
½ red onion, finely sliced
large handful of fresh coriander or coriander micro greens, finely chopped
salt

TAHINI DRESSING
2 tablespoons tahini
1 garlic clove, crushed or finely chopped
pinch of salt
juice of ½ lemon

I hoard butternut squash in autumn and winter. It will keep on a windowsill or cupboard for a month or two without spoiling (until you cut it, then you need to refrigerate it) so it's perfect to buy in season and store for later in the year. I'm not a fan of steamed butternut squash but roasted squash? UH, 1,000 times YES. It's a pretty sweet vegetable so I love love love it with salty, squeaky halloumi and earthy tahini dressing. The pomegranates add a pop of colour, but you can just use raisins or even cubed apple for the same effect.

1 Preheat the oven to 180°C fan, 200°C, Gas Mark 6.

2 Toss the squash with the oil and a pinch of salt on a baking tray. Roast in the oven for 45 minutes, turning it halfway though cooking, until it starts to brown.

3 If starting with uncooked brown rice, place the rice in a medium pan and pour in enough water until well covered. Season with salt and bring to the boil. Reduce the heat and simmer for 20 minutes for long-grain brown rice or 30 minutes for short-grain brown rice, adding more water if needed. Once cooked, drain the rice and return it to the pan. Cover with a lid and leave for 5 minutes to absorb the excess moisture.

4 Mix all the dressing ingredients together in a small bowl or jar. Add enough water to make a drizzle-able sauce and set aside.

5 Heat a dry, nonstick frying pan over a medium heat. Add the sliced halloumi and fry for 2–4 minutes until it is light golden, then flip over and fry on the other side. Remove from the pan.

6 Mix the pomegranate seeds or raisins and roasted squash into the cooked rice. Arrange a bed of spinach in each bowl, top with the rice mixture, drizzle with the tahini sauce and top with the halloumi, red onion and coriander.

Vegan Leave out the halloumi or replace with Sun Feta (see page 219).

LEFTOVERS: see pp228–233

- Butternut squash (raw or roasted)
- Brown rice (cooked or uncooked)
- Tahini
- Red onion
- Baby spinach
- Fresh coriander
- Halloumi
- Pomegranate
- Lemon juice

TIPS & SWAPS

Use gem lettuce, mixed salad leaves, rocket or pea shoots instead of baby spinach.

Swap the pomegranate seeds for some apple! Leave the skin on, just core and roughly chop before using.

Use cooked pearl barley or quinoa instead of the rice.

Replace the squash with an equal weight of cubed sweet potato or carrots cut into 3mm coins.

CHICKPEA, DATE & GINGER TAGINE WITH HUMMUS

Serves 2–3

4 tablespoons olive oil
1 medium aubergine, cut into about 3cm cubes
1 red onion, cut into about 3mm thick slices
1 red, yellow or orange pepper, deseeded and cut into eighths
1 tablespoon grated or very finely chopped fresh root ginger
2 teaspoons garam masala
1 teaspoon Chinese five spice
½ teaspoon ground cinnamon
¼ teaspoon cayenne pepper
3 tablespoons water
1 tablespoon miso, any kind, soy sauce or tamari
4–6 dried dates, pitted and roughly chopped (depending on your taste)
400g can chopped tomatoes
360g (1½ cans, drained weight) cooked chickpeas (don't drain, yet)
1 garlic clove, crushed or very finely chopped
1 tablespoon lemon juice
150g uncooked brown rice or 300g cooked, warmed
salt
fresh coriander sprigs, to serve

Loosely based on a tagine, this chickpea dish is packed with flavour thanks to a hit of ginger and spices. The hummus seems to round out the flavours and textures, plus it cuts through the sticky sweetness of the dates.

1 Heat 1 tablespoon of the oil in a large frying pan over a medium heat. Add the aubergine and sauté for 10 minutes until slightly browned. Add another tablespoon of oil, then the onion, pepper and ginger and cook for a further 10 minutes, or until the onion starts to brown. Add the spices and stir for 1 minute, then add the water and cook for 1–2 minutes until the water has evaporated and the onions have softened. Add the miso, dates and tomatoes and stir until combined.

2 Reserve 4 tablespoons of liquid from the canned chickpeas and set aside. Now completely drain the chickpeas and mix half of them into the pan. Simmer the stew for 15–20 minutes until the aubergine has softened.

3 Meanwhile place the other half of the chickpeas in a blender or food processor (or a bowl or jug if using a hand-held blender) with the remaining oil, garlic, lemon juice and a generous pinch of salt and blitz until smooth, thinning with the reserved chickpea liquid.

4 If using uncooked rice, place it in a medium pan and cover with water. Season with salt and bring to the boil. Reduce the heat and simmer for 20 minutes for long-grain brown rice or 30 minutes for short-grain brown rice, adding more water as needed. Once cooked, drain the rice and return it to the pan. Cover with a lid and leave for 5 minutes to absorb the excess moisture.

5 Serve the stew over the rice with the hummus and a handful of coriander.

Gluten Free Make sure that you are using a certified gluten-free tamari or soy sauce.

LEFTOVERS: see pp228–233

- Cooked chickpeas
- Dates
- Miso
- Tomatoes, canned
- Lemon
- Brown rice
- Fresh coriander

TIPS & SWAPS

Double up on the hummus and keep the extra in the refrigerator for another day.

Serve with pitta or flatbreads (see page 215) instead of rice.

Cool and store any extra rice as quickly as possible by rinsing it under cold running water or spreading it out on a plate. Once cooled, keep in the refrigerator for 1 day or in a sandwich bag in the freezer for 2 months. When reheating, make sure it is piping hot before serving.

AUBERGINE, RED LENTIL & COCONUT CURRY

Serves 2–3

1 medium aubergine
3 tablespoons olive oil
½ red onion or 1 shallot, chopped
½ teaspoon chilli flakes
2 teaspoons garam masala
1½ teaspoons ground cinnamon
½ teaspoon ground cumin
1 teaspoon ground turmeric
1 star anise (optional)
100g red lentils, rinsed
100g (½ a block) creamed coconut
　or 200ml (½ a can) coconut milk
600ml vegetable stock
　or 400ml if using coconut milk
1 teaspoon granulated sugar
　or honey or 2 teaspoons Date
　Paste (see page 221)
juice of ½ lemon or lime
salt
cooked brown rice or No-yeast
　Flatbreads (see page 214)

TO GARNISH
large handful of fresh coriander,
　chopped
3 spring onions, sliced
4 tablespoons toasted coconut flakes

I know it looks like a lot of ingredients but trust me, I'm not trying to trick you into making something super-complicated. Most of the ingredients are individual spices – I like making my own spice mixes for curries rather than using pre-mixed 'curry powder' which can become too same-y. The red lentils make this dish easy for a weeknight meal as they cook quickly and are chockablock full of protein and fibre.

1 Cut the top off the aubergine, slice it in half lengthways and then into rough 2cm cubes.

2 Heat 2 tablespoons of the oil in a deep frying pan over a high heat. Add the aubergine and fry, stirring occasionally, for 15 minutes until it has started to become golden. Transfer to a plate and set aside.

3 Reduce the heat to medium-low, add the remaining oil, onion or shallot and all the spices to the pan. Fry for 2 minutes, stirring until the onion has softened.

4 Add the lentils, creamed coconut or coconut milk, stock and sugar to the pan and stir until the creamed coconut has fully melted and mixed into the other ingredients. Bring to the boil, then reduce the heat and simmer for 20–25 minutes, stirring occasionally, until thickened.

5 Remove and discard the star anise, if using, then season the curry with the lemon or lime juice and salt to taste. Stir in the aubergine. Serve the curry piping hot with some cooked brown rice or No-yeast Flatbreads, garnished with plenty of coriander, sliced spring onions and toasted coconut flakes.

Vegan Use granulated sugar or Date Paste.

TIPS & SWAPS

Yellow split peas work well instead of red lentils, but cook the curry for 20 minutes longer and add a little water to stop it getting too dry.

Add extra veggies – stir in 100g baby spinach at the end of cooking.

LEFTOVERS: see pp228–233

● Creamed coconut
　or coconut milk
● Red onion
● Lemon or lime juice
● Fresh coriander
● Spring onions
● Brown rice

ROASTED (SWEET OR WHITE) POTATO 3 WAYS

If you know you're going to be too exhausted to cook during the week, a good habit to get into is to roast floury or sweet potatoes at the weekend to keep in the refrigerator. When it comes to crunch time, just reheat your potato in the microwave or oven and make one of the easy fillings overleaf OR use the leftovers table on pages 228–233.

1. Preheat the oven to 180°C fan, 200°C, Gas Mark 6.

2. Sweet potato (200–300g): Prick all over with a fork, then wrap in a piece of foil and roast in the oven for 1–1¼ hours (depending on size and shape) until completely tender.

3. Regular potato (200–300g): Prick all over with a fork, rinse with water but don't dry, then rub with sea salt. Place on a baking tray and bake in the oven for 1–1¼ hours (depending on size and shape) until knife tender.

4. Speed it up: Preheat the oven to 180°C fan, 200°C, Gas Mark 6. Prick either potato all over with a fork, place on a plate and microwave on high for 5 minutes. Rub with salt, place on a baking tray and finish in the oven for 20–30 minutes.

CANNELLINI BEANS, TOASTED BREADCRUMBS & SPINACH

LEFTOVERS: see pp228–233

- Whole sweet potato (baked)
- Whole white potato (baked)

MISO, MUSHROOMS
& CRISPY CAVOLO NERO

SALSA & COUSCOUS

TIPS & SWAPS

Bake some extra potatoes and
keep them in the refrigerator for up
to 3 days. Reheat in the microwave or
oven. See the leftovers table on pages
228–233 for other recipes to use
them in.

MISO, MUSHROOMS & CRISPY CAVOLO NERO

Serves 1

2 large cavolo nero leaves, tough stems removed
  and leaves cut into bite-sized pieces
1 tablespoon olive oil or rapeseed oil
1 tablespoon sesame seeds
75g (around 5) button or chestnut mushrooms, sliced
1 teaspoon miso, any kind
salt

1 Preheat the oven to 120°C fan, 140°C, Gas Mark 1.

2 Place the cavolo nero on a baking tray. Drizzle with half
the oil and sprinkle with salt then toss and massage
together until all the leaves are coated. Bake in the oven
for 12–15 minutes until crisp.

3 Place the sesame seeds in a frying pan over a high heat
and stir until golden, then transfer to a bowl and set aside.

4 Return the pan to the heat over a medium heat and add
the remaining oil. Add the mushrooms and sauté for
5–7 minutes until darkened and soft. Add the miso and
a good splash of water – smush the miso into the water
with the back of a spoon to make a miso sauce, then
stir to coat the mushrooms and remove the pan from
the heat.

5 Cut the sweet potato in half and mash the flesh roughly
with a fork. Top with the mushrooms, crispy cavolo nero
and sesame seeds and serve.

LEFTOVERS: see pp228–233

- Cavolo nero
- Miso
- Mushrooms

CANNELLINI BEANS, TOASTED BREADCRUMBS & SPINACH

Serves 1

3 teaspoons olive oil
2 tablespoons dried breadcrumbs (see page 218)
about 100g (less than ½ can, drained weight) cooked
   cannellini beans, drained and rinsed
1 garlic clove, crushed or very finely chopped
2 handfuls of baby spinach
few basil leaves, roughly chopped
salt

1 Drizzle 1 teaspoon of the oil over the halved baked (sweet) potato, sprinkle with some salt and slightly mash it into the flesh with a fork.

2 Toast the breadcrumbs in a frying pan with another teaspoon of the oil over a medium heat, stirring constantly for 1–2 minutes until golden. Pour into a bowl and set aside. Wipe out the pan and return it to the heat.

3 Add the remaining oil to the pan over a medium heat. Add the beans and garlic and sauté for a minute. Add the spinach, reduce the heat to low and stir until wilted. Season with salt to taste.

4 Pour the beans over the halved (sweet) potato and garnish with the breadcrumbs and basil.

SALSA & COUSCOUS

Serves 1

2 tablespoons couscous
3 tablespoons boiling water
4–5 cherry tomatoes, finely chopped
juice of ½ lime
handful of fresh coriander, finely chopped
1 spring onion, finely sliced
   or ¼ red onion, finely chopped
pinch of chilli flakes
1 tablespoon pumpkin or sunflower seeds,
   roughly chopped
salt

1 Place the couscous in a small bowl with the measured boiling water, cover with a plate and set aside for 5 minutes. Fluff up with a fork.

2 Meanwhile, mix the tomatoes, lime juice, coriander, spring onion or red onion, chilli flakes and a pinch of salt together in a bowl.

3 Spoon the couscous and tomato salsa over the halved (sweet) potato and sprinkle on the chopped seeds.

LEFTOVERS: see pp228–233

● Cannellini beans
● Basil leaves
● Baby spinach

LEFTOVERS: see pp228–233

● Lime juice
● Cherry tomatoes
● Spring onions or red onion
● Fresh coriander

TIPS & SWAPS

Serve with a side of vegetables or a simple salad for a hearty main meal.

If you have cubed, roasted sweet potato to hand, you can use that. Skip steps 2 and 3 and scatter the potato over the spinach in step 6, before baking.

Double up on the pastry and keep half of it in the refrigerator or freezer for another day.

VG option

PESTO, SPINACH & SWEET POTATO GALETTE

**Makes 1 galette
(serves 3–4 as a main)**

1 recipe Half-oat Pastry (see page 217)
    or Olive Oil Pastry (see page 217)
    or 250g shop-bought pastry
1 large or 2 small sweet potatoes
    (about 300g total)
plain white flour, for dusting
3 tablespoons homemade Pesto
    (see pages 224–225)
    or shop-bought
100g baby spinach, rinsed
1 teaspoon olive oil
20g feta, crumbled
salt and freshly ground pepper

Galettes are a godsend when you don't have a tart tin or pie dish (of which I had neither for a few months at uni). They also look fancy and, as far as handling pastry goes, they are simple to master, as you don't have to worry about the pastry shrinking or cracking inside a tin. This recipe is quick to make if you have a microwave (or a little bit slower if you don't!) and, thanks to the fancy fanned pattern of the sweet potatoes, makes you look like a boss at tart making.

1 Prepare the pastry according to the recipe on page 217.

2 Prick the sweet potato all over with a fork. Microwave it on full power for 4 minutes or wrap in foil and place in an oven preheated to 180°C fan, 200°C, Gas Mark 6 for 30 minutes. It should be slightly softened, but it will cook more when you bake the tart. Leave the oven on.

3 Slice the sweet potato in half lengthways and remove the skin. Cut each half into 3mm thick slices so they look like little half-moons. If your oven isn't already on, preheat it to 180°C fan, 200°C, Gas Mark 6.

4 Cut a piece of baking paper slightly larger than the size of your baking tray. Lightly dust the baking paper with flour and roll the dough out to a roughly 25–30cm circle. Spread the pesto in the centre of the pastry, leaving a 3cm border around the edge bare.

5 Place the spinach in a heatproof bowl and either microwave it for 1 minute or cover with boiling water to wilt. Drain and rinse under cold running water, then squeeze to remove any excess moisture. Tear into clumps and spread out over the pesto.

6 Arrange the sweet potato in semicircles over the spinach. It's fine if bits are overlapping. Fold the bare edges of the pastry up around the tart, folding in pleats as needed. Drizzle over the oil, then season with salt and pepper.

7 Bake for 25–30 minutes, then remove from the oven and serve with the crumbled feta.

LEFTOVERS: see pp228–233

● Half-oat Pastry
● Sweet potatoes (raw or roasted)
● Pesto
● Baby spinach
● Feta

Vegan Use the Olive Oil Pastry (see page 217). Make sure your pesto is vegan or use one of the recipes on pages 224–225. Use Sun Feta (see page 219) instead of the feta.

CAULIFLOWER
MISO MAC & CHEESE

Serves 2

1 medium head of cauliflower
(about 350g when leaves are
removed), outer leaves removed
and head cut into medium florets
150g dried wholewheat pasta
(I like penne here) or 300g cooked
1 tablespoon olive oil
3 tablespoons plain white flour
350ml milk or non-dairy milk
¼ teaspoon smoked paprika
1 garlic clove, crushed or
very finely chopped
120g mature Cheddar
cheese, grated
1 tablespoon miso, any kind
salt

You might be wondering whether putting miso into cheese sauce is going to work, but trust me, it's great! I know I do use miso a lot, but here it makes the sauce special as that salty, umami twang brightens the flavour. I add cauliflower in two ways here – whole chunks and puréed. The whole chunks help to bulk up the dish and, for me, bring back memories of the incredibly indulgent cauliflower cheese that my dad used to make. The purée is mixed into the cheese sauce because, hey, it's always good to have more vegetables.

1 Bring a large pan of salted water to the boil. Add the cauliflower and simmer for 5 minutes. Scoop the cauliflower out and set aside.

2 If using dried pasta, add the pasta to the same pan, bring to the boil, then reduce the heat and simmer for 4 minutes less than the time instructed on the packet, then drain and return to the pan.

3 Mix half the cooked cauliflower into the cooked pasta then pour this into a medium casserole dish and set aside.

4 Preheat the oven to 180°C fan, 200°C, Gas Mark 6.

5 Return the pan to the hob with the oil over a medium heat. Add the flour and stir for about 1 minute. Add the milk, drizzling it in a little at a time and stirring well between additions. Add the smoked paprika, crushed garlic and 100g of the cheese.

6 If using a hand-held blender, place the reserved, cooked cauliflower and miso into a jug with a few tablespoons of the hot milk mixture and blend until smooth. Return to the pan, stir until smooth then pour over the pasta and cauliflower in the casserole dish.

7 If using a freestanding blender or food processor, pour the hot milk mixture into the blender together with the reserved, cooked cauliflower and miso and blend carefully until smooth. Pour over the pasta and cauliflower in the casserole dish.

8 Top with the remaining Cheddar cheese and bake in the oven for 30–40 minutes until the cheese on top has melted and browned.

LEFTOVERS: see pp228–233

● Cauliflower
● Pasta (cooked or dried)
● Miso

V GF

VG option

POTATO, HALLOUMI & COURGETTE BAKE

Serves 2

400g (about 3 medium) white potatoes
  (e.g. Maris Piper, King Edward),
  unpeeled
1 tablespoon olive oil
2 medium courgettes, cut into chunks
2 red peppers, stalks removed, deseeded,
  halved then cut into 4–5 strips
125g halloumi, cut into 3mm-thick slices
salt

BASIL OIL

large handful of basil, leaves and
  stalks (save a few leaves to scatter
  over the veg)
80ml extra virgin olive oil

I remember being at my friend's house for dinner when her mum brought this out of the oven, much to my delight, covered in bronzed halloumi. It's a simple traybake meal, which is jazzed up by a vibrant basil oil.

1   Cut the potatoes into about 3cm chunks and place in a medium pan. Cover with boiling water and a generous pinch of salt, then bring to the boil. Reduce the heat and simmer for 5 minutes. Drain the potatoes, then return them to the pan and cover with a plate or a lid. Leave for 5 minutes to remove any excess moisture.

2   Preheat the oven to 180°C fan, 200°C, Gas Mark 6.

3   Tip the cooked potatoes out on to a large baking tray or roasting tin and toss in the olive oil, then bake in the oven for 40 minutes. Add the courgette and pepper and toss until coated in the oil. Return to the oven for a further 20–25 minutes. Finally, lay the sliced halloumi over the veg, turn the oven grill on and leave for a few minutes until the halloumi is golden.

4   Blitz the basil and olive oil together*. Drizzle 2 tablespoons of this over the roasted vegetables and halloumi. Scatter the reserved basil leaves over the top and serve.

Vegan   Omit the halloumi and roast the veg for 40 minutes, then top with Sun Feta (see page 219) or roughly chopped pitted olives and drizzle with the basil oil, before returning the tray to the oven.

TIPS & SWAPS

Serve with 'Chorizo' Dip (see page 47)
or some crusty bread for dipping.

*If you don't have a blender, chop the basil as finely
as possible and mix with the olive oil.

Double up on the roasted vegetables and use them in
another recipe (see the leftovers table, pages 228–233)
or wrap in tortillas for a quick lunch the next day.

Use sweet potatoes instead of white potatoes. Peel
them and skip step 1. Reduce the initial roasting time
to 15 minutes.

Store leftover basil oil in the refrigerator and use
for pesto, pasta or salad dressings.

LEFTOVERS: see pp228–233

● Halloumi
● Peppers
● Courgettes
● White potatoes
● Basil

LENTIL & YOGURT PITTA DIP

Serves 2

90g Puy or green lentils, rinsed
  or 110g cooked
2 peppers, deseeded and cut
  into wide strips
1 teaspoon olive oil
2 wholemeal pitta breads, homemade
  (see page 215) or shop-bought
150g natural yogurt
1 garlic clove, crushed
1 tablespoon tahini
  (optional but really good)
handful of mint leaves, finely chopped
1 tablespoon sesame seeds
½ teaspoon sweet smoked paprika
salt

I made this based on a Middle Eastern dish called 'fatteh', of which there are many versions. Some include cooked chicken or minced lamb, chickpeas, aubergine and pine nuts, but this is my own version with roasted pepper, lentils and sesame seeds. It sounds more like a side dish but believe me it is quite filling. If you serve this as a main with a side of cooked vegetables or a simple dressed salad, you should be content. Conversely, you could make a big batch to serve at a dinner party as a fun, shared starter.

1 Preheat the oven to 180°C fan, 200°C, Gas Mark 6.

2 If starting with uncooked lentils, place them in a small pan and pour in enough water to cover. Bring to the boil and cook for 20–25 minutes until soft. Drain and set aside.

3 Meanwhile, toss the peppers in the oil on a baking tray. Roast in the oven for 20 minutes.

4 Cut the pitta bread in half as if you were going to fill it then split each half into 2 thin pieces. Cut each thin piece into around 6 strips.

5 Once the peppers have been roasting for 20 minutes, add the pitta bread pieces to the tray and toss to coat the bread in some of the oil. Return to the oven and bake for a further 5–8 minutes until the pitta pieces are crisp.

6 Mix the yogurt, garlic, tahini and a pinch of salt together in a small bowl.

7 Place the pitta pieces and peppers in a serving bowl. Spoon the yogurt mixture and lentils over the top (I like to leave some pitta chips exposed around the edges for some crunch). Sprinkle over the chopped mint, sesame seeds and smoked paprika and serve immediately.

Vegan Use unsweetened soya yogurt instead of the yogurt.

LEFTOVERS: see pp228–233

- Peppers
- Yogurt
- Tahini
- Mint

TIPS & SWAPS

Extra lentils can be kept for
5 days in the refrigerator and are
great cold in salads or stirred into
a pasta sauce or soup.

Roast extra vegetables, such as sweet
potato or some cauliflower florets, or
make some pitta chips (see page
42) for another meal.

V EF NS

VG option

SQUASH, CAULIFLOWER & ROASTED GARLIC GRATIN

Serves 2–3

450g (1 small or ½ large) butternut squash, peeled, deseeded and cut into 3cm chunks
½ large head of cauliflower (about 250g, once outer leaves are removed), outer leaves removed and cut into florets
1 head of garlic, pointy tip sliced off
2 tablespoons olive oil or rapeseed oil
salt

SAUCE
1½ tablespoons olive oil
3 tablespoons plain white flour
300ml vegetable stock
1 bay leaf
4 sprigs of thyme, leaves picked

TOPPING
1 tablespoon olive oil
30g dried breadcrumbs
10g grated Parmesan*

Classic comfort food right here – caramelized, roasted veg snuggled into a bubbling sauce with a crispy breadcrumb topping. There's a whole head of garlic in there too which is roasted so it mellows into a soft, sticky, sweet pulp. This is great as a main dish with crusty bread and some steamed vegetables. I sometimes tip in cooked cannellini beans to make it heartier or replace the butternut squash with an equal weight of sweet potato.

1 Preheat the oven to 180°C fan, 200°C, Gas Mark 6.

2 Toss together the squash, cauliflower, garlic head, oil and a pinch of salt in a large, deep baking dish and roast in the oven for 30 minutes, flipping halfway through. Once cooked leave to cool a little, then squeeze the cooked garlic cloves out of their papery casing and into the roasted vegetables. Discard the papery casing and leave the oven on.

3 To make the sauce, heat the oil and flour in a medium pan over a medium heat and stir into a paste, cooking for 1 minute. Reduce the heat and gradually drizzle in the stock, stirring until smooth between additions, until it's all added. Add the bay leaf and reduce the heat to low. Cook, stirring occasionally, for 15 minutes. Pour the sauce over the cooked vegetables and squeezed garlic in the baking dish and sprinkle over the thyme leaves.

4 To make the topping, heat the oil in a small frying pan over a medium heat. Add the breadcrumbs and stir for 1 minute. Mix in the Parmesan and remove the pan from the heat. Sprinkle over the saucy veg in the baking dish and bake for 20 minutes.

Vegan Leave the Parmesan out of the breadcrumb topping and season with salt instead.

TIPS & SWAPS

Add 120g (½ can) cooked cannellini beans after the veg is roasted or serve with wholemeal bread for a more substantial meal.

Replace the butternut squash with an equal weight of peeled and cubed sweet potato. The roasting time will remain the same.

*Parmesan isn't technically vegetarian – choose a vegetarian alternative hard cheese.

LEFTOVERS: see pp228–233

● Butternut squash
● Cauliflower
● Thyme

PESTO CRUMB COURGETTES WITH WEEKNIGHT FOCACCIA

Serves 2–3

FOCACCIA
190ml lukewarm water*
1 teaspoon fast-action dried yeast
2 tablespoons olive oil, plus
   extra for greasing
125g plain or strong wholemeal flour
100g plain or strong white flour
pinch of granulated sugar
½ teaspoon salt
1 teaspoon mixed dried herbs
   or dried thyme or dried oregano

FOR THE COURGETTES
20g pumpkin seeds
20g basil (stalks and leaves)
finely grated zest and juice of ½ lemon
3 medium courgettes
1 teaspoon olive oil
1 garlic clove, crushed
finely grated Parmesan,
   for sprinkling (optional)**
salt

My friend Rhiannon and I often eat this as a comforting, easy weeknight dinner when we have a friend date. It gets so cold in Leeds, where we are at uni, so this is the perfect solution. The focaccia dough is extremely wet, which means it requires little kneading. The pesto-crumb courgettes are my solution to the courgettes becoming too watery when grated and sautéed – the crumb has no liquid in it, so it absorbs all the moisture and becomes a chunky pesto.

1 Mix the measured water and yeast together in a medium bowl. Add 1 tablespoon of the oil, the flours, sugar and salt and mix well. Shape your hand like a claw and use it to beat the mixture in the bowl for 1 minute.

2 Grease a 20cm square tin well with some oil. Using oiled hands, press and stretch the dough into the tin. Cover with clingfilm or a clean tea towel and set aside in a warm place for 30–45 minutes, or until almost doubled in size.

3 Preheat the oven to 180°C fan, 200°C, Gas Mark 6.

4 Uncover the dough and use your fingers to gently poke a few dimples into the surface. Drizzle with the remaining 1 tablespoon oil and sprinkle on the dried herbs. Bake in the oven for 30–35 minutes, then tip out on to a board and cut into 6 pieces.

5 Meanwhile, chop the pumpkin seeds finely – around the size of a grain of couscous is best, then sweep them to the side of the chopping board. Finely chop the basil together with a generous pinch of salt and the lemon zest. Mix the chopped seeds and basil on the board and run through chopping once more with your knife.

6 Lay a box grater on its side with the large holes facing towards the ceiling. Drag each courgette along the large holes of the grater in long strokes to create ribbons of courgette. Repeat with the other courgettes.

7 Heat the oil in a frying pan over a medium heat. Add the courgettes and garlic and sauté for a few minutes until they have just softened and released a little liquid. Add the pesto crumb and stir to combine. Remove from the heat and season with salt and the lemon juice, to taste. Top with the Parmesan, if using, and serve with the focaccia.

Vegan Don't serve with Parmesan.

LEFTOVERS: see pp228–233

● Courgettes
● Basil
● Lemon juice

TIPS & SWAPS

*Ensure the water is just slightly
warm to the touch.

**Parmesan isn't technically vegetarian – choose
a vegetarian alternative hard cheese.

Pulse together the pesto crumb ingredients in a food
processor until finely chopped but not pasty.

Use cashews, almonds or sunflower seeds instead of
pumpkin seeds. Rinse salted cashews before using.

For garlic bread, heat 2 tablespoons butter or
olive oil with 2 crushed garlic cloves for 1
minute in a small frying pan and brush
over the baked focaccia.

V VG LS

GF option

CRISPY BROCCOLI & BARLEY BOWL WITH TAHINI DRESSING

Chewy pearl barley meets crunchy fronds of roasted broccoli in a simple, quick bowl meal. The tahini dressing is creamy and tangy and the sweet crunch of the pumpkin seeds adds a pop of texture.

Serves 2

150g uncooked pearl barley
    or 375g cooked, warmed
1 large head of broccoli,
    cut into medium florets
1 tablespoon olive oil
3 tablespoons pumpkin seeds
    or sunflower seeds
1 teaspoon soy sauce or tamari
¼ teaspoon granulated sugar
    or maple syrup
handful of fresh coriander, chopped
salt

TAHINI DRESSING
2 tablespoons tahini
juice of ½ lemon
1 garlic clove, crushed
pinch of salt

1 Preheat the oven to 180°C fan, 200°C, Gas Mark 6.

2 If starting with uncooked pearl barley, place the pearl barley in a medium pan and pour in enough water to cover. Bring to the boil, then reduce the heat and simmer for 35–40 minutes until chewy but soft. Drain, rinse and return to the pan and cover with a tea towel and a lid for 10 minutes.

3 Meanwhile, toss the broccoli in the oil and a sprinkle of salt on a baking tray. Roast in the oven for 20–30 minutes until golden and crispy.

4 Toast the pumpkin seeds in a nonstick frying pan over a medium heat, stirring frequently, until they start to pop. Add the soy sauce or tamari and sugar or syrup, then stir until the seeds clump together. Tip out on to a plate or chopping board and leave to cool.

5 Stir the tahini, lemon juice, garlic and salt together in a small bowl. Add enough water to make a drizzle-able dressing.

6 Divide the cooked pearl barley, crispy broccoli, pumpkin seeds and tahini dressing between 2 bowls, scatter over the coriander and serve warm.

Gluten Free Cook an equal weight of quinoa or rice instead of the pearl barley. Make sure that you are using a certified gluten-free tamari or soy sauce.

TIPS & SWAPS
Use cauliflower instead of broccoli and roast for 30–40 minutes.

Any extra broccoli and cooked pearl barley can be stored in the refrigerator in a container for up to 3 days.

LEFTOVERS: see pp228–233

- Pearl barley, raw or cooked
- Fresh coriander
- Tahini
- Lemon juice

LAZY POTATO HASH
WITH KALE, PESTO & EGGS

(V) (GF) (DF) (NS)

Serves 2

2 medium white potatoes* (about 400g), cut into 1cm-thick coins
2 tablespoons light olive oil or rapeseed oil
4 large leaves of cavolo nero, tough stems removed and leaves shredded into thumb-sized strips
120g (½ can, drained weight) cooked cannellini beans, drained and rinsed
4 tablespoons homemade Pesto (see pages 224–225) or shop-bought
2 eggs
salt and freshly ground pepper

I'm one of those people who likes to use the same pan as much as possible when cooking so I have less washing up to do. Here, I slice the potatoes before parboiling because then it's possible to parboil them in the frying pan, which is then used for sautéeing them, so one less pot to wash up, TICK! Back in the frying pan I whack in cavolo nero until it wilts and becomes a lil crispy, and add in pesto for flavour, beans for texture and eggs for those saucy yolks!

1 Arrange the potatoes in a deep, nonstick frying pan and pour in enough water to cover. Salt well and bring to the boil. Once boiling reduce the heat and simmer for 5 minutes, then drain and set aside.

2 Rinse and wipe out the frying pan and return it to the heat. Add half the oil and place over a medium heat. Add the potato slices, season well with salt and pepper and break them up into bite-sized chunks with a wooden spatula. Leave to turn golden underneath (resist any temptation to nudge them around), then flip over and cook until the other side is golden, about 10 minutes in total.

3 Add the cavolo nero strips to the pan with the remaining oil and sauté until it starts to wilt a little, then add the beans and pesto and stir to coat. Make 2 fist-sized wells in the hash and crack an egg into each. Cover with a lid or large plate, reduce the heat and cook until the whites are set and the yolk is still runny, about 2–3 minutes. Season with more salt and pepper, then divide between plates and serve.

Gluten Free If using shop-bought pesto, make sure it is certified gluten free.

Dairy Free If using shop-bought pesto, make sure it is dairy free.

LEFTOVERS: see pp228–233

- White potatoes
- Cavolo nero
- Cannellini beans
- Pesto

TIPS & SWAPS
*I like Russet or King Edward potatoes for this recipe.

TIPS & SWAPS

Quinoa, pearl barley, cooked soba,
udon or rice noodles will also work well.

Use creamed coconut instead of coconut milk.
Stir 30g into 4 tablespoons hot water.

Cool and store any extra rice as quickly as possible
by rinsing it under cold running water or spreading
it out on a plate. Once cooled, keep in the
refrigerator for 1 day or in a sandwich bag
in the freezer for 2 months. When
reheating, make sure it is piping hot
before serving.

RICE BOWL WITH GREENS & CORIANDER-COCONUT DRESSING

Serves 2

100g brown rice, rinsed
    or 180g cooked
2 eggs
100g tenderstem broccoli
    or ½ head of regular broccoli,
    cut into medium florets
50g frozen petits pois or peas
3 large cavolo nero leaves
handful of sesame seeds
1 spring onion, finely sliced

CORIANDER-COCONUT DRESSING
20g (2 handfuls) fresh coriander leaves
10g piece of fresh root ginger, peeled
    and very finely chopped or grated
juice of 1 lemon or lime
2 tablespoons soy sauce or tamari
1 tablespoon granulated sugar
    or honey or 2 tablespoons Date
    Paste (see page 221)
80ml coconut milk

This is the type of simple meal I like to make on a stressful weekday. It has greens to keep me feeling my best, a wicked dressing and, of course, an oozy soft-boiled egg. I have used broccoli, cavolo nero and frozen petits pois here but any greens will work. Try sautéeing your greens briefly in a drizzle of toasted sesame oil and a crushed garlic clove after cooking for a flavour punch.

1   If using uncooked rice, place it in a medium pan and cover with water. Season with salt and bring to the boil. Reduce the heat and simmer for 20 minutes for long-grain brown rice or 30 minutes for short-grain brown rice, adding more water as needed. Drain the rice and return it to the pan. Cover with a lid and leave for 5 minutes to absorb the excess moisture.

2   Blend all the dressing ingredients together using either a hand-held blender or a freestanding blender. If you don't have a blender, chop the coriander leaves as finely as possible and stir into the rest of the dressing ingredients.

3   Bring a medium pan of water to the boil. Gently lower in the eggs and simmer over a medium-low heat for 5–6 minutes. Use a spoon to scoop the eggs out of the pan (leave the pan on the heat) and place in a bowl of cold water. Set aside. Add the broccoli to the pan and cook for 2 minutes, then stir in the frozen peas and cavolo nero and cook for 3–5 minutes until the cavolo nero is softened. Drain the vegetables and return to the empty pan; cover with a lid or plate to keep warm.

4   Gently fracture the egg shells and carefully peel them.

5   Toast the sesame seeds in a dry frying pan over a medium heat, stirring constantly until golden. Transfer to a plate or bowl.

6   Divide the rice among 2 bowls. Top with the vegetables, a drizzle of the dressing, the sliced spring onion and the sesame seeds. Halve the eggs and add to the bowl.

Gluten Free   Make sure that you are using a certified gluten-free tamari or soy sauce.

LEFTOVERS: see pp228–233

- Brown rice (cooked or uncooked)
- Cavolo nero
- Peas or petits pois
- Fresh coriander
- Coconut milk
- Spring onions
- Lemon or lime juice

MISO-GARLIC-CHILLI BROCCOLI 3 WAYS

I love to display the versatility of miso. It has an umami salinity that works well in many types of dishes. Using it with chilli and garlic makes a simple, sauced-up broccoli side dish, which can then be turned into a main dish by adding a few more ingredients (see overleaf).

Serves 2 as a side

1 medium head of broccoli, cut into medium florets, or about 250g tenderstem broccoli
1 tablespoon olive oil or rapeseed oil
2 garlic cloves, crushed
½–1 red chilli (depending on strength) or few pinches of chilli flakes
1 tablespoon miso, any kind, mixed with 4 tablespoons water to make a paste

1 Steam the broccoli in a small amount of water in a deep frying pan covered with a lid for 5 minutes. Drain and set the broccoli aside.

2 Return the pan to a medium heat, add the oil, garlic and chilli and sauté for 30 seconds, then add the drained broccoli. Sauté for a further 30 second then add the miso-water mixture to the pan. Stir until the broccoli is coated and cook for a further 1–2 minutes until the liquid has reduced by half.

3 Serve on its own as a side or turn into a main meal by leaving it in the pan and using one of the recipes overleaf.

LEFTOVERS: see pp228–233
- Miso
- Red chilli

SOY SAUCE & GINGER & RICE

PASTA & TOMATOES
& SPINACH

ONION & CUMIN
& BEANS

WITH SOY SAUCE & GINGER & RICE

1 If starting with uncooked brown rice, place the rice in a medium pan and pour in enough water until well covered. Season with salt and bring to the boil. Reduce the heat and simmer for 20 minutes for long-grain brown rice or 30 minutes for short-grain brown rice, adding more water if needed. Once cooked, drain the rice and return it to the pan. Cover with a lid and leave for 5 minutes to absorb the excess moisture.

2 Add the oil, ginger, soy sauce or tamari and sugar to the frying pan with the Miso-chilli-garlic Broccoli. Cook over a medium heat for 1 minute to take the raw edge off the ginger, then serve over the cooked rice.

Serves 2

150g uncooked brown rice, rinsed or 270g cooked
1 teaspoon toasted sesame oil
2 teaspoons grated or very finely chopped fresh root ginger
1 tablespoon soy sauce or tamari
good pinch of granulated sugar or a small squeeze of honey
1 recipe for Miso-garlic-chilli Broccoli (see page 118), keep it in the pan

Gluten Free Make sure that you are using a certified gluten-free tamari or soy sauce.

Vegan Use granulated sugar.

TIPS & SWAPS

Not enough of a meal? Add a sweet potato, steamed or mashed with lime juice and a pinch of salt, on the side.

Cool and store any extra rice as quickly as possible by rinsing it under cold running water or spreading it out on a plate. Once cooled, keep in the refrigerator for 1 day or in a sandwich bag in the freezer for 2 months. When reheating, make sure it is piping hot before serving.

LEFTOVERS: see pp228–233

- Brown rice (raw or cooked)

- Cannellini, black or kidney beans
- Fresh coriander
- Yogurt or crème fraîche
- Lime juice

- Pasta (dried or cooked)
- Lemon juice
- Baby spinach
- Cherry tomatoes
- Basil

WITH ONION & CUMIN & BEANS

Serves 2

1 red onion, thinly sliced
1 recipe for Miso-garlic-chilli Broccoli
   (see page 118), keep it in the pan
1½ teaspoons ground cumin
1 teaspoon sweet smoked paprika
juice of ½ lime
240g (1 can, drained weight) cooked
   black, cannellini or kidney beans,
   drained and rinsed
salt

TO SERVE
2 tablespoons plain yogurt
   or crème fraîche
large handful of fresh coriander,
   roughly chopped

1 Add the thinly sliced onion to the frying pan with the Miso-chilli-garlic Broccoli. Stir and cook for 2 minutes to soften the onions. Add the cumin, paprika, lime juice, beans and a good splash of water to the pan and cook over a medium-low heat, stirring gently to mix everything together for 5 minutes. Season with salt to taste and divide between 2 plates. Serve with the yogurt and fresh coriander.

Vegan Use unsweetened soya yogurt or Avocado Cream (see page 219) instead of the yogurt.

TIPS & SWAPS
Poached, soft-boiled or fried eggs are amazing with this dish.

WITH PASTA & TOMATOES & SPINACH

Serves 2

150g dried wholewheat or spelt
   spaghetti or 300g cooked
1 recipe for Miso-garlic-chilli Broccoli
   (see page 118)
finely grated zest and juice of ½ lemon
2 large handfuls of baby spinach
handful of basil leaves, roughly chopped
5–6 cherry tomatoes, quartered
finely grated Parmesan, to serve
   (optional)*

1 If starting with dried pasta, place the pasta in a medium pan and cover with just-boiled water from the kettle. Bring to the boil and cook until al dente (this will generally be the shorter cooking time on the packet). Drain, reserving a small mugful of the pasta water.

2 Add the pasta to the frying pan with the Miso-chilli-garlic Broccoli together with a good splash of the reserved pasta water, the lemon juice and zest and the spinach and cook over a medium heat, stirring until the spinach has wilted and there is still some liquid left in the pan (you can add more pasta water if needed).

3 Remove from the heat and stir in the basil and tomatoes. Divide between 2 bowls and serve with Parmesan, if you like.

TIPS & SWAPS
*Parmesan isn't technically vegetarian – choose a vegetarian hard cheese instead. Omit if vegan.

Cook some extra pasta and keep it in the refrigerator in a container for up to 3 days – handy for a quick lunch.

SPINACH & FETA BALLS
WITH SPAGHETTI

Serves 2–4

400g baby spinach or 240g frozen,
  cooked spinach, defrosted
100g feta, crumbled
1 tablespoon mixed dried herbs
  (I like herbes de Provence)
1 egg
55g Oat Flour (see page 216)
  or dried breadcrumbs
4 tablespoons olive oil, for cooking
  (optional)
300g dried spaghetti
  or 600g cooked
a knob of unsalted butter or 2
  tablespoons extra virgin olive oil
2 tablespoons soy sauce or tamari
1 medium courgette, grated
freshly ground pepper

You may look at me with squinted, questioning eyes when I tell you to use soy sauce, butter and grated courgette to coat your pasta but it does taste good. This recipe makes around 20 spinach and feta balls, enough for 4 people, so if you are only cooking for 1–2 people the leftovers can be repurposed as a kind of falafel substitute the next day in a sandwich!

1 If using fresh baby spinach, tip it into a large pan with a small splash of water. Place over a medium-low heat and cover with a lid. Leave for 3–5 minutes until wilted, then rinse under cold running water. Squeeze the spinach out over the sink to remove as much liquid as possible, then roughly chop and set aside.

2 Mix the feta, dried herbs, a generous amount of pepper, the egg and flour or breadcrumbs together in a medium bowl. Stir in the chopped spinach, then scoop heaped tablespoons of the mixture and roll into balls. You should get about 20 balls. You can either place them on a baking tray lined with nonstick baking paper and bake in an oven preheated to 180°C fan, 200°C, Gas Mark 6 for 20–25 minutes, or you can fry them over a medium heat in 2 batches in 2 tablespoons oil per batch for 3–4 minutes, turning until golden on both sides.

3 If starting with dried pasta, place the pasta in a medium pan and cover with just-boiled water from the kettle. Bring to the boil and cook until al dente (this will generally be the shorter cooking time on the packet). Drain, reserving a small mugful of the pasta water.

4 Return the pasta to the pan off the heat, then stir in the butter, soy sauce or tamari and grated courgette. Serve the pasta with the spinach balls.

Gluten Free If you can tolerate oats, make sure you use certified gluten-free oats in your Oat Flour. Use gluten-free pasta (e.g. brown rice pasta) and make sure your tamari or soy sauce is certified gluten free.

LEFTOVERS: see pp228–233

- Baby spinach
- Feta
- Breadcrumbs, if using
- Pasta (dried or cooked)
- Courgette

TIPS & SWAPS

For 2 people, make the whole recipe but only serve half. Keep the extra pasta (without courgette) in the refrigerator for up to 3 days. Warm up the spinach and feta balls for lunch the next day; serve stuffed into pitta with Quick Pickled Red Onion (page 223), Tahini Dressing (page 226) and salad leaves.

Instead of using grated courgette and soy, make the No-cook Pizza Sauce (see page 220) and heat in a pan over a low heat until reduced by half.

GF option

CRISPY TORTILLA STRIPS WITH CORN & QUINOA

Serves 2–3

1 large or 2 small corn or wholewheat
  tortillas, homemade (see page 214)
  or shop-bought
2 tablespoons olive oil or rapeseed oil
120g quinoa, rinsed or 250g cooked
2 ears fresh corn,* kernels cut off
juice of ½ lemon
pinch of granulated sugar
pinch of salt
½ teaspoon sweet smoked paprika
4–5 sun-dried tomatoes, packed
  in oil**, roughly chopped
½ avocado, pitted, peeled and cubed
handful of fresh coriander, roughly
  chopped
2 spring onions, thinly sliced

Crispy tortilla strips are something that can be sprinkled on to anything and immediately make it better. I like to use corn tortillas when I can as they have a better colour and flavour than wheat ones but either will do. The most important thing is that you make extra strips for snacking on while you cook because, trust me, you'll want them.

1 Preheat the oven to 180°C fan, 200°C, Gas Mark 6.

2 Cut the tortillas in half and then into strips about 5mm wide. Toss with half the oil on a baking tray and place in the oven for 3–4 minutes until just turning golden. Remove and leave to cool and crisp up.

3 If starting with uncooked quinoa, place the quinoa in a medium pan and pour in enough water to cover. Bring to the boil, then reduce the heat and simmer for 10 minutes. Drain, return to the pan and cover with a lid or plate. Set aside for 5 minutes to absorb any excess moisture.

4 Heat the remaining oil in a medium frying pan over a medium heat. Add the corn kernels and sauté for 2 minutes until hot, then remove the pan from the heat.

5 Mix the lemon juice, sugar, salt and paprika into the quinoa and transfer to a serving plate. Top with the cooked corn, sun-dried tomatoes, cubed avocado, chopped coriander, sliced spring onions and crispy tortilla strips.

Gluten Free Use gluten-free corn tortillas.

TIPS & SWAPS

*You can use about 250g canned or defrosted frozen sweetcorn.

**If using sun-dried tomatoes that aren't packed in oil, cover with boiling water and set aside for 15 minutes to rehydrate, then drain.

Replace the sun-dried tomatoes with cherry tomatoes. Halve and roast in a little olive oil in an oven preheated to 140°C fan, 160°C, Gas Mark 3 for 40–60 minutes.

Instead of avocado, top with 30–40g crumbled feta.

LEFTOVERS: see pp228–233

● Sun-dried tomatoes
● Avocado
● Lemon juice
● Spring onions

GF option

ORZO WITH SQUASH, CHILLI, LEMON & PEAS

Serves 2–3

300–400g butternut squash
  (½ small or ¼ large), peeled
  and cut into bite-sized chunks
3 tablespoons olive oil or rapeseed oil
1 teaspoon fennel seeds
½ red chilli, deseeded and finely chopped
100g frozen petits pois or peas
1 red onion, sliced about 3mm thick
1 tablespoon balsamic vinegar
150g dried orzo pasta
  (or any small-shaped pasta)
finely grated zest and juice of ½ lemon
handful of fresh basil, roughly chopped
salt

Orzo is probably the cutest pasta shape around. The little rice-like grains are perfect additions to brothy soups, hearty leaf salads or just simply dressed with some vegetables like this. Eat warm for dinner today and save the rest to have cold for lunch tomorrow.

1 Preheat the oven to 180°C fan, 200°C, Gas Mark 6.

2 Toss the squash with 1 tablespoon of the oil and a pinch of salt on a baking tray. Roast in the oven for 35–45 minutes, flipping halfway through, until golden and soft.

3 Dry-toast the fennel seeds in a frying pan over a medium heat for 2 minutes, or until they pop. Pour in 1 tablespoon of the oil, then add the chilli and frozen peas. Cook for 2 minutes to warm the peas through then tip out into a small bowl and set aside. Return the pan to the heat.

4 Add the onion to the frying pan with the remaining oil and a pinch of salt and cook for 10 minutes over a low heat. Splash in a few tablespoons water and cook for a further 10 minutes, or until the water has evaporated and the onion is soft. Stir in the balsamic vinegar and remove the pan from the heat.

5 If using dried orzo, bring a medium pan of salted water to the boil. Add the orzo and cook until al dente (this is usually the shorter cooking time on the back of the packet). Drain, then add the pasta to the frying pan with the onion and stir together. Stir in the roasted squash and the fennel-chilli-pea mixture from the bowl. Finally, stir through the lemon zest and juice, the basil and a pinch of salt and serve warm.

Gluten Free Use quinoa instead of the orzo.

Omnivores Chuck 125g cooked, shelled prawns (fresh or frozen) into the pan with the onion right at the end of cooking and cook until warmed through. Stir into the pasta together with the other ingredients.

LEFTOVERS: see pp228–233

● Butternut squash (raw or roasted)
● Basil
● Pasta (dried or cooked)
● Lemon juice

TIPS & SWAPS

Swap the butternut squash for roasted
sweet potato.

Replace the orzo with cooked quinoa or giant
couscous (sometimes called Israeli or pearl couscous).

Swap the squash for cubed sweet potato or carrots,
cut into 3mm coins. Roast the sweet potato in oil and
salt for 30 minutes in an oven preheated to 180°C
fan, 200°C, Gas Mark 6 or the carrots in oil and
salt for 20 minutes in an oven preheated
to 200°C fan, 220°C, Gas Mark 7.

QUICKIE CHILLI

MINESTRONE

SHAKSHOUKA

CHICKPEA STEW 3 WAYS

Serves 2–3

BASE STEW

2 tablespoons olive oil
1 carrot, finely diced
1 celery stick, finely diced
1 red onion, finely diced
3 garlic cloves, crushed or finely minced
240g (1 can, drained weight) cooked
   chickpeas, drained and rinsed
400g can chopped tomatoes
200ml water or vegetable stock
½ tablespoon granulated sugar
   or honey or 1 tablespoon
   Date Paste (see page 221)
salt

Having a simple stew recipe like this is super-useful for weekday batch cooking. You can double or triple this base stew, then keep it in the refrigerator or freezer to use throughout the week. It can easily become boring if you're always eating the same flavour combos again and again so by simply adding a couple of extra ingredients (see overleaf) you can have a completely different meal!

1 Heat the oil in a large pan over a medium-low heat. Add the carrot, celery, onion, garlic and a generous pinch of salt and cook, stirring frequently, for 15–20 minutes until the vegetables are softened.

2 Tip the chickpeas, tomatoes, measured water and sugar into the pan. Stir together then bring to the boil. Reduce the heat to a simmer and continue according to one of the recipes overleaf.

Vegan Use granulated sugar or Date Paste.

TIPS & SWAPS

Use an equal weight of fresh tomatoes, instead of canned.

Make a double or triple batch of stew base and store in the freezer in a container for up to 2 months. Defrost to use in one of the recipes on pages 130–131.

LEFTOVERS: see pp228–233

- Cooked chickpeas
- Tomatoes, canned
- Celery
- Carrots

QUICKIE CHILLI

Serves 2

1 tablespoon olive oil or rapeseed oil
3 teaspoons ground cumin
2 teaspoons ground coriander
1 teaspoon ground cinnamon
¼ teaspoon smoked paprika
½ teaspoon cayenne pepper
1 recipe for Chickpea Stew (see page 129)
1 teaspoon mixed dried herbs
2 tablespoons soy sauce or tamari
fresh coriander, finely chopped

TO SERVE
tortillas or cooked rice
natural yogurt or Avocado Cream (see page 219)

1 Heat the oil in a small frying pan over a low heat. Mix in the spices and cook, stirring constantly, for 1 minute.

2 Tip this mixture into the pan of Chickpea Stew and stir through along with the mixed herbs and soy sauce or tamari. Simmer for 15 minutes to thicken. Scatter the chopped coriander over and serve with tortillas or cooked rice and yogurt.

Vegan Serve with Avocado Cream.

Gluten Free Use certified gluten-free tamari or soy sauce. Serve with gluten-free corn tortillas or brown rice.

MINESTRONE

GF & VG options

Serves 4

2 teaspoons fennel seeds
600ml vegetable stock
1 bay leaf
1 tablespoon mixed dried herbs
1 recipe for Chickpea Stew (see page 129)
75g small dried pasta (e.g. macaroni) or 150g cooked
2 handfuls of baby spinach or 2 cavolo nero leaves, stalks removed and leaves roughly chopped
salt

TO SERVE
Parmesan shavings (optional)

1 Dry-toast the fennel seeds in a frying pan over a medium heat for 2 minutes, or until they pop, then remove from the heat.

2 Mix the fennel seeds, stock, bay leaf and dried herbs into the pan of Chickpea Stew. If using dried pasta, add that in now. Bring to the boil, then reduce the heat and simmer until the pasta is al dente. If you're using pre-cooked pasta, simmer the stew for 10 minutes, then stir in the cooked pasta. Remove and discard the bay leaf then stir in the spinach or cavolo nero and season with salt to taste. Divide between 4 bowls and serve topped with shavings of Parmesan, if you like.

Vegan Serve without the Parmesan cheese.

Gluten Free Use certified gluten-free pasta.

SHAKSHOUKA

DF option

Serves 2–3

1 teaspoon olive oil
1 red, yellow or orange pepper,
 deseeded and cut into thick strips
2 teaspoons smoked paprika
½ teaspoon chilli flakes
1 recipe for Chickpea Stew (see page 129)
3–4 eggs
30g feta, crumbled, or Sun Feta (see page 219)
handful of fresh coriander, roughly chopped
salt

TO SERVE
crusty bread

1 Heat the oil in a large frying pan over a medium heat. Add the pepper and cook for 5 minutes. Stir in the paprika and chilli flakes and cook for a further minute.

2 Tip in the Chickpea Stew and stir together. Bring to the boil, then reduce the heat and simmer for 10 minutes.

3 Once thickened, make 3 or 4 wells in the mixture. Crack an egg into each well then cover with a lid (I often just use a large plate or another frying pan) and cook over a low heat until the egg whites are set and the yolks are still runny.* Scatter over the feta and coriander. Serve with crusty bread, for dipping.

Dairy Free Use Sun Feta or chopped olives instead of the feta, or just omit the feta.

TIPS & SWAPS

*If you don't have a lid or large plate to cover the pan, cook the mixture on the hob for 5 minutes, then place under a hot preheated grill with the rack at the top. Cook until the whites are set and the yolks are still runny. Alternatively, carefully cover the pan with foil.

LEFTOVERS: see pp228–233

- Feta
- Pepper
- Fresh coriander

- Pasta (dried or cooked)
- Baby spinach or cavolo nero

TIPS & SWAPS

Just make the filling and serve as
a stew with thick wholemeal bread.

If you have roasted cauliflower to hand
use about 300g instead of raw cauliflower
and skip step 1.

Double up on the pastry and store half in the
refrigerator or freezer for another day.

Use cooked kidney beans or chickpeas
instead of the cannellini beans.

CAULIFLOWER, LEEK & SAGE PIE

Serves 4

1 recipe for Half-oat Pastry
   (see page 217) or Olive Oil Pastry
   (see page 217)
1 large cauliflower, outer leaves
   removed, cut into medium florets
   (about 500g once leaves are
   removed)
2 tablespoons olive oil
6 sage leaves, finely sliced
2 leeks
1 carrot, finely chopped
1 celery stick, finely chopped
3 tablespoons plain white flour,
   plus extra for dusting
500ml vegetable stock
2 teaspoons miso, any kind
240g (1 can, drained weight) cooked
   cannellini beans, drained and rinsed
salt

When you live somewhere that gets pretty cold from October to April, like I do, you're gonna need a hearty pie recipe to pull you through. This is my veggie-friendly version of a chicken and leek pie, with cauliflower and cannellini beans instead of the meat. My special trick here is to stir miso into the sauce, which seasons it and brings in an extra layer of flavour.

1 Prep the pastry according to the recipe on page 217.

2 Preheat the oven to 180°C fan, 200°C, Gas Mark 6.

3 Place the cauliflower in a deep roasting tin or casserole dish (you'll be baking the pie in this later) and toss with 1 tablespoon of the oil, the sage leaves and a pinch of salt. Roast in the oven for 30 minutes. Remove and leave the oven on.

4 Cut the leeks in half and rinse under cold running water to remove any dirt, then shake dry. Chop the leeks into short 2cm wide strips.

5 Heat the remaining oil in a medium pan over a medium heat. Add the leeks, carrot and celery and cook for 10 minutes, stirring frequently, until the leeks have softened. Add the flour and stir for 1 minute. Pour in the stock and stir together.

6 Mix the miso with about 3 tablespoons of the liquid from the pan to thin it out then pour it into the pan. Cook over a medium-low heat, stirring occasionally until thickened. Stir in the cannellini beans, then pour the mixture over the roasted cauliflower in the roasting tray or casserole dish.

7 Cut a piece of nonstick baking paper a little bigger than the size of your roasting tray or casserole dish. Dust the baking paper lightly with flour and place your pastry on to it, dusting the pastry with some flour too. Roll it out so it's a little larger than the size of your tray or dish. Lift the baking paper up and invert it over the tray or dish then peel the baking paper off. Cut a few slits in the centre of the pastry so the steam can escape and bake the pie in the oven for 40–50 minutes until the pastry is dry.

Vegan Use Olive Oil Pastry.

Omnivores Cut 1–2 chicken breasts into 3cm chunks and cook together with the leeks, carrot and celery in the pan. Use chicken stock instead of the vegetable stock. Another delicious tip is to roast the cauliflower with 100g smoked pancetta cubes.

LEFTOVERS: see pp228–233

● Sage
● Leeks
● Celery
● Carrots
● Cannellini beans
● Pastry (Half-oat or Olive Oil)
● Miso

GF option

PAPRIKA BEAN STEW

Serves 2

1 tablespoon olive oil
1 red onion, finely diced
1 carrot, finely diced
1 celery stick, finely diced
about 100ml water
1 orange, yellow or red pepper,
  deseeded and cut into thin strips
1 garlic clove, crushed or very finely
  chopped
½–1 red chilli, finely chopped (keep
  the seeds in if you like it spicy)
2 tablespoons plain white flour
1 tablespoon smoked paprika
1 tablespoon miso, any kind, or
  2 tablespoons soy sauce or tamari
400ml vegetable stock
240g (1 can, drained weight) cooked
  kidney beans, rinsed and drained
½ teaspoon granulated sugar or honey
  or 1 teaspoon Date Paste (see
  page 221)
juice of ½ lemon
salt

One night when my flatmate, Anna, and I were craving something substantial and comforting, we cooked up this stew by cobbling together what we had in the refrigerator. We served it with a huge Yorkshire pudding, of course. The next time we made it, we added some chorizo, which really amped up the rich, smoky flavour, so omnivores take note.

1 Heat the oil in a large pan over a medium heat. Add the onion, carrot and celery and cook, stirring frequently for 5 minutes until the onion is translucent. Add a good splash of water to the pan and stir until evaporated.

2 Add the pepper, garlic and chilli and cook for a further 5 minutes, stirring frequently. Sprinkle over the flour and paprika then cook for 2 minutes, stirring constantly.

3 Stir in the miso, stock, beans, sugar and lemon juice and stir to combine. Reduce the heat to low and simmer for 30 minutes, stirring occasionally to prevent it from burning. The stew should be quite thick now. Season with salt to taste and divide the stew between 2 bowls to serve.

Vegan Use granulated sugar or Date Paste.

Gluten Free Use gram (chickpea) flour or cornflour instead of the plain white flour. Make sure you are using a certified gluten-free tamari or soy sauce.

Omnivores Chop about 50g chorizo into chickpea-sized chunks and sauté them with the vegetables at the beginning of the recipe.

LEFTOVERS: see pp228–233

- Miso
- Pepper
- Cooked kidney beans
- Lemon
- Celery
- Carrots
- Chilli

TIPS & SWAPS
Serve with chunky brown bread or mashed potatoes and cauliflower.

RICOTTA GNOCCHI

Serves 2

80g plain white flour,
   plus extra for dusting
250g ricotta cheese
1 egg
10g grated Parmesan*

I find making my own fresh pasta extremely gratifying. I love the flavour but sometimes I find it a bit too much effort to make tagliatelle due to the time required for kneading, resting and rolling it out. Ricotta gnocchi is an exception and although making it can look like an arduous task, it's actually pretty speedy.

1 Dust a baking tray lightly with flour and set aside.

2 Line a plate with 3 layers of kitchen paper. Place the ricotta on the kitchen paper and top with another 3 layers of paper. Press down and pat the ricotta out into a circle about 1cm thick. Remove the top layers of kitchen paper then tip the ricotta into a bowl.

3 Add the egg and Parmesan to the ricotta and stir to combine. Add the flour and gently mix in until just combined.

4 Dust a work surface or a large chopping board with some flour. Scoop the dough on to the floured surface and sprinkle a little more flour over it and on your hands. Flatten the dough slightly and cut into quarters. Roll one of the quarters out gently into a 2cm wide rope then cut it into 2cm pieces. Carefully place the gnocchi on to the prepared baking tray and repeat with the remaining dough.

5 If your sauce is ready to go, cook the gnocchi immediately by dropping them gently into a pan of boiling water and cooking for 2–3 minutes. Otherwise place the tray into the freezer for about 2 hours until the gnocchi are frozen, then tip them all into a re-sealable plastic bag. Date and label it and freeze for up to 3 months. You don't have to defrost them before cooking, just dump them straight into a pan of boiling water and cook as usual for 2–3 minutes until they puff up and float to the surface.

TIPS & SWAPS

*Parmesan isn't technically vegetarian – choose a vegetarian alternative hard cheese.

Replace half the plain white flour with Oat Flour (see page 216) to increase the fibre content.

LEFTOVERS: see pp228–233

● Ricotta

RICOTTA GNOCCHI
WITH PESTO & COURGETTES

Serves 2

2 tablespoons olive oil
2 medium courgettes, cut
  into 1cm-thick coins
1 recipe for Ricotta Gnocchi
  (see page 137)
3 tablespoons Basil & Rocket Pesto
  (see page 224) or shop-bought
salt

TO GARNISH
handful of basil leaves
Parmesan, shaved*

Simple and quick to make, this is the main way I serve gnocchi. I like to let it brown in the pan a little before stirring in the wet ingredients because that crispy shell it gains is to die for.

1 Heat 1 half of the oil in a large frying pan over a medium heat. Add the courgettes and season with salt. Cook until golden underneath then flip the coins over and cook until the other side is golden, about 10–15 minutes in total.

2 Meanwhile, bring a large pan of salted water to the boil. Once the courgettes are cooked, remove them from the pan to a plate and take the pan off the heat.

3 Add the gnocchi to the boiling water and cook for 2–3 minutes until they puff up and start to float to the surface. Reserve a mugful of the water from the pan of gnocchi, then drain the gnocchi.

4 Add the gnocchi to the frying pan with the remaining oil and return to the heat. Allow the gnocchi to sit undisturbed in the frying pan until they start to colour and crisp up, then add the courgettes, pesto and a splash of the reserved pasta water to the pan. Gently stir to coat the gnocchi, then remove from the heat and divide between 2 plates. Top with fresh basil and Parmesan shavings and serve.

TIPS & SWAPS

*Parmesan isn't technically vegetarian – choose a vegetarian alternative hard cheese.

LEFTOVERS: see pp228–233

- Courgettes
- Pesto
- Basil

TIPS & SWAPS

*Parmesan isn't technically vegetarian – choose a vegetarian alternative hard cheese.

Don't have sage? Don't worry! Leave it out or sprinkle with fresh thyme or chopped basil.

Most vegetables will work – try cubed courgettes fried in a little olive oil, roasted butternut squash or steamed broccoli.

V NS

VG option

PASTA WITH MUSHROOMS, CRISPY SAGE & GARLIC BREADCRUMBS

Serves 2

125g dried pasta or 250g cooked
4 tablespoons olive oil or rapeseed oil
1 tablespoon plain white flour
300ml vegetable or chicken stock
20g Parmesan*, finely grated
  (or other hard cheese)
1 bay leaf
4 large sage leaves
100g chestnut or button mushrooms,
  sliced
3 tablespoons dried breadcrumbs
1 garlic clove, crushed or
  very finely chopped
salt

As I have an Italian-American mum, I've grown up eating lots of pasta, and it is my go-to food for a weeknight when I don't feel like cooking. This is a cupboard-friendly meal as you can use whatever veg you have around (top tip: use frozen peas if you don't have any fresh veggies) and you don't even need to have milk as you use vegetable stock for the sauce. The garlic breadcrumbs are not to be missed – they amp up the dish and make it feel special.

1 If starting with dried pasta, place the pasta in a medium pan and cover with just-boiled water from the kettle. Bring to the boil and cook until al dente (this will generally be the shorter cooking time on the packet). Drain, reserving a small mugful of the pasta water.

2 Heat 1 tablespoon of the oil in a medium pan over a medium heat. Add the flour and stir for 1 minute then reduce the heat to low and gradually pour in the stock, stirring well between additions, until all the stock has been added. Stir in the Parmesan and add the bay leaf. Simmer for 5 minutes, stirring occasionally, then season with salt to taste.

3 Heat the remaining oil in a small frying pan over a medium-high heat. Add the sage leaves and fry until crisp. Drain on kitchen paper and set aside.

4 Add the sliced mushrooms to the pan and cook over a medium heat for 5–7 minutes until dark and soft. Pour the cooked mushrooms into the sauce and return the frying pan to the heat.

5 Add the breadcrumbs, garlic and a pinch of salt to the frying pan and toast, stirring constantly but gently, for 2 minutes so the garlic cooks and the breadcrumbs are crisped.

6 Remove the bay leaf from the sauce and pour it over the cooked pasta. Stir together and splash in a little of the reserved pasta water to loosen the mixture, if needed. Divide between dishes then top with the mushrooms, breadcrumbs and crispy sage and serve.

Vegan Use vegetable stock. Replace the cheese in the sauce with 2 tablespoons nutritional yeast flakes.

Omnivores This is a great recipe to add prawns to! Omit the Parmesan from the sauce and don't use sage, just sprinkle chopped fresh parsley over the finished dish. If using frozen, peeled, cooked prawns just chuck them into the sauce in the last minute of simmering to defrost them. If using fresh, cooked, peeled prawns just stir them into the sauce right at the end.

LEFTOVERS: see pp228–233

- Mushrooms
- Pasta (dried or cooked)
- Sage leaves
- Breadcrumbs

ROASTED CAULIFLOWER & GARLIC SOUP

Serves 3–4

1 large head of cauliflower, outer
  leaves removed (about 500g
  once leaves are removed)
2 tablespoons olive oil
1 red onion, thickly sliced
3 garlic cloves, crushed
250ml vegetable stock
500ml milk or non-dairy milk
2 teaspoons miso, any kind, or
  2 tablespoons soy sauce or tamari
¼ teaspoon ground cayenne
¼ teaspoon smoked paprika
½ teaspoon ground turmeric
120g (½ can, drained weight) cooked
  cannellini beans, drained and rinsed
4 sprigs of thyme, leaves picked
1 tablespoon lemon juice
2 tablespoons natural or unsweetened
  soya yogurt or crème fraîche
  (optional)
handful of chive sprouts or finely
  chopped chives
salt and freshly ground pepper

If you've never had roasted cauliflower before, you're about to meet a game changer. The bitterness fades away to leave a deep and cosy flavour, while the cannellini beans make the soup more filling while keeping the creamy texture. It's even dairy free if you opt for non-dairy milk, which I usually do.

1   Preheat the oven to 180°C fan, 200°C, Gas Mark 6.

2   Cut the cauliflower into large florets and toss in 1 tablespoon of the oil in a roasting tin or on a rimmed baking tray. Roast in the oven for 30 minutes, tossing occasionally until soft and starting to turn golden.

3   Meanwhile, heat the remaining oil in a large pan over a medium heat. Add the sliced onion and sauté for 5 minutes until translucent. Add the garlic and cook for 1 minute. Add the stock, milk, miso, cayenne, smoked paprika, turmeric and drained beans. Bring to the boil then remove from the heat.

4   Add the roasted cauliflower, thyme and lemon juice to the pan. Blend the soup. This can either be done straight in the pan using a hand-held blender or you can transfer the soup to a freestanding blender and blitz it in there. Just be careful not to overfill your blender, so you may need to blend in batches. Season with salt and pepper to taste.

5   Divide between bowls then top with the yogurt, if using, and the chive sprouts or chopped chives.

Vegan Use non-dairy milk and unsweetened soya yogurt (if using).

Gluten Free Make sure that you are using a certified gluten-free tamari or soy sauce.

LEFTOVERS: see pp228–233

● Cannellini beans
● Yogurt or crème fraîche
● Lemon juice
● Thyme
● Miso

TIPS & SWAPS

Make a quick, creamy pasta sauce from leftover soup – thin it out with a little vegetable stock and some butter or olive oil.

If you have roasted cauliflower to hand use about 300g. Skip step 1 and continue with the recipe.

THAI GREEN CURRY PEA SOUP

Serves 3–4

280g frozen petits pois or peas
250ml coconut milk
   (or 100g creamed coconut stirred
   into 250ml hot water), reserve
   a little for drizzling later
100g baby spinach or
   30g frozen spinach
juice of 1 lime
1–3 tablespoons Thai green curry
   paste, homemade (see page 221)
   or shop-bought
handful of fresh coriander leaves,
   roughly chopped
1 spring onion, finely sliced

I like to make my own curry paste because I can control the heat and salt levels, but you can buy some pretty good shop-bought green curry pastes now. If I'm buying it I usually go to Asian grocers as the paste in supermarkets seems more expensive and less flavoursome. My top tip for making this soup is to make excess and freeze it – I like to repurpose it into a riff on Thai green curry by serving it with cooked rice, potatoes, runner beans or mangetout and broccoli.

1 Place the frozen peas and coconut milk or creamed coconut and hot water mixture in a medium pan and cook over a medium heat until the peas have defrosted and the mixture is gently steaming.

2 Stir in the spinach until wilted and cooked (or defrosted, if using frozen spinach) and lime juice then blend the soup. This can either be done straight in the pan using a hand-held blender or you can transfer the soup to a freestanding blender and blitz it in there. Just be careful not to overfill your blender, so you may need to blend in batches.

3 Blend or stir in the curry paste. Start with 1 tablespoon and add more if needed. I recommend this because if you're using shop-bought paste it can vary wildly in strength of flavour, level of heat and salinity. Serve the soup hot, drizzled with the reserved coconut milk, the coriander and spring onion.

Vegan The recipe for the Thai curry paste is vegan but if using shop-bought paste, then make sure you check the label.

TIPS & SWAPS

Turn leftover soup into curry! Boil chopped white or sweet potatoes, broccoli and green beans and mix them into the soup when reheating it. You could also add roast veggies, frozen prawns or cold chicken from a roast. Serve with cooked brown rice and fresh coriander.

LEFTOVERS: see pp228–233

● Baby spinach
● Thai green curry paste
● Coconut milk
● Fresh coriander
● Spring onions

VG option

CURRIED TOMATO-COCONUT SOUP

Serves 2–3

1 tablespoon olive oil
1 small red onion, diced
1 tablespoon grated or finely
    chopped fresh root ginger
2 garlic cloves, crushed
    or very finely chopped
50g creamed coconut or 200ml
    (½ a can) coconut milk
200ml boiling water (if using the
    creamed coconut)
400g can chopped tomatoes
1 tablespoon miso, any kind,
    or soy sauce or tamari
½ teaspoon granulated sugar
    or honey or 1 teaspoon Date
    Paste (see page 221)
about 100g red lentils, rinsed
200ml cold water
½ teaspoon garam masala
½ teaspoon ground turmeric
2½ teaspoons sweet smoked paprika
1 teaspoon coriander seeds, ground

TO SERVE
handful of fresh coriander, chopped

This is a humble tomato soup, jazzed up with coconut milk
and spiced and thickened with red lentils. It's a thrifty, filling
recipe for cold evenings, and is a lot more special than your
usual tomato soup.

1   Heat the oil in a medium pan over a medium heat. Add the onion and sauté
    for 7–10 minutes until translucent. Add the ginger and garlic, reduce the
    heat and sauté for a further minute.

2   If using creamed coconut, place the creamed coconut in a mug and pour
    over the measured boiling water. Stir until melted and combined.

3   Set aside 2 tablespoons of the creamed coconut-water mixture or coconut
    milk for drizzling at the end. Add the remaining coconut mixture or milk to
    the pan together with the chopped tomatoes, miso, sugar, red lentils and
    the measured cold water. Stir, then bring to the boil. Reduce the heat and
    simmer for 20 minutes, stirring occasionally. Add the spices, stir and cook
    for a further 2 minutes.

4   Blend the soup until smooth or leave as is for something more like dahl.
    Serve drizzled with the reserved coconut mixture or milk and some
    chopped coriander.

Vegan Use sugar or Date Paste.

Gluten Free Make sure that you are using a certified gluten-free tamari
or soy sauce.

LEFTOVERS: see pp228–233

● Coconut milk or creamed
    coconut
● Fresh coriander
● Miso

ONE-PAN CREAMY PASTA WITH ASPARAGUS, LEMON & BASIL

(V)

Serves 2

150g dried wholewheat pasta,
    such as spaghetti*
1 tablespoon olive oil
2 garlic cloves, crushed
    or very finely chopped
600ml boiling water
100g asparagus
¼ white cabbage, sliced into
    5mm-wide ribbons
handful of basil leaves,
    finely chopped
1 egg, lightly beaten
finely grated zest of 1 lemon
30g Parmesan, Grana Padano
    or Cheddar cheese, grated
salt and freshly ground pepper

This pasta dish is a dream come true – the method cooks the pasta by water absorption so you don't have to drain it at the end. What you're left with is perfectly cooked pasta and vegetables coated in a slick of starchy water. By vigorously stirring a beaten egg into the pasta just as it finished cooking, you create a luscious yet light sauce in a matter of seconds.

1   Place the pasta, oil, garlic and measured boiling water into a deep frying pan over a medium heat. Bring to the boil then reduce the heat and simmer, pushing the pasta into the pan to submerge it as it softens, for 6 minutes, stirring occasionally to prevent clumping.

2   Snap the woody ends off the asparagus then cut into small pieces. Place the asparagus and cabbage on top of the pasta in the pan. Cover with a lid or a large plate and cook for 5 minutes.

3   Carefully uncover and take the pan off the heat. Immediately add the basil and egg into the frying pan and quickly toss and stir into the pasta with a couple of forks until the egg has thickened into a lovely, creamy sauce. If the egg doesn't look like it's thickening up place the pan back on the heat briefly, while still mixing, to help it cook through. At this point you can splash some water into the pan to thin the sauce out a little, if needed.

4   Stir the lemon zest and cheese into the pasta, reserving some for sprinkling, and season with salt and pepper. Divide between 2 plates and top with more cheese, lemon zest and a small squeeze of lemon juice.

LEFTOVERS: see pp228–233

● White cabbage

TIPS & SWAPS

*Use wholemeal spaghetti to help you feel fuller for longer.

If asparagus isn't in season, replace with an equal quantity of broccoli, runner or broad beans.

Grana Padano is often cheaper than Parmesan and works just as well!

TIPS & SWAPS

*Parmesan isn't technically vegetarian – choose a vegetarian alternative hard cheese.

This dish works with any pasta shape you like!

Use a spiralizer, vegetable peeler or box grater to create long ribbons of raw courgette, then toss in with the pasta at the end to bulk up the dish and add more vitamins.

GF option

CREAMY CAVOLO NERO, LEEK & PEA PASTA

Serves 2

1 large or 2 small leeks
150g cavolo nero (weighed with stems)
1 tablespoon olive oil
150g dried wholewheat
  tagliatelle or 300g cooked
100g frozen petits pois or peas
4 sprigs of thyme, leaves picked
4 tablespoons crème fraîche
  or ricotta cheese
salt
grated Parmesan, to serve (optional)*

Cavolo nero is my favourite leaf to cook. Its texture is better than curly kale in my opinion and it doesn't wither away into nothingness like spinach tends to do. Combined with the soft sweetness of leeks and peas plus the zing of crème fraîche, this is a light, fresh pasta dish packed with veggies. If you own a spiralizer, tossing in some raw, spiralized courgette will add even more vitamins and bulk to this dish.

1 Cut the leek in half lengthways and wash under cold running water to remove any dirt between the layers. Shake off the excess water and place on a chopping board and cut into 2cm thick strips, then rinse again in a colander.

2 Strip the leaves off the stems of the cavolo nero and roughly chop the leaves, discarding the stems. Set aside.

3 Heat the oil in a large frying pan over a medium-low heat. Add the leek with a generous pinch of salt and cook for 15 minutes, stirring frequently so they soften but don't colour.

4 Meanwhile, if starting with dried pasta, place the pasta in a medium pan and cover with just-boiled water from the kettle. Bring to the boil and cook until al dente (this will generally be the shorter cooking time on the packet). Drain, reserving a small mugful of the pasta water.

5 Add the cavolo nero and frozen peas to the pan with the leeks and stir over a medium heat until the cavolo nero has softened a little. Add the thyme, a good splash of the reserved pasta water (or just some tap water if you're using precooked pasta) and the creme fraîche. Stir until the cavolo nero is fully softened then stir in the pasta. Season with salt to taste and add more pasta water if needed to make it saucier. Divide between plates and top with Parmesan, if using.

Gluten Free Use gluten-free pasta (e.g. brown rice pasta) instead of the tagliatelle.

LEFTOVERS: see pp228–233

- Cavolo nero
- Leeks
- Pasta (dried or cooked)
- Crème fraîche or ricotta
- Frozen petits pois or peas
- Thyme

EASY SUMMER PASTA

Serves 2

300g cherry tomatoes, halved
2 medium courgettes
1 aubergine, cut into 2cm cubes
1 tablespoon olive oil or rapeseed oil
2 teaspoons mixed dried herbs
    (I like herbes de Provence)
75g fresh mozzarella cheese,
    torn into medium strips
150g dried wholewheat penne
    pasta or 300g cooked
3 tablespoons crème fraîche
    or ricotta cheese
salt

By roasting tomatoes, aubergine and courgettes together you end up with a ratatouille-like mixture. Just whack it all in the oven for an hour and come back when you are ready to cook the penne. Throw on some torn mozzarella near the end so that it melts over the vegetables and combine with the pasta and some crème fraîche.

1 Preheat the oven to 180°C fan, 200°C, Gas Mark 6.

2 Reserve roughly 70g of the cherry tomatoes for later. Pour the rest on to a roasting tray. Cut the courgettes in half along their lengths, then cut the lengths into half-moons about 2cm thick and add them to the roasting tray with the aubergine, oil, herbs and a pinch of salt. Toss together and roast in the oven for 1 hour, tossing halfway through cooking. In the last 15 minutes, scatter the torn mozzarella over the top of the vegetables and return to the oven so the cheese melts.

3 Meanwhile, if starting with dried pasta, place the pasta in a medium pan and cover with just-boiled water from the kettle. Bring to the boil and cook until al dente (this will generally be the shorter cooking time on the packet). Drain, reserving a small mugful of the pasta water.

4 Once the vegetables and mozzarella have finished roasting scoop them into the pan of drained pasta along with the crème fraîche or ricotta and a splash of reserved pasta water (or tap water if using precooked pasta). Season with salt to taste and divide between 2 plates. Scatter the reserved cherry tomatoes over the pasta and serve.

Vegan Omit the mozzarella and replace the crème fraîche with 2 tablespoons extra virgin olive oil and a squeeze of fresh lemon juice.

Gluten Free Use gluten-free pasta (e.g. brown rice pasta).

TIPS & SWAPS

Roast some extra tomatoes and cook extra pasta to use for lunch or dinner the next day. Keep in the refrigerator in a container for up to 3 days. See the leftovers table, pages 228–233, for how to use them.

LEFTOVERS: see pp228–233

- Aubergine
- Courgette
- Cherry tomatoes
- Mozzarella cheese
- Pasta (dried or cooked)
- Crème fraîche or ricotta cheese

LENTIL & FENNEL RAGU WITH BALSAMIC ONIONS

V

VG & GF options

Serves 4

2 tablespoons olive oil
1 red onion, cut into 2mm thick slices
about 100ml water, plus 1 tablespoon
2 tablespoons balsamic vinegar
1 bulb of fennel
3 garlic cloves, roughly chopped
   or crushed
2 teaspoons coriander seeds, ground
1 tablespoon fennel seeds
2 teaspoons mixed dried herbs
2 teaspoons granulated sugar
   or honey or 1 tablespoon Date
   Paste (see page 221)
400g can chopped tomatoes
800ml vegetable stock
125ml white or red wine or water
90g Puy lentils, rinsed
50g walnuts, finely chopped (optional)
1 tablespoon miso, any kind, or
   2 tablespoons soy sauce or tamari
3 tablespoons Worcestershire sauce*
300g dried pasta or 600g cooked
salt
grated Parmesan, to serve**

Even if you don't think you'd enjoy a vegetarian ragu, this one might surprise you... in a good way. I don't really like fennel bulb raw as I find the anise flavour too intense and the texture a bit tough. But when, on impulse, I cooked it down into a stewy sauce, it softened in flavour and texture. I'm such a fan of the tomato and fennel combo with the lentils and walnuts.

1 Heat half of the oil in a large pan over a medium heat. Add the sliced onion and pinch of salt and cook for 5 minutes, stirring frequently. Pour in 50ml of the water and stir until the water has evaporated, then reduce the heat to low and cook for a further 3 minutes. Add in another 50ml water and cook for a further 3 minutes. Stir in half the balsamic vinegar, transfer the onions to a plate and set aside.

2 Heat the rest of the oil in the same pan over a medium-low heat. Trim the base of the fennel then cut in half from top to base. Slice each half into about 3mm-thick slices then add to the pan together with the garlic. Cook, stirring constantly for 1 minute to cook the garlic. Add the coriander and fennel seeds and stir through for a further minute. Add the herbs, sugar, tomatoes, stock and wine or water. Stir in the lentils and walnuts then bring the mixture to the boil. Reduce the heat to low, cover and simmer for 40–50 minutes, or until the lentils are tender but not mushy.

3 Uncover the pan. Mix the miso with the tablespoon of water in a small bowl or mug then tip into the pan and stir through with the remaining tablespoon of balsamic vinegar and the Worcestershire sauce. Taste the sauce and add salt, if needed. Cook, uncovered, until it is reduced to a thick sauce.

4 Meanwhile, if starting with dried pasta, place the pasta in a medium pan and cover with just-boiled water from the kettle. Bring to the boil and cook until al dente (this will generally be the shorter cooking time on the packet). Drain, reserving a small mugful of the pasta water.

5 Stir most of the thickened sauce into the cooked pasta together with a good splash of the reserved pasta water. Divide between 4 bowls, top with more sauce and some of the onions and serve with Parmesan, if you like.

Vegan Use granulated sugar or Date Paste. Make sure your wine (if using) is vegan. Use vegan Worcestershire sauce or Marmite or vegemite instead. Don't serve with Parmesan.

Gluten Free Use gluten-free pasta (e.g. brown rice pasta). Make sure your tamari or soy sauce is certified gluten free.

LEFTOVERS: see pp228–233

● Pasta (dried or cooked)
● Miso

TIPS & SWAPS
*Conventional Worcestershire sauce contains fish — find vegetarian or vegan alternatives online or in health-food shops, or use Marmite or vegemite instead.

**Parmesan isn't technically vegetarian — choose a vegetarian alternative hard cheese.

Replace the fennel with 2 sticks of chopped celery.

This sauce also makes a great pie filling.

Make a double batch and store in the freezer in a container for up to 3 months.

TIPS & SWAPS

Replace the mango with thinly sliced apple, cubed pineapple or peach.

Use frozen (then defrosted) mango cubes instead of fresh.

For the dressing use creamed coconut instead of coconut milk. Stir 30g into 4 tablespoons hot water. This is much more convenient than using a small amount of canned coconut milk which goes off within a few days.

HALLOUMI & MANGO NOODLE SALAD

Serves 2

100g frozen, shelled edamame beans
150g soba or udon noodles
125g halloumi, cut into
    3mm-thick slices
½ large ripe mango, peeled and cubed
2 spring onions, thinly sliced
handful of basil, roughly chopped
handful of cashews or peanuts,
    roughly chopped

CORIANDER-COCONUT DRESSING

20g fresh coriander leaves
10g piece of fresh root ginger, peeled
    and very finely chopped or grated
juice of 1 lemon
2 tablespoons soy sauce or tamari
1 tablespoon granulated sugar or
    honey or 2 tablespoons Date Paste
    (see page 221)
1–2 pinches of chilli flakes
80ml coconut milk

**Halloumi and mango may seem an unlikely pairing but it's
a good combo, trust me. Sweet and salty, chewy and juicy,
this is a light meal for a summery day. If you don't eat dairy
then I have good news – the baked tofu from page 75 swaps
in perfectly in place of the halloumi!**

1 Place the frozen edamame beans in a colander in the sink. Place the noodles
in a pan of boiling water over a medium heat. Cook for the length of time
indicated on the packet then pour the contents of the pan over the frozen
edamame beans in the colander. Leave to stand for 30 seconds (to defrost
the edamame) then rinse under cold running water to prevent the noodles
from clumping.

2 Heat a dry, nonstick frying pan over a medium heat. Add the sliced halloumi
and fry for 2–4 minutes until it is light golden, then flip over and fry on the
other side. Remove from the pan.

3 Blend all the dressing ingredients together. This can be done in a jug using a
hand-held blender or in a freestanding blender. If you don't have a blender,
just chop the coriander leaves as finely as possible and stir into the rest of
the dressing ingredients.

4 Toss the noodles and edamame beans with the cubed mango, spring onion,
basil and cashews or peanuts. Divide between 2 plates and top with the
dressing and halloumi slices.

Vegan Replace the halloumi with the baked tofu from the recipe on page 75.
Use granulated sugar or maple syrup in the dressing.

Gluten Free If you can find gluten-free soba noodles, use those, otherwise
use flat rice noodles (the ones usually used for pad Thai) instead. Make sure
your soy sauce or tamari is certified gluten free.

LEFTOVERS: see pp228–233

● Halloumi
● Basil
● Fresh coriander
● Coconut milk
● Spring onions
● Mango

ORANGE, FENNEL, OLIVE & PEARL BARLEY STEW

Serves 2–3

1 bulb of fennel
2 tablespoons olive oil
2 teaspoons fennel seeds
2 red onions, roughly diced
1 red, yellow or orange pepper, stalk
  removed, deseeded and thinly sliced
5 garlic cloves, crushed
  or very finely chopped
½ teaspoon smoked paprika
½ teaspoon ground cinnamon
½ teaspoon ground turmeric
1 bay leaf
1 large orange (finely grated zest
  of ½, juice of whole)
400g can chopped tomatoes
70g black or green pitted olives,
  roughly chopped
1 litre vegetable stock or chicken stock
80g pearl barley
120ml white or red wine or more stock
1 tablespoon sherry vinegar or apple
  cider vinegar or balsamic vinegar
2 teaspoons granulated sugar
  or 1 tablespoon Date Paste
  (see page 221)
salt
basil leaves, torn, to serve

My dad makes a chicken stew with olives, lots of orange juice and a cinnamon stick thrown in. It's a surprising combination of flavours but it works. This is my university version of it (basically just minus the meat) with some chewy pearl barley and fennel added in. It's a salty, sweet and fragrant stew, which is light enough to suit a slightly cold summer's evening.

1 Trim the tough base off the fennel then cut in half from top to base. Slice each half into about 3mm-thick slices.

2 Heat the oil in a large pan over a medium heat. Add the fennel seeds and onion and cook for about 5 minutes, stirring frequently, until the onions are translucent. Add the fennel to the pan with the pepper and garlic and continue to cook for 7–10 minutes, stirring occasionally, until the fennel starts to soften.

3 Stir in the paprika, cinnamon, turmeric, bay leaf and orange zest and cook for 30 seconds, then pour in the orange juice, tomatoes, olives, stock, pearl barley and wine. Stir together, then bring to the boil. Once boiling, cover with a lid, reduce the heat and simmer for 20 minutes.

4 Uncover and stir in the vinegar and sugar or Date Paste, then season with salt to taste. If the mixture seems too watery, cook uncovered for 5–10 minutes until it is your preferred consistency. Serve with torn basil.

Vegan If using wine, make sure it's vegan, otherwise use more stock.

LEFTOVERS: see pp228–233

● Pepper
● Pearl barley
● Basil

TIPS & SWAPS
If fresh fennel is out of season,
use 2 sticks of roughly chopped
celery instead.

V GF

VG option

ZINGY CARROT & RICE NOODLE SALAD

Serves 2

2 large carrots, peeled into ribbons
100g rice vermicelli (thin rice noodles)
200g frozen sweetcorn, defrosted
    or canned, drained corn
large handful of fresh coriander,
    roughly chopped
handful of cashews, roughly chopped
2 spring onions, finely sliced
handful of Quick Pickled Red Onion
    (see page 223)

DRESSING
½ teaspoon salt
juice of 2 limes
4 tablespoons apple cider vinegar
    or rice vinegar
2 tablespoons honey or granulated sugar
2 teaspoons freshly grated or very finely
    chopped fresh root ginger
1 garlic clove, crushed or very
    finely chopped
½ red chilli, deseeded and finely chopped
1 star anise (optional)

In this dish a hot, spicy and punchy dressing is heated up and poured over ribboned carrots, effectively quick pickling them. They are tossed into rice vermicelli (which only require a quick soak to 'cook' them) and some other flavoursome additions to make an incredibly fast meal. You don't have to spend much time at the hob, so this recipe is ideal for when it's too hot to bear being in the kitchen for too long.

1   To make the dressing, heat all the ingredients together in a small pan until it begins to steam. Remove from the heat and pour the hot dressing over the carrots. Leave to cool.

2   Place the rice vermicelli in a medium heatproof bowl and pour in enough just-boiled water to cover them well. Leave to stand for 5 minutes, then drain.

3   Remove and discard the star anise, if using, from the bowl of carrots, then toss the noodles, dressing, carrots and sweetcorn together. Tip out on to a plate and garnish with the coriander, cashews, spring onion and Quick Pickled Red Onion.

Vegan   Use granulated sugar.

TIPS & SWAPS

Replace the rice vermicelli with cooked soba or udon noodles. You can also use wide, flat rice noodles (like the ones in pad Thai).

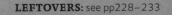

LEFTOVERS: see pp228–233

● Carrots
● Red chilli
● Fresh coriander

Clear the Fridge

At the end of the week, my once bountiful refrigerator is usually looking bare. There will be scraps of raw or cooked vegetables, cut lemons, wilting herbs and the likes, and so it can be very uninspiring to try and cook. This is where these template recipes come in. Use them as guides for how to use up all those random pieces of food that you have left. For each of the templates I have also included three structured recipes so you can see how I use the templates as a guide. Hopefully they can spark some creativity and give you and your refrigerator an end-of-the-week boost to get you through to your weekend food shop.

PIZZA TEMPLATE

Makes 3 medium pizzas

1 recipe for Pizza Dough (see page 220)
plain flour, for dusting
olive oil, for drizzling
salt

SAUCE
(2–4 TABLESPOONS PER PIZZA)
1 recipe for No-cook Pizza Sauce
  (see page 220)
Pesto (see pages 224–225)
puréed, cooked sweetcorn
puréed, roasted butternut squash
  or sweet potato

VEGETABLES
(A HANDFUL PER PIZZA)
puréed cooked sweetcorn
puréed roasted butternut squash
  or sweet potato
raw courgette or asparagus, peeled
  into ribbons
diced courgette or aubergine, sautéed in
  olive oil with a pinch of salt until golden
roasted cubed sweet potato or
  butternut squash
roasted sliced carrots
roasted cherry tomatoes
wilted spinach or cavolo nero
small florets of steamed or roasted
  broccoli or cauliflower
thinly sliced and parboiled white
  potatoes
frozen peas, defrosted
pepper, deseeded and thinly sliced
mushrooms, thinly sliced and sautéed
  in olive oil with a pinch of salt

This template makes enough for 3 medium pizzas. If you are cooking for one or two people, just divide the recipe quantities as needed.

1 Place a medium frying pan over the highest heat. Heat the oven grill to the highest setting and place the rack in the top third of the oven.

2 Take one-quarter of the pizza dough, flour it and stretch it into a circle roughly the size of your frying pan. To do this I lift the pizza dough up, hold it with both my hands and stretch it all the way around the perimeter of the dough. Once the dough is the right size, carefully lay it into the hot frying pan. Reduce the heat to medium and let the pizza dough cook until it starts to change colour and looks dry in patches on top.

3 Spread on the pizza sauce and sprinkle on any vegetables you are using. Dot or sprinkle with any 'special additions' (see page 161) – I personally put mozzarella followed by a grating of Parmesan on to my pizzas.

4 Drizzle your pizza with some olive oil and sprinkle with some salt. Place under the grill with the door ajar and the frying pan handle sticking out. Leave for 4–6 minutes until the crust is browned and, if using mozzarella, the cheese is browned.

5 Remove from the grill (make sure you use a tea towel or oven glove to grab the handle as it may be hot) and leave to cool on a heatproof surface for a second. Slide the pizza out on to a chopping board, top with any 'uncooked sprinkles' (see page 161) and slice into wedges. Repeat with the remaining pizza dough and toppings, as desired.

TOP LEFT: POTATO, CARAMELIZED ONION & THYME
TOP RIGHT: EGG, SPINACH & CHERRY TOMATO
BOTTOM: BLITZED CORN, CORIANDER & SPRING ONION

(V)

PIZZA: BLITZED CORN, CORIANDER & SPRING ONION

Makes 2

about 150g cooked sweetcorn
(if canned, drained, if frozen,
defrosted)
½ recipe for Pizza Dough (see page 220)
½ recipe for 'Chorizo' Dip (see page 47)
150g mozzarella cheese, torn
finely grated Parmesan, for sprinkling
olive oil, for drizzling
handful of fresh coriander, finely chopped
1 spring onion, thinly sliced
2 radishes, thinly sliced
salt

A slightly unusual sauce here. It's so simple to do though and my boyfriend, Andy, loves it. The vibrant sweetcorn base is offset by shards of thinly shaved radish, pungent spring onion and fresh coriander. Don't forget about the smoky 'Chorizo' Dip (see page 47) – you will be a fan of it if you usually go for a meaty pizza.

1   Blitz the sweetcorn in a blender or in a jug with a hand-held blender to form a rough paste.

2   Follow the pizza template method on page 158 to make and cook the pizzas. Blob the 'Chorizo' Dip and blitzed sweetcorn over the pizzas along with the mozzarella cheese and Parmesan, but don't put the coriander, spring onion and radishes on yet. Once the pizzas have been cooked, sprinkle them on top.

(V)

PIZZA: POTATO, CARAMELIZED ONION & THYME

Makes 2

1 floury potato (about 100g),
thinly sliced
2 tablespoons olive oil,
plus extra for drizzling
1 red onion, cut into about
2mm-thick slices
about 4 tablespoons water
1 tablespoon balsamic vinegar
½ recipe for Pizza Dough
(see page 220)
½ recipe for No-cook Pizza Sauce
(see page 220) or 200ml of
your favourite tomato sauce
4 sprigs of thyme
150g mozzarella cheese, torn
finely grated Parmesan*, for sprinkling
salt

Carbs on carbs! This is my idea of heaven. I love putting sliced potatoes on pizza because in my eyes, you can never have too many carbs on one plate. Some balsamic-tangy caramelized onion sets it off beautifully and the thyme adds freshness.

1   Place the potato in a small pan and cover with water. Bring to the boil, then reduce the heat to a simmer and cook for 5 minutes. Drain and set aside.

2   Heat the olive oil in a medium frying pan over a medium heat. Add the red onion and a pinch of salt and cook, stirring frequently, over a medium-low heat until softened, about 5–10 minutes. Add the water and stir until it has evaporated then cook for a further 5 minutes until the onion is completely soft. Stir in the balsamic vinegar then remove from the heat and set aside.

3   Follow the pizza template method on page 158 to make and cook the pizzas, sprinkling on the thyme and mozzarella and adding the potato and onions. Serve with a sprinkling of Parmesan.

PIZZA: EGG, SPINACH & CHERRY TOMATO

Makes 2

1 tablespoon olive oil, plus a little
    extra for drizzling
2 garlic cloves, crushed
    or very finely chopped
150g baby spinach
½ recipe for Pizza Dough
    (see page 220)
½ recipe for No-cook Pizza Sauce
    (see page 220) or 200ml of your
    favourite tomato sauce
150g mozzarella cheese, torn
finely grated Parmesan*, for sprinkling
2 eggs
100g cherry tomatoes, halved or
    quartered
torn basil, for sprinkling

Whoever came up with baking an egg right on top of a pizza was a genius. That runny yolk just gives you more sauce to mop up with each slice. Technically, I think this also makes this a brunch-appropriate pizza – yes...?

1   Heat the oil in a large pan over a medium heat. Add the garlic, reduce the heat to low and cook, stirring for 1 minute, then add the spinach. Continue to stir until the spinach has wilted. Remove from the heat and set aside. Give the spinach a little squeeze to remove any excess water before using on the pizzas.

2   Follow the pizza template method on page 158 to cook the pizzas but don't put the eggs, cherry tomatoes or basil on yet. Once the pizza has been under the grill for 2 minutes, crack an egg on to the pizza then place back under the grill for the remaining 3 minutes, or until cooked.

3   Once the pizza is cooked, top it with the cherry tomatoes and a sprinkling of torn basil.

TIPS & SWAPS

*Parmesan is not technically vegetarian – choose an alternative vegetarian hard cheese.

SPECIAL ADDITIONS

Choose between 1 and 3 and use 2–3 tablespoons each per pizza:
'Chorizo' Dip (see page 47), Pea Hummus (see page 46), sliced chillies, sun-dried tomatoes, pitted black olives, feta cheese or Sun Feta (see page 219), balsamic onions (see Lentil & Fennel Ragu on page 150), ricotta, mozzarella, Parmesan, Cheddar cheese, sage leaves, thyme leaves

UNCOOKED SPRINKLES

Use 1–2 tablespoons per pizza:
Basil or fresh coriander, spring onions, Avocado Cream (see page 219), crème fraîche, cherry tomatoes, rocket or pea shoots, Parmesan, Quick Pickled Red Onion (see page 223)

LEFTOVERS: see pp228–233

- Mozzarella
- Basil
- Tomatoes
- Baby spinach

- Mozzarella
- Thyme

- Fresh coriander

FRITTATA TEMPLATE

Serves 2–3

BASE
6–8 eggs
¼ teaspoon salt
2 garlic cloves crushed (optional)
100–200g ricotta cheese (optional)
olive oil, for cooking
freshly ground pepper

1 Whisk the eggs in a large bowl with the salt and some black pepper. If using garlic and/or ricotta, mix that in now. Set aside.

2 Heat a large, nonstick frying pan with 2 tablespoons olive oil over a medium heat. Sauté slow-cooking vegetables first until soft, then add medium-cooking vegetables and lastly any quick-cooking vegetables and sauté until soft. If using any cooked starch ingredients, add them to the pan now.

3 Heat the oven grill to the highest setting and place the rack into the top of the oven.

4 Reduce the heat under the pan to low and pour the beaten egg mixture over the vegetables. Cook on the stove until you can see the egg at the edges of the pan beginning to turn opaque. Sprinkle or dollop on any 'extra' ingredients, then place the frittata under the grill, leaving the handle poking out and the oven door slightly ajar. Cook until puffed and golden.

Gluten Free   Don't use pasta for the 'starch'.

STARCH
(100–200G, SEE
COOKING TIMETABLE ON PAGE 11)

cooked chickpeas
cooked cannellini beans
cooked pasta (spaghetti works well)
sliced, parboiled white or sweet
  potatoes (boil for 5 minutes)
roasted cubed sweet potato
grated raw sweet potato
cooked brown rice

VEGETABLES
(2–3 HANDFULS)

Quick cooking:
roasted, cubed butternut squash or
  sweet potato
roasted sliced carrot
roasted or steamed florets of broccoli
  or cauliflower
roasted cherry tomatoes
sliced and steamed cabbage
baby spinach
kale (stems removed, leaves chopped),
peas (fresh, shelled or frozen)
sweetcorn (fresh, canned or frozen),
green beans (chopped and steamed)

Medium cooking:
diced courgette
diced aubergine
thinly sliced pepper
grated raw sweet potato
chopped asparagus
sliced leeks
sliced mushrooms

Slow cooking:
sliced onions
diced carrot
diced celery

'CHORIZO' DIP
& RED PEPPER

CAULIFLOWER,
SWEET POTATO
& THYME

PEAS, POTATO
& MOZZARELLA

FRITTATA: CAULIFLOWER, SWEET POTATO & THYME

Serves 2

½ large head of cauliflower, outer leaves removed and cut into medium florets (about 250g when leaves are removed)
1 medium sweet potato (200–300g), peeled and cut into 3cm chunks
2 tablespoons olive oil
1 red onion, cut into about 3mm-thick slices
4 sprigs of thyme, leaves picked
6 eggs
salt

My favourite way to use up leftover roasted veg is in a frittata. This recipe is perfect for leftover roasted cauliflower and sweet potato – just skip steps 1 and 2 and continue with the recipe.

1 Preheat the oven to 180°C fan, 200°C, Gas Mark 6.

2 Toss the cauliflower and sweet potato together with 1 tablespoon of the oil and a pinch of salt on a baking tray. Roast in the oven for 45 minutes, flipping halfway through, until starting to brown.

3 Heat the remaining oil in a medium, nonstick frying pan over a medium heat. Add the onion and a pinch of salt and cook, stirring frequently until the onion is beginning to turn translucent. Reduce the heat to low and add the roasted vegetables and thyme leaves in an even layer.

4 Heat the oven grill to the highest setting and place the rack into the top of the oven.

5 Beat the eggs together with ¼ teaspoon salt in a bowl, then pour over the vegetables in the pan. Cook on the stove until you can see the egg at the edges beginning to turn opaque. Place under the grill, leaving the handle poking out and the oven door slightly ajar and cook until puffed and golden.

FRITTATA: PEAS, POTATO & MOZZARELLA

Serves 2

1 medium floury potato (200–300g), unpeeled and cut into about 3mm-thick slices
1 tablespoon olive oil
100g frozen petits pois or peas
2 garlic cloves, crushed or very finely chopped
6 eggs
¼ teaspoon salt
½ ball mozzarella, torn
handful of basil, roughly chopped

Classic Spanish tortillas are potato and onion heavy. Here, I've layered potatoes with sweet peas and gooey mozzarella.

1 Bring a small pan of water to the boil. Add the potato, reduce the heat and simmer for 10 minutes, then drain and set aside.

2 Heat the oil in a medium, nonstick frying pan over a medium heat. Add the petits pois or peas and garlic and cook for a minute or so to defrost the peas. Reduce the heat to low and arrange the slices of cooked potato in the pan.

3 Heat the oven grill to the highest setting and place the rack into the top of the oven.

4 Beat the eggs and salt together in a medium bowl, then pour over the vegetables in the frying pan. Top with the mozzarella and cook on the stove until the egg at the edges of the pan begins to turn opaque. Place under the grill, leaving the handle poking out and the oven door slightly ajar and cook until puffed and golden. Sprinkle the basil over before serving.

FRITTATA:
'CHORIZO' DIP & RED PEPPER

Serves 2

1 red pepper
6 eggs
¼ teaspoon salt
1 tablespoon olive oil or rapeseed oil
2 spring onions, finely sliced
½ recipe for 'Chorizo' Dip (see page 47)

If you have made the 'Chorizo' Dip (see page 47) and are wondering what to do with the rest of it, this is a tasty, unexpected way to use it. Along with the smoky roasted red pepper it's a perfect match of flavours.

1   Either, place the pepper directly over the flame of a gas hob, turning occasionally until the whole skin of the pepper has been blackened. Or, place the pepper on a baking tray, turn on your oven grill to the highest setting and place the rack in the top of the oven. Place the pepper until the grill and turn occasionally until blackened all over.

2   Place the hot, cooked pepper into a bowl, cover with a plate and leave for 10 minutes to steam. Pierce the peppers with a knife to let any steam escape, then rub the pepper under cold running water to remove the skin. Remove the stalk and seeds with your hands and tear the pepper into about 6 strips.

3   Heat the oven grill to the highest setting and place the rack into the top of the oven.

4   Beat the eggs and the salt together in a medium bowl.

5   Heat the oil in a medium nonstick frying pan over a medium heat. Once the oil is hot reduce the heat to low and arrange the torn pepper strips over it. Scatter over the spring onions and pour the beaten egg over, too. Dot with spoonfuls of the 'Chorizo' Dip and cook on the stove until you can see the egg at the edges of the pan beginning to turn opaque. Place the frittata under the grill, leaving the handle poking out and the oven door slightly ajar and cook until puffed and golden.

LEFTOVERS: see pp228–233

● Cauliflower
● Thyme

● Frozen petits pois or peas
● Mozzarella
● Basil

● Pepper
● Spring Onions

V

GF & VG options

TACO TEMPLATE

Serves as many as you want!

Pick a few different fillings. I usually do 1 starchy, 1 creamy, 2 vegetables and 1 extra or salsa. Layer them up in a soft or crunchy tortilla and eat!

small tortillas, homemade (see page 214) or shop-bought, warmed
OR crunchy corn tortillas, shop-bought

STARCHY
(2–3 TABLESPOONS PER TACO, SEE COOKING TIMETABLE ON PAGE 11)
cooked chickpeas
cooked cannellini beans
cooked black beans
cooked kidney beans
cooked green or Puy lentils
cooked brown rice
cooked couscous
cooked quinoa

CREAMY
(1 TABLESPOON PER TACO)
yogurt
crème fraîche
ricotta
cooked sweet potato, puréed
cooked butternut squash, puréed
'Chorizo' Dip (see page 47)
Pea Hummus (see page 46)
Pesto (see pages 224–225)
mashed or cubed avocado
Avocado Cream (see page 219)

VEGETABLES
(A SMALL HANDFUL PER TACO)
mixed salad leaves, baby spinach, rocket or pea shoots
finely sliced gem lettuce or chicory
roasted, cubed squash, sweet potato or white potato
roasted carrots
roasted or steamed broccoli or cauliflower florets
roasted cherry tomatoes
sliced pepper, raw or sautéed in olive oil until soft
balsamic onions (see Lentil & Fennel Ragu on page 150)
fresh corn, cut off the cob, raw or sautéed
raw bean sprouts or grated carrot
steamed cavolo nero or asparagus
thinly sliced cabbage or Brussels sprouts
sweetcorn (defrosted if frozen, drained if canned)

EXTRAS
(A SPRINKLE, PER TACO)
tortilla chips, crushed, for texture
toasted pumpkin seeds
toasted sesame seeds
roughly chopped cashews
roughly chopped walnuts
roughly chopped almonds
halloumi, dry-fried until golden
firm tofu, baked according to recipe on page 75
Cheddar cheese, grated
feta or Sun Feta (see page 219), crumbled
spring onion, finely chopped
Quick Pickled Red Onion (see page 223)
chopped mint, coriander or basil
Slaw (see pages 54–55)
thinly sliced radishes

SALSA
(MIX TOGETHER)
3 parts cherry tomatoes, finely chopped
2 parts fruit (peach, mango, pineapple, grape, apple are all good)
1 part red onion, finely chopped
lime or lemon juice, to taste
pinch of salt
pinch of chilli flakes or a splash of hot sauce
roughly chopped coriander, mint or basil

Vegan Avoid the dairy options in the 'creamy' and 'extras' sections.

Gluten Free Use certified gluten-free corn tortillas.

TACOS: HALLOUMI TACOS WITH MANGO SALSA & RICE

**Serves 2
(2 large or 4 small tacos)**

80g brown rice or 160g cooked
125g halloumi, cut into about
   3mm-thick slices
4 soft tortillas, warmed
a few Quick Pickled Red Onions
   (see page 223)
salt

MANGO SALSA
½ ripe mango, cubed
juice of ½ lime
4 cherry tomatoes, finely chopped
handful of fresh coriander,
   finely chopped
pinch of chilli flakes

I usually end up basing tacos around dry-fried halloumi. It's got that 'meaty' factor and a heavy salt level to balance with the juicy salsa and sharp, pretty pickled red onions. Brown rice bulks them up with starch but I also like filling them with crunchy shredded lettuce and sautéed peppers if I'm craving a veg-ful taco.

1 If starting with uncooked rice, place the rice into a medium pan and cover well with water and a pinch of salt. Bring to the boil then reduce the heat to a simmer and cook for 20 minutes if using long-grain brown rice or 30 minutes if using short-grain brown rice. Check on the rice as it cooks and add more water as needed to prevent it from drying out and burning. Once cooked, drain and return to the pan then cover with a lid or plate and leave for 5 minutes to absorb any excess water.

2 Lay the halloumi slices in a dry nonstick frying pan over a high heat and fry for 2–4 minutes until the slices are light golden, then flip over and fry on the other side. Remove from the pan.

3 Mix all the salsa ingredients together in a medium bowl and set aside.

4 Divide the rice, salsa and halloumi between warmed tortillas. Top with a few strips of Pickled Red Onion.

Gluten Free Use certified gluten-free corn tortillas.

TIPS & SWAPS
Cool and store any extra rice as quickly as possible by rinsing it under cold running water or spreading it out on a plate. Once cooled, keep in the refrigerator for 1 day or in a sandwich bag in the freezer for 2 months. When reheating, make sure it is piping hot before serving.

LEFTOVERS: see pp228–233

- Mango
- Lime juice
- Fresh coriander
- Halloumi
- Brown rice (cooked)
- Cherry tomatoes

VG option

TACOS: CRISPY BROCCOLI TACOS WITH 'CHORIZO' DIP

**Serves 2
(2 large or 4 small tacos)**

2 tablespoons olive oil or rapeseed oil
½ head of broccoli, cut into medium
 florets
about 100g plain flour
about 125ml milk or non-dairy milk
about 100g breadcrumbs
 (I like panko here)
4 small or 2 large wholemeal tortillas,
 shop-bought or homemade
 (see page 214)
½ recipe for 'Chorizo' Dip (see page 47)
1 recipe for Avocado Cream
 (see page 219) or a few tablespoons
 natural yogurt
handful of mixed salad leaves
salt

Coating broccoli in breadcrumbs and baking it makes it super-crispy and is a lot less hassle than frying it. With a little smear of 'Chorizo' dip, you get a spicy bite, which is delicious with some cooling Avocado Cream.

1 Preheat the oven to 180°C fan, 200°C, Gas Mark 6 and grease a baking tray with half the oil.

2 Place the broccoli in a medium pan with a few centimetres of water and bring to the boil. Cover with a lid, reduce the heat to low and cook for 3 minutes, then drain and set aside.

3 Place the flour, milk and breadcrumbs in separate shallow bowls. Dip the broccoli florets into the flour, turning to coat, followed by the milk and then in the breadcrumbs. Lay the coated florets on the prepared baking tray, drizzle over the remaining oil and sprinkle with some salt. Bake in the oven for 20 minutes until golden underneath, then flip over and cook on the other side for 5 minutes.

4 Warm the tortillas then spread with some of the 'Chorizo' Dip and Avocado Cream. Top with a few salad leaves and the crispy baked broccoli.

Vegan Use non-dairy milk and Avocado Cream.

LEFTOVERS: see pp228–233

● Breadcrumbs

TACOS: SCRAMBLED EGG, PEA, ONION & BASIL

Serves 2
(2 large or 4 small tacos)

1 tablespoon olive oil or rapeseed oil
1 red onion, cut into about
    3mm-thick slices
about 50ml water
100g frozen petits pois or peas
4 eggs
4 small soft tortillas, warmed
a small chunk of Cheddar cheese,
    to serve (optional)
handful of basil leaves, torn
salt and freshly ground pepper

**This is a perfect breakfast/brunch taco. Easy and quick
to whip up but also a little more impressive than standard
scrambled eggs on toast!**

1 Heat half the oil in a large frying pan over a medium heat. Add the onion
   with a pinch of salt and cook, stirring frequently, until the onions begin to
   look translucent. Pour in the measured water and stir it through, then cook
   until it has evaporated. Cook the onions for a further 5–10 minutes, or until
   they are completely soft, then transfer to a plate.

2 Return the pan to the heat and add the frozen petits pois or peas. Cook
   over a medium-high heat for about 1 minute, shaking the pan until they are
   defrosted and warmed through. Transfer them to the plate with the onions
   and set aside. Rinse out the pan and return to a low heat to dry.

3 Meanwhile, crack the eggs into a medium bowl and, using a fork, whisk with
   a generous pinch of salt and some black pepper.

4 Add the remaining oil to the pan and, once hot, pour in the eggs and cook,
   stirring frequently until cooked to the texture you prefer. Remove from the
   heat and stir through the onions and peas. Divide the mixture between the
   warmed tortillas and top with grated Cheddar, if you like, and torn basil.

Gluten Free Use gluten-free corn tortillas.

LEFTOVERS: see pp228–233

● Frozen petits pois or peas
● Basil

V

GF option

STIR FRY TEMPLATE

Serves as many as you want!

Use this template like you would one of those supermarket 'meal deal' stir fry mixes. Just remember to get the pan SUPER HOT and prep all the ingredients before you start cooking.

1 Place a wok or large frying pan over a high heat with 1 tablespoon rapeseed oil. If using crumbled tofu as an extra, toss it in a little cornflour and add to the wok. Cook, stirring occasionally until golden, then transfer to a plate. Add another tablespoon of oil to the wok, if needed.

2 Pick 2–4 different vegetables to add to the wok. Start with the slow-cooking ones and stir-fry until they have softened and are starting to colour, then repeat with the medium-cooking ones, and lastly the quick-cooking vegetables.

3 If using an egg as an extra, make a hole in the middle of the vegetables and pour in the whisked egg. Leave for 10 seconds then stir everything together.

4 Reduce the heat to medium. Mix a sauce together and add it to the wok along with the portion(s) of starch. Divide between plates and sprinkle on any toppings.

Vegetarian Use soy sauce or tamari instead of fish sauce.

Gluten Free Use rice noodles, rice, quinoa or certified gluten-free soba noodles for the 'starch'. Make sure you use certified gluten-free tamari or soy sauce in the sauces.

TIPS & SWAPS

EXTRAS: rapeseed oil, for cooking; cubed firm tofu, tossed in cornflour (100g tofu plus ½ teaspoon cornflour per person); whisked egg (1 per person).

VEGETABLES
(A GOOD HANDFUL PER PERSON):

slow-cooking:
sliced carrots
pepper
diced courgette
diced aubergine
quartered red onion

medium-cooking:
chopped asparagus
chopped bok choy or pak choi
chopped green beans
chopped or sliced red onion
thinly sliced pepper

quick-cooking:
frozen peas
frozen shelled edamame
frozen or canned sweetcorn
bean sprouts
thinly sliced Brussels sprouts or cabbage
spinach, chopped kale or cavolo nero
sliced mushrooms
grated broccoli or cauliflower
finely chopped chillies

require steaming before sautéing (once steamed are quick-cooking):
broccoli florets
cauliflower florets
sweet potato

SAUCES
(EACH ONE MAKES ENOUGH FOR 2 PEOPLE)

2 tablespoons soy sauce or tamari + 1 teaspoon grated ginger + 1 crushed garlic clove + 1 teaspoon toasted sesame oil

100ml orange juice + 2 tablespoons soy sauce or tamari + 2 crushed garlic cloves + 1 teaspoon cornflour + 2 tablespoons water

2 tablespoons Thai curry paste + 150ml coconut milk + pinch of granulated or soft brown sugar + juice of 1 lime

juice of 1 lime + 3 tablespoons fish sauce or 3 tablespoons soy sauce or tamari + 2 teaspoons granulated or soft brown sugar or honey

1 tablespoon sugar or honey + 3 tablespoons mirin + 2 tablespoons soy sauce or tamari + 1 crushed garlic clove + 2 tablespoons rice vinegar or lemon juice + 1 teaspoon cornflour + 2 tablespoons water

2 tablespoons miso + 2 crushed garlic cloves + 1 teaspoon grated ginger + 1 tablespoon granulated or soft brown sugar or honey + 3 tablespoons water

3 tablespoons Date Paste (see page 221) + 2 tablespoons ketchup + ½ teaspoon Chinese five spice + 2 tablespoons rice vinegar + 2 tablespoons soy sauce or tamari + 2 tablespoons water

3 tablespoons apricot jam + 3 tablespoons ketchup + 2 tablespoons soy sauce or tamari + 1 teaspoon grated ginger + juice of 1 lime + 1 teaspoon cornflour + 2 tablespoons water

STARCH
(A CUPPED HANDFUL, ABOUT 100–200G, PER PERSON, SEE COOKING TIMETABLE ON PAGE 11)
cooked quinoa
cooked brown rice
cooked udon or soba or rice noodles
cooked pearl barley

TOPPINGS
(A SPRINKLE)
thinly sliced spring onion
toasted sesame seeds
chopped cashews, peanut or almonds
toasted sunflower seeds
toasted pumpkin seeds
chopped fresh coriander, basil,
    Thai basil or mint
thinly sliced chillies
grated raw carrot
Quick Pickled Red Onion (see page 223)

STIR FRY: QUINOA, PEA & BROCCOLI

Serves 2

90g quinoa, rinsed or 300g cooked
1 tablespoon toasted sesame oil
½ head of broccoli, coarsely grated
   or pulsed in a food processor
2 teaspoons finely grated fresh
   root ginger
2 garlic cloves, crushed or very
   finely chopped
100g frozen petits pois or peas
2 tablespoons soy sauce or tamari
1 spring onion, finely chopped

TO SERVE
mixed salad leaves or steamed
   vegetables dressed with
   Miso Dressing (see page 226)

I never truly like the whole 'substitute starches with vegetables' thing... I'm looking at you, 'courgetti' and 'cauliflower rice'. However, these can be used to bulk up wholegrain starches while adding more fibre and some micronutrients. Here I used grated broccoli to bulk up a dish of simple stir-fried quinoa. It's a good basic stir-fry to know as you can change the grain (obviously brown rice would be great but couscous or pearl barley also work) and add other proteins, such as a whisked egg while you fry everything together or cooked prawns.

1 If starting with uncooked quinoa, place the quinoa in a small pan and cover with water. Bring to the boil then reduce the heat and simmer for 10 minutes. Drain and return to the pan, cover with a lid or large plate and leave for 5 minutes to absorb excess water.

2 Heat the oil in a wok or large frying pan over a high heat. Add the quinoa, grated broccoli and ginger and stir-fry for 30 seconds. Add the garlic and stir-fry for a further 30 seconds. Add the frozen petits pois or peas and soy sauce or tamrai and stir until the peas are defrosted and warmed through. Stir through the spring onion.

3 Serve with a simple side of mixed salad leaves or steamed vegetables dressed with Miso Dressing.

Gluten Free Make sure that you are using a certified gluten-free tamari or soy sauce.

Omnivores Add cooked, peeled frozen or fresh prawns together with the peas at the end.

LEFTOVERS: see pp228–233

● Frozen petits pois or peas

TIPS & SWAPS
Start by pouring a beaten egg into the sesame oil, then immediately add the quinoa and broccoli on top and continue with the recipe.

Use frozen edamame or corn instead of the peas.

QUINOA, PEA & BROCCOLI

NOODLES, CRISPY CRUMBLED TOFU, BEAN SPROUTS

SPICY COCONUT RICE WITH BRUSSELS SPROUTS

V VG

GF option

STIR FRY: NOODLES, CRISPY CRUMBLED TOFU, BEAN SPROUTS

Serves 2

120g dried soba or udon or rice noodles or about 175g cooked
200g firm tofu
5 tablespoons soy sauce or tamari
1 tablespoon granulated sugar
juice of ½ lime
½ teaspoon Chinese five spice
100ml water
1 tablespoon cornflour
1 tablespoon toasted sesame oil
100g bean sprouts
handful of fresh coriander leaves

I learnt about this technique for crumbling firm tofu and frying it with cornflour on *Bon Appetit* magazine's website. There the author was talking about how this method of cooking tofu kind of makes it seem like minced meat so is a good introductory recipe for tofu haters or meat lovers. I think I still would say this isn't very meat-like but I prefer tofu in small pieces like this so that it gets nice and saucy.

1 If starting with dry noodles, cook the noodles according to the packet instructions, then drain and rinse with cold water. Set aside.

2 Press the tofu. Wrap the tofu in a clean tea towel and place on a flat surface. Cover with a chopping board and then weigh the chopping board down with something heavy, such as a stack of cookbooks or a pan full of water and leave for 30 minutes to drain.

3 Mix the soy sauce or tamari, sugar, lime juice, Chinese five spice and measured water together in a small bowl.

4 Crumble the pressed tofu into another small bowl and toss with the cornflour.

5 Heat the oil in a wok or large frying pan over a high heat. Add the tofu and cook, stirring occasionally until it starts to colour. Add the cooked noodles and bean sprouts and stir together for 30 seconds. Reduce the heat to medium, pour in the soy sauce mixture and stir to coat the noodles. Once everything is coated remove from the heat and serve with fresh coriander leaves on top.

Gluten Free Use wide, flat rice noodles instead of the wheat noodles or, use certified gluten-free soba noodles. Make sure that you are using a certified gluten-free tamari or soy sauce.

LEFTOVERS: see pp228–233

● Fresh coriander
● Lime juice
● Firm tofu

STIR FRY: SPICY COCONUT RICE WITH BRUSSELS SPROUTS

Serves 2 as a side

100g uncooked brown rice or 200g cooked

1 tablespoon olive oil or rapeseed oil

100g Brussels sprouts, thinly sliced

100g white or red cabbage, thinly sliced

1–3 teaspoons Thai green curry paste (see page 220) or shop-bought

100ml coconut milk or 2 tablespoons creamed coconut mixed with 100ml water

a pinch of cayenne pepper (if your curry paste is mild)

juice of ½ lime

The idea here is it's like a slightly better-for-you version of coconut rice that you might order with your takeaway. It's bulked up with veggies and uses brown rice to keep you full. I add a little green curry paste too, but not so much to make it taste of a Thai green curry, more to just add heat and a little boost of flavour.

1 If starting with uncooked rice, place the rice in a medium pan and cover with water. Bring to the boil then reduce the heat to a simmer and cook for 20 minutes if using long-grain brown rice or 30 minutes if using short-grain brown rice. Check on the rice as it cooks and add more water as needed to prevent it from drying out and burning. Once cooked, drain and return to the pan then cover with a lid or plate and leave for 10 minutes to absorb any excess water.

2 Heat the oil in a wok or large frying pan over a medium heat. Add the Brussels sprouts and cabbage and cook until softened and starting to colour. Add the rice and stir for a minute.

3 Add the curry paste (start with 1 teaspoon and add more later if you need to) and the coconut milk or creamed coconut to the pan and cook until most of the liquid has evaporated. Remove from the heat and stir in the cayenne pepper, if using, and lime juice.

Vegan The recipe for the Thai curry paste is vegan but if using shop-bought paste, then make sure you check the label.

TIPS & SWAPS

Hate Brussels sprouts? Sub in more cabbage or grated, raw cauliflower.

Cool and store any extra rice as quickly as possible by rinsing it under cold running water or spreading it out on a plate. Once cooled, keep in the refrigerator for 1 day or in a sandwich bag in the freezer for 2 months. When reheating, make sure it is piping hot before serving.

LEFTOVERS: see pp228–233

- Cabbage (red or white)
- Coconut milk or creamed coconut
- Lime juice
- Brown rice (raw or cooked)

Cheeky Treats

Gotta love a baked good, eh! I'm a baker at heart so of course I needed to showcase a selection of sweet treats for you. The great news is that none of the recipes require a freestanding mixer or electric beaters – they are all pretty much a one bowl stir-and-bake job. The most complex recipe is probably the Cinnamon Knots, purely because the shaping of them is difficult to explain. However, if you have made bread dough before, it'll be quite simple (and there are pictures to help you with the shaping).

As I'm a bit of a lazy person, I prefer to bake with oil rather than butter most of the time as butter requires time to soften and is usually more effort to mix into batters and doughs (unless it's melted butter). I do use olive oil in a lot of the baking recipes just because it seems to be the healthiest oil to use. Some people might be horrified by this but I'm just gonna say that I use refined olive oil (sometimes called 'light' olive oil) which has barely any flavour and a high smoke point. I only ever use extra virgin olive oil in my Easy Freezer Chocolate Chip Cookies (see page 204) if I'm in the mood for that deep, savoury flavour. If you still are not jamming with the olive oil thing, use an unflavoured oil such as rapeseed oil or just melted butter (yum!) instead.

COOKIE DOUGH BALLS

Makes 20–24

2 tablespoons olive oil
  or 3 tablespoons nut butter
75g Date Paste (see page 221)*
1 tablespoon soft brown sugar
1 teaspoon vanilla extract
pinch of salt
100g porridge oats
4 tablespoons plain wholemeal flour
  or Oat Flour (see page 216)
20g plain dark chocolate, chopped,
  or mini dark chocolate chips

You know when you're just having a bad day and all you want to do is watch Netflix while eating cookie dough? Yeah, same. I think that's all I need to say to introduce this recipe to you...

1 Mix the oil, Date Paste, brown sugar, vanilla and salt together in a medium bowl. Stir in the oats, flour and chocolate chips until well mixed.

2 Roll heaped teaspoons of the dough into balls and place on a plate. Leave to stand for 30 minutes to dry a little before transferring them to a lidded container. Store in the refrigerator for 3–5 days.

Vegan Make sure your chocolate is suitable for vegans.

Gluten Free Use buckwheat flour instead of the wholemeal flour. If you can tolerate oats, make sure they're certified gluten free. If not, use millet flakes instead.

TIPS & SWAPS

*Make a smaller batch of date paste. Soak 50g pitted dried dates in boiling water for 15 minutes. Drain and blend with 2–3 tablespoons water until smooth, using a hand-held blender in a jug or a freestanding blender. Store in an airtight container in the refrigerator for up to 2 days.

LEFTOVERS: see pp228–233

● Nut butter, if using

SINGLE-SERVE CHOCOLATE CHIP COOKIE

Serves 1

1 tablespoon nut butter, such as
  cashew butter or peanut butter
pinch of salt (if nut butter is unsalted)
1½ teaspoons honey, maple syrup
  or golden syrup
pinch of bicarbonate of soda
splash of vanilla extract
1½ tablespoons ground almonds
  or Ground Almond Alternative
  (see page 218) or 1 teaspoon plain
  wholemeal flour
1–2 squares of plain dark chocolate,
  chopped into chunks

People need to stop with the mug cakes. They are rubbery and weird and oh, often leak in the microwave. If you're craving a chocolatey dessert just for yourself, try this. It's easier to make (there's no 'half an egg' involved) and tastes much better. Eat it warm while it's still soft and melty.

1 Preheat the oven to 180°C fan, 200°C, Gas Mark 6.

2 Place the nut butter, salt (if using), honey or syrup, bicarbonate of soda and vanilla extract in a small, ovenproof bowl, mug or ramekin (I use a 7cm ramekin) and stir together until combined. Mix in the ground almonds and top with the chocolate chunks.

3 Place the ovenproof bowl, mug or ramekin on a baking tray and bake in the oven for 6–8 minutes until set around the edges but still soft in the middle. Eat while warm with a spoon.

Vegan Use maple syrup or golden syrup. Make sure your chocolate is suitable for vegans.

Gluten Free Use ground almonds or Ground Almond Alternative.

TIPS & SWAPS

If your ovenproof vessel for baking is larger than 7cm , just check the cookie after 6 minutes, as it will cook more quickly.

LEFTOVERS: see pp228–233

● Nut butter

V EF

VG option

INDIVIDUAL APRICOT SUGAR BUNS

Makes 6

PASTE
2 tablespoons plain
   or strong wholemeal flour
80ml water

DOUGH
6 tablespoons water
2 tablespoons granulated or caster sugar
1 teaspoon fast-action dried yeast
1½ tablespoons olive oil, plus a little
   extra for greasing
130g strong wholemeal flour,
   plus extra for dusting
¼ teaspoon salt
4 ripe apricots, pitted and
   roughly chopped

DIP
30g unsalted butter
4–6 tablespoons caster sugar
1 teaspoon ground cinnamon

TIPS & SWAPS
Replace the apricots with 150g
seasonal or frozen fruit, such as
rhubarb (cooked with
2 tablespoons granulated sugar),
blueberries, blackberries,
peaches or plums.

Did you ever play that game where you had to eat a doughnut without licking your lips? That's the reason behind these doughnut-bun hybrids. Dipping them in cinnamon-sugar gives that throwback doughnut flavour.

1   Mix the paste ingredients together in a small pan and set over a medium-low heat. Stir for 5–10 minutes until it is a thickened, smooth paste, then remove from the heat and set aside to cool.

2   For the dough, mix 4 tablespoons water, half the sugar and the yeast together in a medium bowl and set aside for 5 minutes.

3   Add the slightly warm paste mixture to the bowl with the yeast mixture and stir together. Mix in the oil, then add the flour and salt and stir until it is a sticky dough. Shape your hand like a claw and use it to beat the dough for about 1 minute. Pour a little oil over the dough and turn it to coat it. Cover with clingfilm and leave to rise in a warm place for 1 hour.

4   Meanwhile, place the apricots with 2 tablespoons water and the remaining sugar in a small pan. Cook for 10 minutes over a medium heat, stirring occasionally, until softened and jammy. Leave to cool.

5   Grease a baking tray with oil. Punch the dough down, tip out on to a work surface and dust with flour. Divide into 6 equal pieces and roll each piece into a ball. Dust the balls of dough with flour. Take 1 ball of dough and press down in the middle of it with your thumb to make a roughly 3cm wide well in the centre of the ball of dough. Repeat this with the remaining pieces of dough and place on to the prepared baking tray. Fill the indents with the jammy apricots and leave the buns to rise again in a warm place for 30 minutes.

6   Preheat the oven to 180°C fan, 200°C, Gas Mark 6.

7   Once the buns have risen, bake them in the oven for 20 minutes until golden.

8   To make the dip, place the butter in a small, heatproof bowl and place in the oven for the final 2 minutes of the buns baking. Alternatively, melt the butter in a small pan on the hob or in a microwave-safe bowl in the microwave.

9   Brush the baked buns all over with the melted butter. Mix the sugar and cinnamon together on a plate and roll the buttery buns around in it until they are coated. The buns are best the day they're made but will keep for 2 days in a container in the refrigerator. Just warm them up on a baking tray in an oven preheated to 140°C fan, 160°C, Gas Mark 3 for a few minutes before eating.

Vegan Swap the butter for melted vegan spread or coconut oil.

CHOCOLATE PEANUT FUDGE CAKE BARS

Makes 8

oil, for greasing
160g unsalted peanut butter
50g granulated sugar or 4 tablespoons honey or maple syrup
1 egg
20g unsweetened cocoa powder, plus extra for dusting
1 teaspoon baking powder
pinch of salt
120g carrot, grated

TIPS & SWAPS

*Fold a piece of foil in half and use it as a divider in a large 900g loaf tin.

Replace the carrot with grated courgette.

Change the flavour with a different nut butter (hazelnut butter is expensive but it's amazing in this recipe).

This cake batter will probably seem like the weirdest you have ever made. There's no flour or butter, it's thick, and it may seem the carrot will just make it too 'healthy'. Just trust me; this will probably be one of the richest, fudgiest chocolate cakes you will ever have. The peanut butter provides the fat and, along with the carrots, brings bulk to the mixture. I dust the baked cake with extra cocoa to balance the richness and, as the cake doesn't rise too much, cut it into 'bars'.

1 Preheat the oven to 180°C fan, 200°C, Gas Mark 6. Grease and line the base and sides of a mini 450g loaf tin* with nonstick baking paper.

2 Heat the peanut butter in a medium pan over a low heat until loosened, then stir in the sugar, honey or maple syrup. Remove from the heat and leave until it is only slightly warm. Quickly mix in the egg, then stir in the cocoa, baking powder and salt. Fold in the carrots.

3 Spread the mixture into the prepared loaf tin and bake in the oven for 30 minutes.

4 Leave the loaf to cool in the tin, then tip it out on to a plate, dust with cocoa powder and slice into 8 bars. Store in an airtight container for up to 3 days.

LEFTOVERS: see pp228–233

● Nut butter
● Carrots (raw)

V DF

VG & GF options

BROWNIES

There are many different types of brownie – cakey, fudgy, gooey – in the world. I'm not one for a cakey brownie, I must say, and this recipe is my current favourite. They are not super-gooey but are dense and fudgy. I love adding chopped hazelnuts or even walnuts to the top for texture and to balance the sweetness but I know lots of people don't like to add nuts to brownies so I will leave the addition up to you.

Makes 12–16

100g plain dark chocolate
    (at least 70% cocoa solids)
80ml olive oil or rapeseed oil
    or melted butter
¼ teaspoon baking powder
1 teaspoon vanilla extract
½ teaspoon salt
30g unsweetened cocoa powder
2 eggs
150g granulated sugar
125g plain wholemeal flour
    or Oat Flour (see page 216)
30g hazelnuts, any other nut or dark
    chocolate, roughly chopped (optional)

1   Preheat the oven to 180°C fan, 200°C, Gas Mark 6 and line the base and sides of a 20cm square baking tin with nonstick baking paper.

2   Break the chocolate into a few large chunks and place in a bowl in a medium pan of simmering water, over a low heat. Stir constantly until the chocolate has melted, then remove from the heat. Add the oil or butter, baking powder, vanilla, salt and cocoa powder and mix.

3   Crack in the eggs and mix well to combine. Mix in the sugar and stir vigorously for 2 minutes – this helps to dissolve the sugar into the liquids so you get a nice fudgy brownie. Stir in the flour then pour the batter into the prepared baking tin and smooth it out into an even layer. Scatter over the chopped hazelnuts, if using, then bake the brownies in the oven for 20–25 minutes until set around the edges but still very soft in the middle.

4   Remove from the oven and leave to cool slightly before cutting into 12–16 brownies. Store in an airtight container at room temperature for up to a week.

Vegan Replace the eggs with 2 tablespoons ground flaxseed or chia seeds mixed with 6 tablespoons water or 4 tablespoons puréed silken tofu. Use olive oil or rapeseed oil. Make sure your chocolate is suitable for vegans.

Gluten Free Use gluten-free oats to make the Oat Flour or use buckwheat flour instead (this also works when making the vegan version).

VG option

NO-ROLL SCONES

Makes 4

80g plain white flour
80g Oat Flour (see page 216)
    or wholemeal flour
2 tablespoons granulated sugar,
    plus extra for sprinkling
1½ teaspoons baking powder
¼ teaspoon salt
50g unsalted butter, cubed
1 egg
3 tablespoons milk

I'm pretty lazy when it comes to baking. I hate having to drag out a freestanding mixer or dig through drawers to find cookie cutters. I'm more of a mix, pour and bake kind of gal than a super-involved baker. That's why these scones are a godsend for me. You don't need to dirty cookie cutters or rolling pins when making them as you just pat the dough out into a circle and cut it into wedges. Simple as that!

1 Preheat the oven to 180°C fan, 200°C, Gas Mark 6 and line a baking tray with nonstick baking paper.

2 Mix the flours, sugar, baking powder and salt together in a large bowl. Add the butter and rub it into the dry ingredients with your fingertips until no large chunks of butter remain. Crack in the egg and add the milk, then stir gently until you have a soft, rough dough.

3 Tip the dough out on to the prepared baking tray and pat out into a circle about 2cm thick. Sprinkle over some sugar and cut into quarters. Don't separate the quarters out, leave it as one mega-scone.

4 Bake in the oven for 20–22 minutes until golden and risen. Remove from the oven and cut through the mega-scone where you cut through earlier to separate it into quarters. Store any leftovers in an airtight container for up to 2 days.

Vegan Replace the butter with 50ml olive oil or rapeseed oil. Replace the egg with 1 tablespoon ground flaxseed mixed with 3 tablespoons water. Use 4 tablespoons non-dairy milk instead of the milk.

ANY-FRUIT FREE-FORM GALETTE

Makes 1 galette

1 recipe for Half-oat Pastry (see page
   217) or Olive Oil Pastry (see page
   217) or 250g shop-bought
   shortcrust pastry
plain white flour, for dusting
500g fresh or frozen fruit, such as
   plums and peaches (see method)
2–5 tablespoons granulated sugar
   (depending on sweetness of fruit)

FRANGIPANE

50g granulated sugar or 4 tablespoons
   Date Paste (see page 221)
50g unsalted butter, softened
1 egg
60g ground almonds or Ground Almond
   Alternative (see page 218)
2 tablespoons plain white
   or wholemeal flour
pinch of salt
1 teaspoon almond or vanilla extract

TO SERVE

natural yogurt, whipped cream or ice
   cream (optional)

Picture this: it's the weekend, you want to make a tart but you don't have a fancy dish to bake in and the idea of trying to line a tart tin makes your fists clench in stress. Now, let me tell you about free-form galettes. They are versatile as you can use any fruit, you don't need any fancy tins (just a regular baking tray) and, best of all, they are meant to look rustic so the messier it looks the more... umm... artisanal it is.

1 Preheat the oven to 180°C fan, 200°C, Gas Mark 6.

2 Roll the pastry out on a piece of slightly floured nonstick baking paper into a large rectangle about 3mm thick and roughly as big as your baking tray. Lift the piece of baking paper up, bringing the pastry with it, and put it down on the baking tray so the pastry is still on top.

3 To make the frangipane, cream the sugar or Date Paste and butter together in a medium bowl with a spoon until smooth. Mix in the egg followed by the ground almonds, flour, salt and almond or vanilla extract. Spread the mixture over the rolled pastry, leaving a border of about 3cm around the edge.

4 Prepare the fruit(s) you are using. Here are my seasonal suggestions:
SPRING: Rhubarb cut into 3cm lengths with a little finely grated orange zest.
SUMMER: Peaches or plums or apricots, pitted and flesh cut into quarters or eighths.
AUTUMN: Pears, cored and cut into eighths mixed with blackberries.
WINTER: Peeled, cored cooking apples or dessert apples tossed in the juice of 1 lemon and cut into eighths.
ALL YEAR: Frozen blueberries, raspberries and strawberries – no need to defrost, just chuck them in a bowl!

5 Put the fruit into a bowl with 2 tablespoons sugar and stir to coat. Taste and add a further 1–3 tablespoons sugar, as needed. (Peaches, strawberries and blueberries will usually need only 2 tablespoons sugar, whereas rhubarb, plums, cooking apples and underripe raspberries may need more.

6 Lay the fruit over the frangipane and fold over the border of the pastry (as shown opposite). Bake in the oven for 40–50 minutes until bubbling with a golden crust. Leave to cool slightly and serve warm with yogurt, whipped cream or ice cream, if you like.

LEFTOVERS: see pp228–233

● Fresh or frozen fruit
● Pastry, Half-oat or Olive Oil

Vegan Use Olive Oil Pastry. Use almond butter, cashew butter or vegan spread instead of butter in the frangipane and replace the egg with 1 tablespoon ground flaxseed mixed with 3 tablespoons water.

TIPS & SWAPS

If you want to omit the frangipane, spread a few tablespoons of your favourite jam over the pastry before topping with the fruit and baking.

Double up on the pastry and keep half in the refrigerator or freezer for another day.

TOP RIGHT: OATY SNACK CAKE
MIDDLE: PEAR & HAZELNUT
BOTTOM: LEMON POPPY SEED

OATY SNACK CAKE

Makes 1 small loaf

60g rolled oats, Oat Flour
(see page 216) or plain
wholemeal flour
5 tablespoons granulated sugar
2 teaspoons baking powder
¼ teaspoon salt
½ teaspoon ground cinnamon
240g (1 can, drained weight) cooked
chickpeas, drained and rinsed
2 eggs
4 tablespoons olive oil or rapeseed oil

TIPS & SWAPS
*Fold a piece of foil in half
and use it as a divider in a large
900g loaf tin.

You may have seen recipes for chickpea blondies or black
bean brownies and felt doubtful. I was also a bit unsure about
adding beans to desserts but seriously, if you're still adding
fat and sugar, you will end up with an incredibly tasty treat
(with no chickpea flavour, I promise). This cake is not overly
sweet, is adaptable and has lots of protein and fibre from the
oats and chickpeas so it keeps me feeling fuller for longer.

1 Preheat the oven to 180°C fan, 200°C, Gas Mark 6 and line the base and
sides of a mini 450g loaf tin* or 20cm cake tin with nonstick baking paper.

2 If using a blender or food processor, blend the oats or flour, sugar, baking
powder, salt and cinnamon until fine. Tip into a small bowl and set aside.
Blend together the chickpeas, eggs and oil until completely smooth. Return
the bowl of oat mixture to the blender and blend until smooth.

3 If using a hand-held blender, place the chickpeas in a large bowl and blitz
them up a little. Add the oil and eggs, blitzing again until smooth. Add the
oats or flour, sugar, baking powder, salt and cinnamon. Blitz again until the
mixture is as smooth as possible.

4 Pour the batter into the prepared tin, level the surface and bake in the oven
for 30–35 minutes in the mini loaf tin or 20–25 minutes in the cake tin.
The cake will still look quite pale but a toothpick or cocktail stick inserted
into the middle should come out clean. Leave to cool for 20–30 minutes
before serving. Store in an airtight container for up to 5 days.

LEMON POPPY SEED VARIATION
Replace the cinnamon with the finely grated zest of 1 lemon and 1 tablespoon
poppy seeds. Once the cake has baked, mix 50g icing sugar with a little freshly
squeezed lemon juice to form a thick liquid and pour it over the cake, and then
sprinkle over the poppy seeds.

PEAR & HAZELNUT VARIATION
Replace the cinnamon with 1 teaspoon vanilla extract. Halve a pear and scoop
out its seedy core, then thinly slice it. Roughly chop 20g hazelnuts. Pour the
batter into the tin, then top with the pear slices and hazelnuts.

Gluten Free If you can tolerate oats, make sure you use certified
gluten-free oats in your Oat Flour. If not, use an equal weight of ground
almonds, gram (chickpea) flour or buckwheat flour instead.

DOUBLE CHOCOLATE COOKIES

Makes 18–20

125g plain dark chocolate
  (at least 70% cocoa solids)
5 tablespoons nut butter, such
  as cashew, peanut or almond
240g (1 can, drained weight) cooked
  kidney beans, drained and rinsed
100g granulated sugar
50g unsweetened cocoa powder
¾ teaspoon baking powder
¼ teaspoon salt
20g pistachios or any nut or seed
  (optional)

I've made black bean cookie recipes before which relied on cocoa powder for the chocolate flavour and found them quite lacking. By mixing in melted dark chocolate you are adding cocoa along with cocoa butter, which is quite flavourful in itself and, as it's a fat, makes the cookies rich and soft.

1 Preheat the oven to 180°C fan, 200°C, Gas Mark 6 and line a baking tray with nonstick baking paper.

2 Break the chocolate into small chunks and place in a bowl in a small pan of simmering water, over a low heat. Stir constantly until the chocolate has melted, then remove from the heat. Pour 50g of the melted chocolate into a small bowl and set aside for later, keeping the rest in the pan.

3 If using a hand-held blender, add the beans and nut butter to the pan and blitz into a smooth paste. Stir in the remaining ingredients, except the reserved chocolate and pistachios, if using.

4 If using a food processor, pour the melted chocolate from the pan into it along with the nut butter and beans. Blend until smooth, scraping down the sides of the bowl as needed. Add the sugar, cocoa powder, baking powder and salt and blend again.

5 Place heaped tablespoons of the dough on to the prepared baking tray. You can put them fairly close together as they don't spread much when baking. Wet your hands slightly and flatten the dough with the palm of your hand.

6 Bake in the oven for 6–8 minutes. The cookies should still be soft in the centre but set around the edges. Leave them on the baking tray for a minute, then transfer to a wire rack to cool.

7 Place the reserved chocolate in a sandwich bag (you may need to re-melt it), cut the tip off of the corner of the bag and use it like a piping bag to drizzle the melted chocolate over the cookies. Finely chop the pistachios, if using, and sprinkle over the cookies while the chocolate is still molten. Leave to cool and set. Store in an airtight container for up to 3 days.

Vegan Make sure your chocolate is suitable for vegans.

TIPS & SWAPS
Use an equal weight of black beans instead of kidney beans.

LEFTOVERS: see pp228–233

● Nut butter

GF option

BANANA BREAD

Makes 1 loaf

3 large ripe bananas, peeled
   (250–280g peeled weight)
90g granulated sugar, plus 1 teaspoon
   for sprinkling
80ml olive oil or rapeseed oil
1 teaspoon vanilla extract
4 tablespoons milk or non-dairy milk
1½ teaspoons baking powder
120g plain wholemeal flour
   or gram (chickpea) flour
90g porridge oats
½ teaspoon ground cinnamon

If you look in my freezer drawer, you'll always find butter, pesto, peas and overripe bananas. I'm an overripe banana hoarder, for sure, because I never know when a banana bread craving will hit. This recipe doesn't include eggs because the bananas provide enough moisture to keep the mixture cakey.

1   Preheat the oven to 180°C fan, 200°C, Gas Mark 6 and line the base and sides of a 900g loaf tin with nonstick baking paper.

2   Mash the peeled bananas on a plate with a fork, then tip into a medium bowl and add the sugar, oil, vanilla and milk and stir well to combine. Add the baking powder, flour and oats and stir until just combined. Tip into the prepared loaf tin.

3   Mix the remaining 1 teaspoon of sugar and the ground cinnamon in a small bowl and sprinkle it over the surface of the loaf.

4   Bake in the oven for 50–60 minutes until a toothpick or cocktail stick inserted into the centre of the loaf comes out clean. Leave to cool in the tin for 10 minutes, then turn out on to a wire rack to cool completely before slicing.

Vegan   Use non-dairy milk.

Gluten Free   Use gram (chickpea) flour. If you can tolerate oats make sure they're certified gluten free. If you can't tolerate oats use quinoa flakes or millet flakes instead.

TIPS & SWAPS
Use whole or cubed, roasted sweet potato or butternut squash (as long as there are no spices on it) instead of the bananas. Remove any skin and blend the flesh until smooth.

LEFTOVERS: see pp228–233

● Bananas

BANANA CHOCOLATE CHIP BLONDIES

Makes 9–12

oil, for greasing
85g nut butter, such as cashew
   or peanut butter
50g unsalted butter
150g soft brown sugar
¼ teaspoon salt (if your nut
   butter is unsalted)
1 overripe banana, peeled and
   mashed with a fork (75–100g,
   peeled weight)
pinch of baking powder
1 teaspoon vanilla extract
70g plain wholemeal flour
90g Oat Flour (see page 216)
   or extra wholemeal flour
50g plain dark chocolate (at least 70%
   cocoa solids), roughly chopped

A few years ago I was walking around East London with my brother when we stopped by a lovely little bakery called E5 bakehouse. My bro went for a ginger cookie but my attention was on a fat, squidgy banana blondie, which I then devoured at an incredible speed. This is my homage to that blondie, with a caramel-banana flavour and a fudgy texture. But be warned, they're rich, so you might want to cut them into small pieces!

1 Preheat the oven to 180°C fan, 200°C, Gas Mark 6 and lightly grease a 20cm cake tin with oil.

2 Melt the nut butter and unsalted butter together in a small pan over a low heat until completely smooth. Remove from the heat and stir in the sugar, salt (if using), banana, baking powder and vanilla extract. Add the both flours and stir in until just combined.

3 Tip the dough into the prepared cake tin. Use damp hands to press the dough out into an even layer, then press the chopped chocolate on to the surface.

4 Bake in the oven for 20–25 minutes until it is set around the edges but still quite soft in the centre. Leave to cool slightly in the tin before slicing into 9–12 pieces. Store any leftovers in an airtight container for 3–4 days.

Vegan Replace the butter with 50ml olive oil or rapeseed oil. Make sure your chocolate is suitable for vegans.

Gluten Free If you can tolerate oats, use certified gluten-free oats to make the Oat Flour and replace the wholemeal flour with buckwheat flour. If you can't tolerate oats, omit the wholemeal flour and oat flour and use 170g buckwheat flour instead.

LEFTOVERS: see pp228–233

● Bananas
● Nut butter

V VG

GF option

OLIVE OIL ANY-FRUIT CRUMBLE

I think everyone should know how to make a fruit crumble. They are versatile – you can use frozen fruit or fruit which might otherwise be destined for the bin, and you can mix up the flavours. My mum always uses oats, which helps the clump-factor of the topping, and I add sunflower seeds for more crunch.

Serves 4–6

500g mixed fruit (e.g. apples, apricots,
   blackberries, blueberries, peaches,
   plums, apricots, nectarines, rhubarb)
2–6 tablespoons brown
   or granulated sugar
juice of ½ lemon (optional)

TOPPING
4 tablespoons olive oil or rapeseed oil
2 tablespoons honey or maple syrup
2 tablespoons brown or granulated sugar
pinch of salt
55g plain wholemeal flour, Oat Flour
   (see page 216) or gram flour
100g porridge oats
¼ teaspoon ground cinnamon
20g roughly chopped sunflower
   seeds (or any nut/seed you want!)

TO SERVE
natural yogurt, ice cream or cream
   (optional)

1 Preheat the oven to 180°C fan, 200°C, Gas Mark 6.

2 Prepare the fruit. For apples and pears, peel, core and cut into 2cm chunks. For berries, remove the stems and leaves. For rhubarb, discard the leaves and cut the stalks into 2cm lengths. For peaches, plums, apricots and nectarines, remove the stones and cut the fruit into quarters or eighths. Taste the fruit to gauge its sweetness then toss with 2 tablespoons sugar and taste again, adding more sugar if needed. If you are using dessert apples, pears, peaches or nectarines it's nice to add the lemon juice. If you are using cooking apples or rhubarb, err on the side of adding more sugar and no lemon juice at all. Tip the fruit into a medium casserole dish and cook in the oven for 10 minutes.

3 Meanwhile, make the topping. Mix the oil, honey, sugar and salt together in a medium bowl. Add the flour, oats, cinnamon and seeds and mix together until clumpy and moist. Scatter the crumble mix over the fruit, cover with foil and bake for a further 30 minutes. Remove the foil from the dish and return to the oven for a final 10 minutes to brown.

4 Serve hot with yogurt, ice cream or cream, if you like.

Gluten Free Use gram (chickpea) flour. If you can tolerate oats, make sure they're certified gluten free. If not, use millet flakes or quinoa flakes instead.

TIPS & SWAPS

Want a richer crumble? If you can tolerate dairy, rub unsalted butter (instead of olive oil) into the crumble topping.

I love adding a handful of dried fruit to the crumble to intensify the flavour and sweetness. Raisins are an obvious choice but you could also try chopped, pitted dates or dried blueberries.

LEFTOVERS: see pp228–233

● Fresh or frozen fruit
● Lemon juice

CARAMELIZED APPLE & PECAN BREAD PUDDING

(V)

Serves 6–8

400–500g peeled and cored apples
   (3–5 apples, depending on size)
6 tablespoons soft brown sugar
60g unsalted butter
500ml milk or non-dairy milk
2 eggs
1 teaspoon vanilla extract
30g plain wholemeal flour
35g pecans, roughly chopped
5–6 pieces of (preferably stale)
   wholemeal bread, cut into about
   3cm squares
salt

TIPS & SWAPS
If using dessert apples, add a
squeeze of lemon juice to the pan
to balance the sweetness.

LEFTOVERS: see pp228–233
● Bread (stale)
● Apples

Stale bread is a blessing. You can turn it into French toast, breadcrumbs, croutons, bread pudding... I like my bread pudding to have a higher ratio of crispy top to gooey middle so I bake it in a large casserole dish to increase the surface area. The topping of pecan streusel makes it more crunchy.

1 Preheat the oven to 180°C fan, 200°C, Gas Mark 6.

2 Chop the peeled, cored apples into 2cm chunks. Place in a large frying pan together with 4 tablespoons of the sugar, 40g of the butter and a pinch of salt. Stir over a high heat until the butter has melted, then reduce the heat to low and leave the apples to soften and caramelize for 20 minutes, stirring occasionally. Remove from the heat.

3 Whisk the milk, eggs, vanilla, 1 tablespoon of the sugar and a pinch of salt together in a large jug or bowl with a fork.

4 Place the flour, remaining butter and the rest of the sugar in a small bowl, and using your fingertips, rub together until it is a crumbly mixture, then mix in the pecans.

5 Layer a third of the caramelized apples in a large casserole dish, then layer half the bread on top, followed by a third of the apples, the remaining bread and then the remaining apples. Pour over the milk and egg mixture and sprinkle over the crumbly pecan mixture. Bake in the oven for 30 minutes.

CINNAMON KNOTS

Makes 12

STARTING PASTE
80ml water
2 tablespoons plain white flour

DOUGH
50g granulated sugar
100ml boiling water
100ml milk or non-dairy milk
7g sachet (2¼ teaspoons)
    of fast-action dried yeast
150g plain or strong white flour,
    plus extra for dusting
280g plain or strong wholemeal flour
80ml olive oil or rapeseed oil,
    plus extra for greasing
1 teaspoon salt
4 tablespoons olive or rapeseed oil
    or melted butter, for brushing over
    the dough

FILLING
4 teaspoons ground cinnamon
10 green cardamom pods, seeds
    removed and ground in a mortar
    and pestle (optional)
pinch of salt
1 tablespoon plain or strong white flour
110g soft brown sugar

GLAZE (OPTIONAL)
2 tablespoons granulated sugar
2 tablespoons water

These probably aren't the cinnamon buns you are used to — these are made with layered strips of dough twisted into a pretty shape, and are spiked with cardamom. Slather with a cream cheese frosting or sugar glaze for extra sweetness.

1   Line a baking tray with nonstick baking paper and set aside. To make the starting paste, heat the water and flour in a small pan over a medium heat and stir until thickened. Set aside.

2   For the dough, mix the sugar, boiling water and milk in a large bowl. Sprinkle in the yeast and stir, then set aside for 5 minutes. Add the starting paste to the bowl with both flours, the oil and salt and stir together to form a sticky dough.

3   Tip the dough out on to a lightly floured work surface. Dust the dough and your hands with flour and knead it until soft and slightly sticky, adding a little more flour as needed.

4   Pour some oil into the bowl and place the dough in it. Turn the dough to coat it in oil, then cover the bowl with a tea towel or clingfilm and set aside in a warm place* for 1 hour to rise.

5   Tip the risen dough on to a lightly floured work surface and dust with flour. Roll it out into a 40 x 60cm rectangle using a floured rolling pin (or even a wine bottle). Brush the dough with more oil or melted butter.

6   Mix all the filling ingredients together in a bowl, then sprinkle it over the surface of the dough in an even layer. Fold the dough into thirds like a business letter so you end up with a 40 x 20cm rectangle. Cut the rectangle in half along the 40cm edge to make 2 x 20cm squares. Cut each square into 6 strips. Twist each strip all along its length (it should stretch a little as you twist it). Coil the strips up like a snail shell, stretching the last few centimetres over the top of the bun and tucking underneath (see picture). Alternatively, simply coil the strips of dough like a snail shell.

7   Place the buns on to the baking tray, spacing them a few centimetres apart, cover with oiled clingfilm and leave in a warm place for 30 minutes.

8   Preheat the oven to 180°C fan, 200°C, Gas Mark 6.

9   Once the buns have risen, uncover and bake them in the oven for 20–25 minutes until golden.

10 Heat the glaze ingredients in a small pan to dissolve the sugar and brush over the buns with a pastry brush. Allow to cool slightly before eating. Store extras in an airtight container at room temperature for up to 3 days.

Vegan   Use non-dairy milk and use oil instead of the melted butter.

TIPS & SWAPS

*Create a perfect rising area for your dough – heat the oven to 90°C fan, 110°C, Gas Mark ¼ for 3 minutes, then switch the oven off, place the dough inside and close the door.

EARL GREY CUPCAKES WITH LEMON GLAZE

Makes 10

230ml strong brewed Earl
  Grey tea, cooled
150g granulated sugar
100ml olive oil, rapeseed oil
  or melted unsalted butter
2 eggs
finely grated zest and juice of 1 lemon
110g plain white flour
100g plain wholemeal flour
  or more plain white flour
1¼ teaspoons baking powder
½ teaspoon bicarbonate of soda
½ teaspoon salt
150g icing sugar

I am an avid Earl Grey tea drinker. I grew up drinking it so it's probably nostalgia that makes me love it so much. The tea has citrusy notes in it due to the addition of bergamot oil, which comes from the bergamot orange. Given this fact, I think that this tea pairs incredibly well with lemon, especially in cake.

1   Preheat the oven to 180°C fan, 200°C, Gas Mark 6 and line a muffin tin with 10 paper cases.

2   Mix the brewed tea with the sugar, oil or butter, eggs and grated lemon zest in a medium bowl until smooth. Dump both flours, the baking powder, bicarbonate of soda and salt on top and stir until just combined. Divide the batter between the paper cases, filling them about three-quarters full.

3   Bake in the oven for 25–30 minutes until a toothpick or cocktail stick inserted into the centre comes out clean. Leave to cool in the tin then transfer to a wire rack or large platter and leave to cool.

4   Mix the icing sugar and 1 tablespoon of the lemon juice in a small bowl. Gradually add more lemon juice until you have a smooth, spoonable icing. Spoon this over the cooled cupcakes and leave to set. Store in an airtight container for up to 4 days.

Vegan Use olive or rapeseed oil. Replace the eggs with 2 tablespoons ground flaxseed mixed with 6 tablespoons warm water.

TIPS & SWAPS

For the strong brewed tea fill a mug with around 350ml just-boiled water, add 2 Earl grey teabags and leave for 10 minutes, before measuring out the liquid as needed.

If you are using wholemeal flour, make sure it's intended for use in cakes and pastries (not wholemeal bread flour)!

SIMPLE LEMON BISCOTTI

Makes 12

170g plain wholemeal flour
1 teaspoon baking powder
5 tablespoons granulated sugar
grated zest of 1 lemon
¼ teaspoon salt
50g mixed seeds, such
   as sunflower, pumpkin, sesame
   and flaxseeds
1 large egg
4 tablespoons milk or non-dairy milk
2 tablespoons olive oil
1 teaspoon vanilla extract
sesame seeds, for sprinkling (optional)

Usually I'm not one to like biscotti (well, cantuccini, as I should call them) as they're often tooth-breakingly dry. I prefer homemade ones which I bake enough to only slightly dry them out. They're not too sweet and are a great pick-me-up.

1 Preheat the oven to 180°C fan, 200°C, Gas Mark 6 and line a baking tray with nonstick baking paper.

2 Mix the flour, baking powder, sugar, lemon zest, salt and seeds together in a medium bowl. Make a well in the middle of the dry ingredients and add the egg, milk, oil and vanilla and mix together to form a dough.

3 Tip the dough out on to the baking tray and make a log about 20cm x 8cm. Sprinkle with sesame seeds, if using, then bake in the oven for 35 minutes.

4 Remove the dough from the oven and leave to cool for 5 minutes. Slice it into 12 even pieces (a serrated knife is useful for this). Lay the biscotti on the baking tray. Return to the oven, reduce the temperature to 140°C fan, 160°C, Gas Mark 3 and bake for 25–30 minutes.

5 Store in a sealed jar for up to 1 month at room temperature. If the biscotti soften up, put them in an oven preheated to 160°C fan, 180°C, Gas Mark 4 for 10–15 minutes to dry them out.

Dairy Free Use non-dairy milk.

LEFTOVERS: see pp228–233

● Lemon juice

VG option

ALMOND COOKIE BAKED PEACHES WITH LEMON YOGURT

Makes 6 peach halves (or serves 3–6)

3 ripe peaches, halved and pitted
20g unsalted butter, softened
20g soft brown sugar or 3 tablespoons
  Date Paste (see page 221)
20g ground almonds or Ground
  Almond Alternative (see page 218)
3 tablespoons plain wholemeal flour
pinch of baking powder
pinch of salt
½ teaspoon almond extract
  or vanilla extract
1 tablespoon milk or non-dairy milk
2 tablespoons roughly chopped almonds
  or pecans

LEMON YOGURT
large pinch of sugar
finely grated zest of ½ lemon
6 tablespoons natural yogurt
  or non-dairy yogurt

There's a French pastry recipe called 'Bostock' which consists of a slice of day-old brioche, soaked with orange syrup, spread with frangipane, sprinkled with flaked almonds and baked until caramelized. It's delicious but I never have brioche around. Frangipane pairs very well with fruit so I subbed peaches in for the brioche. The peaches soften and sweeten while the almond batter becomes crisp and gooey. The lemon yogurt, which is zingy and zesty, cuts through the sweetness.

1 Preheat the oven to 180°C fan, 200°C, Gas Mark 6.

2 Arrange the halved peaches on a baking tray or in a 20cm cake tin.

3 Cream the butter and sugar together in a medium bowl until smooth. Mix in the ground almonds, flour, baking powder and salt, then mix in the almond or vanilla extract and milk. Spread the mixture over the halved peaches and sprinkle with the chopped nuts.

4 Bake in the oven for 25–30 minutes until golden on top.

5 To make the lemon yogurt, place the sugar and lemon zest in a small bowl and rub together with your fingertips to infuse the sugar with the lemon flavour. Mix in the yogurt.

6 Serve the peaches hot with the lemon yogurt.

Vegan Use vegan spread, cashew butter or almond butter instead of the butter. Use non-dairy milk and yogurt.

LEFTOVERS: see pp228–233

● Peaches
● Lemon juice
● Yogurt

TIPS & SWAPS
Use nectarines or ripe plums
instead of peaches.

V DF

VG option

EASY FREEZER CHOCOLATE CHIP COOKIES

Makes 20–24

125ml extra virgin olive oil,
    olive oil or melted unsalted butter
160g granulated or brown sugar
2 teaspoons miso, any kind,
    or ½ teaspoon salt
2 teaspoons vanilla extract
200g plain or strong wholemeal flour
¾ teaspoon baking powder
¾ teaspoon bicarbonate of soda
100g plain dark chocolate
    (at least 70% cocoa solids),
    roughly chopped
100g pecans or walnuts, roughly
    chopped
1 egg
sea salt flakes, for sprinkling (optional)

Ever wanted to make chocolate chip cookies but know that you become an incarnation of The Cookie Monster whenever cookies are around (i.e. have no self control)? Look to this recipe to help! The dough is super easy to make, before being shaped into balls and frozen before baking. This improves the texture of the cookie and means you can bake as many as you need, leaving the rest for when another cookie craving hits.

1   Line a baking tray or large plate with nonstick baking paper.

2   Mix the oil or butter, sugar, miso and vanilla together in a medium bowl. Add the flour, baking powder and bicarbonate of soda and stir until evenly combined. Add the chocolate and nuts and stir through. Crack in the egg and stir until it is a slightly crumbly dough.

3   Scoop heaped tablespoons of dough into balls, then place on the prepared baking tray or large plate and flatten the balls slightly. Freeze for 1 hour, then tip into a labelled and dated sandwich bag and seal. Store in the freezer for up to 3 months.

4   When you are ready to bake, take however many cookie dough balls you want out of the freezer and preheat the oven to 180°C fan, 200°C, Gas Mark 6. Line a baking tray with nonstick baking paper.

5   Place the cookie dough balls on to the prepared baking tray, spacing them about 3cm apart. Sprinkle with salt flakes, if liked, and bake in the oven for 8–10 minutes.

6   Leave the cookies to cool for a few minutes before eating as they're fragile when hot. Leave leftovers to cool completely then transfer to an airtight container and store for up to 5 days.

Vegan Use olive oil instead of the melted butter. Replace the egg with 1 tablespoon ground flaxseed mixed with 4 tablespoons water. Ensure your chocolate is suitable for vegans.

TIPS & SWAPS

If you are going to bake the cookies straightaway, only freeze the dough balls for 10 minutes.

If you enjoy the taste of olive oil opt for extra virgin; use refined olive oil for a neutral taste.

LEFTOVERS: see pp228–233

● Miso

DATE, WALNUT & CHOCOLATE OAT COOKIES

MAKES 20–24

110ml olive oil, rapeseed
  oil or melted, unsalted butter
4 tablespoons honey or maple syrup
50g soft brown sugar
1 egg
160g rolled oats
60g plain wholemeal
  or white flour
¼ teaspoon baking powder
½ teaspoon ground cinnamon
¼ teaspoon salt
50g walnuts, roughly chopped
50g pitted dried dates, roughly chopped
50g plain dark chocolate (at least 70%
  cocoa solids), roughly chopped

Oat cookies are often the rejects out of the cookie choices, especially when they contain raisins, but I have a soft spot for them. The chewy oats add texture and the creamy, toasty flavour that I love. In fear of offending too many people by mixing chocolate and raisins together, I opted for dates instead. They bring pops of chewy, caramel sweetness to offset the bitter chocolate and crunchy walnuts.

1 Preheat the oven to 180°C fan, 200°C, Gas Mark 6 and line a baking tray with nonstick baking paper.

2 Mix the oil, honey, sugar and egg together in a medium bowl until smooth. Add the remaining ingredients and stir together until you have a sticky dough.

3 Scoop heaped tablespoons of the dough on to the prepared baking tray, spacing the balls a few centimetres apart. I usually get about 12 to a tray and bake in the oven for 8–12 minutes until they look dry but are still slightly soft.

4 Leave to cool on the baking tray for 1 minute before transferring to a wire rack to cool completely. Repeat with the rest of the dough. Store the cooled cookies in a sealed container for up to 5 days.

Vegan Use olive oil or rapeseed oil instead of the butter, and maple syrup instead of the honey. Replace the egg with 1 tablespoon ground flaxseed mixed with 3 tablespoons water. Make sure your chocolate is suitable for vegans.

Gluten Free If you can tolerate oats, make sure they're certified gluten free. If not, use millet flakes or quinoa flakes instead. Use gram (chickpea) flour instead of wholemeal flour.

LEFTOVERS: see pp228–233

● Dates

TIPS & SWAPS

Swap the walnuts for toasted desiccated coconut.

Use raisins instead of dates.

TIPS & SWAPS

Bake the cake in a 20cm cake tin
if you don't have a bundt tin.

If you are using wholemeal flour, make sure
it's intended for use in cakes and pastries
(not wholemeal bread flour)!

If you have roasted sweet potato (whole or
cubed) to hand use about 200g of it as long
as there are no spices on it. Skip steps 1
and 2 and continue with the recipe.

V

VG option

ONE-BOWL CHOCOLATE CAKE WITH MAGIC GANACHE

Serves 8–10

80ml olive oil or rapeseed oil, plus extra
  for greasing
30g unsweetened cocoa powder,
  plus extra for dusting
150g courgette (about 1 medium),
  grated
150g granulated sugar
½ teaspoon salt
180ml water
1 teaspoon apple cider vinegar,
  lemon juice or white wine vinegar
180g plain or wholemeal flour
1 teaspoon bicarbonate of soda

MAGIC CHOCOLATE GANACHE

1 large or 2 small sweet potatoes
  (about 300g)
100g plain dark chocolate
  (at least 70% cocoa solids),
  melted (see page 192)
2 tablespoons unsalted butter
1 tablespoon honey or maple syrup
1 teaspoon vanilla extract
pinch of salt
4–6 tablespoons milk or non-dairy milk

TO DECORATE (OPTIONAL)

shaved chocolate
edible flowers

Baked sweet potatoes have such a soft, melty interior and are so tasty in desserts. Mixed with melted dark chocolate and a few other things, you have an A* ganache. You can even chill the ganache, then beat it with a wooden spoon to make more of a buttercream. I like to keep it pourable and drape it over a moist, light chocolate cake. It's so good, no one will ever know you're hiding two types of vegetable in there.

1 Preheat the oven to 180°C fan, 200°C, Gas Mark 6 and grease a 20cm bundt tin well with oil and dust with cocoa powder, tipping out any excess cocoa powder.

2 Start on the ganache: prick the sweet potato(es) all over with a knife. Wrap in foil and bake in the oven for 1–1½ hours until completely tender. Remove and leave to cool. Leave the oven on for the cake.

3 Once the sweet potato is cool, cut in half and scoop the flesh out into a jug. Blend with the melted chocolate, butter, honey, vanilla and salt until smooth, then blend in enough milk to make a thick, spreadable ganache.

4 For the cake, place the grated courgette in a sieve, then hold the sieve over the sink and squeeze the courgette to remove as much moisture as possible from it. Tip the squeezed courgette into a medium bowl. Add the sugar, oil, salt, measured water, vinegar and cocoa powder and stir to combine. Dump the flour and bicarbonate of soda into the bowl and stir in until just combined.

5 Pour the cake batter into the tin and bake in the oven for 35–45 minutes, or until a toothpick or cocktail stick inserted into the centre of the cake comes out clean (the baking time will vary depending on the tin you use).

6 Leave the cake to cool for 10 minutes in the tin before loosening the edges with a knife and tipping the cake out on to a serving plate. Spread with the ganache and decorate with shaved chocolate and flowers, if you like.

Vegan Make sure your chocolate is suitable for vegans. Use 2 tablespoons coconut oil or vegan spread instead of the butter in the ganache. Use maple syrup and non-dairy milk.

LEFTOVERS: see pp228–233

- Sweet potato (raw or roasted)
- Courgette

CHOCOLATE CHIP,
RASPBERRY & ALMOND CAKE

Serves 6

80ml olive oil, rapeseed oil or melted
  unsalted butter, plus extra for greasing
80g Oat Flour (see page 216),
  plus extra for dusting
80g ground almonds or Ground
  Almond Alternative (see page 218)
80g soft brown sugar
¼ teaspoon salt
½ teaspoon baking powder
1 large egg
4 tablespoons milk or non-dairy milk
½ teaspoon almond extract
35g plain dark chocolate
  (at least 70% cocoa solids),
  finely chopped
100g frozen or fresh raspberries

TO SERVE (OPTIONAL)
whipped cream or natural yogurt
fresh raspberries

I have never enjoyed making layer cakes that much. There's too much buttercream involved and I reach maximum stress levels when trying to evenly frost the outside. I find it much more satisfying to bake a flavourful single layer cake. This is one such cake. It's moist and studded with jammy raspberries and deep, dark chocolate chunks. It's the type of cake which you can eat a slice of with a cup of tea at teatime, or with whipped cream and extra raspberries for a special dessert.

1 Preheat the oven to 180°C fan, 200°C, Gas Mark 6 and grease a 23cm cake tin with oil and dust with flour, tipping out any excess flour.

2 Mix the ground almonds, oil, sugar, flour, salt, baking powder, egg, milk and almond extract in a medium bowl until smooth. Pour the batter into the prepared tin. Sprinkle over the chopped chocolate and frozen raspberries and slightly swirl them into the batter with a spoon.

3 Bake in the oven for 30–35 minutes until the middle of the cake springs back when you apply light pressure with your finger.

4 Remove from the oven and leave the cake to cool in the tin. Once completely cooled, slice and serve as is or with whipped cream or yogurt and fresh raspberries, if you like.

Gluten Free If you can tolerate oats, make sure the oats used to make the flour are certified gluten free. If you can't tolerate oats, use gram (chickpea) flour instead.

Dairy Free Use oil not butter in the cake and use non-dairy milk. Make sure the chocolate you use is dairy free.

LEFTOVERS: see pp228–233

● Raspberries (fresh or frozen)

LEMON, BLUEBERRY & CORN CAKE

**Makes 1 loaf cake
(Serves 10–12)**

100ml olive oil or melted butter, plus
    extra for greasing
165g cooked sweetcorn (I used canned)
2 eggs
finely grated zest and juice of 1 lemon
100g granulated sugar, plus 1 tablespoon
180g plain wholemeal
    or white flour
50g Oat Flour (see page 216)
1½ teaspoons baking powder
¼ teaspoon salt
150g blueberries, fresh or frozen

Okay don't get annoyed with me because I keep putting
vegetables into baked goods, but you will love this cake,
especially if you're a lemon cake connoisseur like me. The
sweetcorn here makes the cake taste even more cake-y
somehow, while also adding moisture and obviously sweetness.
There's lemon zest and blueberries in the batter plus a strong
lemon syrup poured over the cake at the end for that zingy,
zesty kick. Go on, I dare you to try it.

1 Preheat the oven to 180°C fan, 200°C, Gas Mark 6 and grease and line
the base and sides of a 900g loaf tin with nonstick baking paper.

2 Blitz the corn into a paste. This can be done in a jug or deep bowl if using
a hand-held blender or in a freestanding blender.

3 Tip the blitzed corn into a medium bowl and stir in the oil, eggs, lemon zest
and the 100g sugar. Add both flours, the baking powder and salt and stir
until just smooth. Fold the blueberries into the batter briefly, then pour the
batter into the prepared loaf tin.

4 Bake in the oven for 50–60 minutes, or until a toothpick or cocktail stick
inserted into the centre of the cake comes out clean (if the toothpick hits
a blueberry, test a different spot).

5 Meanwhile, heat the lemon juice and remaining tablespoon of sugar
in a small pan just until the sugar dissolves.

6 Once the cake is cooked, leave it to cool in the tin for 10 minutes, then turn
out on to a wire rack. Poke it all over with a toothpick and use a spoon to
drizzle the sweetened lemon juice all over the cake. Leave to cool completely
before slicing. Store any leftovers in an airtight container for up to 5 days.

Dairy Free Use oil instead of butter.

TIPS & SWAPS

If you don't like corn, omit it and add
125ml milk or non-dairy milk.

Replace the oat flour with ground almonds
or Ground Almond Alternative (see page
218) for a richer taste.

Use an equal weight of frozen
blackberries or raspberries instead
of the blueberries.

LEFTOVERS: see pp228–233

● Blueberries (fresh or frozen)

DIY

This is the little section at the back of the book with all the cool, nifty recipes which will boost your store cupboard and freezer and make your cooking life easier. All the dressings in the book are listed here so that you don't have to hunt for them if you want to make a specific one. There's also, of course, recipes for things such as pastry, bread dough and pesto, which are always better when they are homemade.

TORTILLAS

Makes 12

180g plain or strong white
  bread flour, plus extra for dusting
200g plain or strong wholemeal flour
½ teaspoon salt
¼ teaspoon baking powder
250ml lukewarm water*
3 tablespoons olive oil

1 Mix the flours, salt and baking powder in a medium bowl. Make a well in the centre of the dry ingredients, then pour in the water and oil. Stir until it is a rough dough, then tip it out on to a lightly floured work surface and dust with a little more flour. Knead together briefly until smooth. Divide in half and cut each half into 6 pieces. Roll each piece into a ball and leave them to rest for 5 minutes at room temperature.

2 Dust each ball with flour and roll it out into a rough circle as thin as possible, dusting with flour as needed.

3 Heat a nonstick frying pan over a high heat. Once the pan is hot place a circle of dough into the pan. It will start to puff up and once golden spots appear underneath, flip it over and cook on the other side until that is also speckled.

4 Keep the tortillas warm by wrapping in a tea towel while you cook the rest of the dough. Store any leftover tortillas in a sandwich bag in the freezer for up to 1 month.

TIPS & SWAPS

Reheat in a frying pan with some oil for 2–3 minutes; in the oven wrapped in foil for 10 minutes; or straight over a gas hob for 30 seconds.

VG option

NO-YEAST FLATBREADS

Makes 6 small flatbreads

150g plain or strong wholemeal
  flour, plus extra for dusting
½ teaspoon baking powder
¼ teaspoon bicarbonate of soda
¼ teaspoon salt
4–6 tablespoons water
4 tablespoons natural yogurt
1 tablespoon olive oil, rapeseed oil
  or melted butter

1 Mix the flour, baking powder, bicarbonate of soda and salt together in a medium bowl. Make a well in the centre of the mixture and pour in the wet ingredients. Mix to form a smooth dough, adding more water if needed.

2 Tip the dough out on to a lightly floured work surface and knead for a few minutes, then return it to the bowl, cover with a clean tea towel and set aside for 10 minutes.

3 Divide the dough into 6 equal pieces and roll into balls. Using a lightly floured rolling pin, roll them out into circles about 3mm thick.

4 Heat a dry frying pan over the highest heat. Place 1–2 circles of dough into the frying pan and cook until the bread is browned underneath. Flip over and cook on the other side until brown. Transfer to a plate and repeat with the remaining dough. Store extra flatbreads in a sandwich bag at room temperature for up to 2 days. When ready to eat, place them in an oven preheated to 180°C fan, 200°C, Gas Mark 6 for a few minutes.

Vegan Use unsweetened soya yogurt instead of the natural yogurt.

WHOLEWHEAT PITTA OR STOVETOP FLATBREADS

(V) (VG) (NS)

Makes 6

1 teaspoon fast-action dried yeast
200ml lukewarm water*
125g plain or strong white flour,
   plus extra for dusting
125g plain or strong wholemeal flour
½ teaspoon salt

I like to make this dough on a Sunday and keep it in the refrigerator for quick, weekday flatbreads, which I can either pan-fry or bake each day. Having a freshly made flatbread doesn't sound like anything special but I find it makes building up a lunch idea much easier!

1 Dissolve the yeast in the measured water in a large bowl and set aside for 5 minutes.

2 Add the flours and salt and mix into a rough dough. Tip the dough out on to a lightly floured work surface, sprinkle with flour and knead for 6–10 minutes until smooth. Return the dough to the bowl and cover with a clean tea towel or clingfilm. If baking immediately, leave the dough in a warm place for 40 minutes to rise. Otherwise, the bowl can be stored in the refrigerator for up to 5 days.

3 Tip the risen dough out on to a lightly floured work surface, punch it down and divide it into 6 equal balls.

4 If making pitta breads: preheat the oven to 220°C fan, 240°C, Gas Mark 9 and lightly flour a baking tray. Roll a ball of dough out into an oval, dusting with flour as needed. The dough should be around 5mm thick. Place on the prepared baking tray and repeat with another ball (depending on the size of your tray). Bake in the oven for 10–12 minutes until puffed and dry.

5 Remove the baked pittas and wrap in a clean tea towel to keep them warm and soft. Repeat the rolling and baking with the remaining dough. Store any leftover flatbreads in the freezer for up to 2 months, placing in the toaster to defrost.

6 If making flatbreads, roll out each ball of dough to a circle about 10cm in diameter. Heat a dry frying pan over the highest heat. Once the pan is hot, reduce the heat to medium-high and place a circle of dough in the pan and cook until it starts to bubble up and brown underneath. Flip over and cook on the other side until it is flecked with spots. Transfer to a plate and cook the remaining dough as before.

TIPS & SWAPS
*Make sure the water is only just slightly warm to the touch.

OAT FLOUR

Oat flour is fabulous to make at home. Oats are very cheap and oat flour is much better for you than refined, white wheat flour as it contains more protein and fibre, while also (in my opinion) being tastier than using all wholemeal flour.

You can use any type of oats as long as 'oats' are the only ingredient on the packet. You don't want to use flavoured oats for this. You also don't want to use pinhead or steel-cut oats unless you have a high-speed blender.

Blend whatever quantity of oats you need in a blender or food processor until it becomes a rough flour. Transfer to a labelled, airtight container and store at room temperature for up to a year.

Gluten Free If you can tolerate oats, use gluten-free certified oats.

TIPS & SWAPS

If you can find unflavoured 'instant', smooth porridge (e.g. Ready Brek) which contains 'oat flour' in the ingredients list, you can use that instead of making oat flour. It's more expensive and isn't as fine as oat flour but, if you have it to hand, it usually works.

INSTANT NUT MILK (FOR BAKING)

Makes 150ml

2 tablespoons smooth unsalted nut butter, any kind (cashew, almond, peanut, creamed coconut...)
150ml hot water

This is a good one to remember when you're out of milk but want to bake, even if you usually use cow's milk.

1 Stir the nut butter and measured hot water together in a bowl until the nut butter has melted and mixed into the liquid. Use in baking recipes where non-dairy milk is called for.

OLIVE OIL PASTRY

Makes enough for 1 galette or 1 pie top

120g plain white flour
120g plain wholemeal flour*
½ teaspoon salt
1 tablespoon granulated sugar
   (for sweet recipes)
80ml olive oil
4–6 tablespoons cold water

1 Stir the flours, salt and sugar, if using, together in a medium bowl. Pour in the oil and stir until the oil is evenly mixed into the dry ingredients. Make a well in the middle of the dry ingredients and pour in 3 tablespoons of the water. Use your hands to work the water into the dry ingredients, drizzling in more water if it seems too dry.

2 Pat the dough into a circle. You can either use it straight away or wrap it in clingfilm and store it in the refrigerator for up to 3 days or in the freezer for up to 3 months.

TIPS & SWAPS
*Make sure you are not using strong wholemeal bread flour in this recipe.

HALF-OAT PASTRY

Makes enough pastry for 1 galette or 1 pie top

100g cold unsalted butter,
   cut into 1cm cubes
100g plain white flour
120g Oat Flour (see page 216)
   or plain wholemeal flour
¼ teaspoon salt
1 tablespoon granulated sugar
   (for sweet pastry only)
2 tablespoons natural yogurt,
   crème fraîche or ricotta
1–3 tablespoons cold water

1 Toss the butter into a medium bowl with both flours, the salt and sugar, if using, and rub the butter into the dry ingredients with your fingertips until it is a coarse, sandy mixture.

2 Make a well in the centre of the mixture and pour in the yogurt, crème fraîche or ricotta and 1 tablespoon of the cold water. Mix together gently with your fingertips until it becomes a dough that holds together when pinched. If it's too dry, dribble in more water as needed.

3 Tip the rough dough out on to a piece of clingfilm, shape it into a ball and flatten it into a disc, then wrap up in clingfilm. Chill in the refrigerator for at least 30 minutes before using. The pastry can be kept in the refrigerator for 3 days or frozen for 3 months.

LEFTOVERS: see pp228–233

● Yogurt, crème fraîche or ricotta

BREADCRUMBS

1 WITH A FOOD PROCESSOR/BLENDER: Preheat the oven to 120°C, fan 140°C, Gas Mark 1. If you have fresh bread, slice it into bite-sized chunks and lay the slices on a baking tray. Bake in the oven for 15–25 minutes until the bread feels dry and crisp. Leave to cool before using.

Pulse the dried or stale bread in a food processor or blender (you may need to do this in batches) until fine.

2 WITH A BOX GRATER: Preheat the oven to 120°C fan, 140°C, Gas Mark 1. Slice the bread and grate it against the coarse side of a box grater. Spread the breadcrumbs out on a baking tray and bake in the oven for 10–20 minutes until dry. You may need to stir the breadcrumbs halfway through their baking time so they dry out evenly.

3 Store the breadcrumbs in a re-sealable sandwich bag for 1–2 weeks at room temperature or in the freezer for up to 3 months.

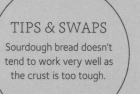

TIPS & SWAPS
Sourdough bread doesn't tend to work very well as the crust is too tough.

GROUND ALMOND ALTERNATIVE

This tip is useful for people with allergies or those on a budget. You can grind up pretty much any nut or seed to make a 'flour', which can be used for baking. However, sunflower seeds and desiccated coconut seem to be the cheapest. Things to be aware of are that sunflower seeds have a mild flavour but sometimes when baked in combination with bicarbonate of soda, will turn things green. This doesn't affect the flavour or safety of the baked good, it's just a visual thing. For desiccated coconut, it does have a coconut flavour so may not be useful for all applications, especially if you don't like the flavour.

Sunflower seeds or desiccated coconut (the unsweetened kind)

1 Place the desired weight of sunflower seeds or desiccated coconut into a food processor or blender and blitz until fine, stopping to scrape down the sides as needed. Don't overblend or you'll start to make sunflower-seed or coconut butter!

2 Store in an airtight container at room temperature for up to 2 months. Use as you would ground almonds in baking recipes.

V VG GF

AVOCADO CREAM

Serves 3–4

1 avocado
juice of ½ lime
pinch of salt

This is a cooling, fatty-yet-light sauce to serve with spicy foods. It's a great vegan alternative to soured cream or natural yogurt.

1   Cut the avocado in half and remove the stone. Use a spoon to scoop the avocado flesh out into a jug if using a hand-held blender or blender jug if using a freestanding blender. Whizz with the remaining ingredients until smooth. Keep the excess in a lidded container in the refrigerator for up to 3 days.

V VG GF

SUN FETA

Makes about 100g

100g sunflower seeds
juice of 1 lemon
½ teaspoon salt
100ml water

I like to sprinkle feta over a simple salad for that salty kick, but when I take a break from dairy (I used to be lactose intolerant and am sensitive of overdoing it on the dairy) I make this. It's cheap to make, and keeps in the refrigerator for a few days.

1   Soak the sunflower seeds in a bowl of water for 8–12 hours, then drain and rinse.

2   Preheat the oven to 120°C fan, 140°C, Gas Mark 1 and line a baking tray with nonstick baking paper.

3   Blend the drained sunflower seeds in a food processor or freestanding blender until chunky, then add the lemon juice, salt and the measured water and blend again until smooth.

4   Pat the mixture into rectangle about 1cm thick on the prepared baking tray and bake in the oven for 1½ hours, or until firm.

5   Leave to cool, then slice into cubes. Store in a sealed container in the refrigerator for up to 3 days.

TIPS & SWAPS

For a vegan alternative to soured cream or crème fraîche, cut the salt down to ¼ teaspoon, use the juice of only ½ lemon and don't bake the mixture. You will be left with a thick, rich and creamy sauce, which you can use for drizzling on tacos, pizza and curry or stirring into pasta or risotto. Add 1 tablespoon maple syrup and only use a pinch of salt if you want a sweet cream for serving with berries, cake, porridge or pancakes.

You can also use almonds instead of sunflower seeds here.

NO-COOK PIZZA SAUCE

Makes enough for 4–6 pizzas (depending on size)

400g can chopped tomatoes
1 tablespoon balsamic vinegar
1 teaspoon mixed dried herbs
1 teaspoon granulated sugar
   or 2 teaspoons Date Paste
   (see page 221)
3 garlic cloves, crushed
generous pinch of salt

1 Blend all the ingredients together, either in a large jug with a hand-held blender or in a freestanding blender or food processor.

2 Keep any excess pizza sauce in a lidded container in the refrigerator for up to 3 days or freeze for up to 3 months.

TIPS & SWAPS
If I have sauce left over from making pizzas, I usually keep the sauce for the next day then cook it until thickened to have with pasta.

This sauce is pretty thin because of the fact it hasn't been cooked down. For this reason, it's best not to use too much on pizzas or things can get soupy, fast! You just need a thin layer on the pizza dough really.

PIZZA DOUGH

Makes enough for 2 large or 3 medium pizzas

210g water
1 teaspoon fast-action dried yeast
1 tablespoon olive oil
150g wholemeal bread flour
150g white bread flour
   or white plain flour
½ teaspoon salt

1 In a large bowl, combine the water and yeast. Let it sit for 2 minutes.

2 Add the oil, both flours and the salt to the bowl and mix together with a spoon until you get a shaggy dough.

3 Shape your hand like a claw and beat the dough in the bowl – try to stretch it up and then slap it back into the bowl – for about 1 minute. Cover the bowl of dough with clingfilm or a clean tea towel.

If making the pizza soon – leave the dough out at room temperature for 1 hour.

If making the pizza later – leave the dough in the refrigerator for 2–10 hours. Remove from the refrigerator at least 30 minutes before using, to bring to room temperature.

DATE PASTE

Makes about 250g

200g dried dates, pitted
4–6 tablespoons hot water

This is a thick, caramel-like paste made simply from dates and water. It adds a lovely subtle sweetness to savoury dishes and is also delicious on toast or pancakes. It can sometimes be used in baking instead of regular sugar. As it is high in fibre it is also healthier than using just straight sugar. Due to its high sugar content, date paste keeps very well in the refrigerator in a lidded container.

1 If the dates aren't soft and sticky, soak them in a heatproof bowl of boiling water for 15 minutes, then drain.

2 Blend the pitted dates with the hot water until smooth. This can be done in a large jug or bowl if using a hand-held blender or in a freestanding blender.

3 Alternatively, place the dates in a small pan and just cover with water. Bring to the boil then reduce the heat and simmer until the water has mostly evaporated. Add 4 tablespoons of the water to the pan and keep cooking the dates over a low heat, stirring and mashing them with the back of a spoon until as smooth as possible. Remove from the heat and cool.

THAI GREEN CURRY PASTE

Makes enough for a curry for 3–4 people

½ onion or 2 shallots, roughly chopped
6 garlic cloves, chopped
1½ tablespoons ground cumin
1½ tablespoons ground coriander
30g fresh coriander, roughly chopped
2 green chillies, finely chopped
3 tablespoons grated or very finely chopped fresh root ginger
2 lemongrass stalks, finely chopped
1 tablespoon salt
2–3 tablespoons water (optional)

1 Blitz everything together in a jug with a hand-held blender or in a free-standing blender until smooth.

2 Store in the refrigerator for up to 3 days. For long-term storage, scoop tablespoons of the paste on to a plate lined with nonstick baking paper and freeze. Once frozen, pop the cubes into a labelled and dated sandwich bag, seal and keep in the freezer for up to 3 months.

NO-BLENDER
RED LENTIL HUMMUS

Serves 2–3

120g red lentils, rinsed
1 garlic clove, very finely chopped
   or crushed
juice of ½ lemon
4 tablespoons extra virgin olive oil
pinch of salt

I use this recipe when I either have no access to a blender or I don't have any cooked chickpeas to hand. Red lentils are very cheap and quicker to cook than chickpeas. They are also more sustainable to grow and make a smoother hummus.

1 Place the lentils in a medium pan and pour in enough water to cover. Bring to the boil then reduce the heat and simmer for 20 minutes until completely soft, adding water if needed to keep the lentils hydrated but not too soupy.

2 After the 20 minutes are up, keep cooking the lentils, stirring frequently, until the remaining water has nearly evaporated and you are left with a thick paste. Remove from the heat and beat in the remaining ingredients until as smooth as possible. Cover and store in the refrigerator for 2–3 days.

3 If you do have a blender, once the lentils have cooked for 12 minutes, drain them, then either blend with the remaining ingredients using a hand-held blender in a large jug or bowl or in a freestanding blender or food processor. Cover and store in the refrigerator for 2–3 days.

CHICKPEA MAYONNAISE

Makes about 12 tablespoons

3 tablespoons liquid from a can
   or pan of cooked chickpeas
juice of ½ lemon
pinch of granulated sugar
¼ teaspoon salt
¼ teaspoon Dijon mustard (optional)
150ml olive oil

Ah the magic of chickpea liquid! It's a strange ingredient, also known as 'aquafaba', which can act in certain recipes as an egg substitute. Here we utilize the emulsifying properties of the aquafaba to blend oil and lemon juice into a creamy, dreamy mayonnaise substitute, which is completely vegan.

1 Put all the ingredients into a jug and use a hand-held blender to blitz until everything is emulsified. It will be thick and creamy. Pour into a clean jar, seal with the lid and refrigerate for up to 1 week.

2 To make it in a freestanding blender, place all the ingredients, except the oil, into the blender then blitz on medium speed and very very slowly stream in the oil until emulsified.

LEFTOVERS: see pp228–233

● Lemon juice

QUICK PICKLED RED ONION

Serves 4–6

1 red onion, thinly sliced into rings
4 tablespoons apple cider vinegar
   or rice vinegar
1 tablespoon granulated sugar
½ teaspoon salt
4 tablespoons water

1 Place the onion rings in a small bowl or a sandwich bag.

2 Heat the vinegar, sugar and salt in a small pan over a medium heat, stirring until the sugar has dissolved. Pour the hot liquid over the onion rings in the bowl or bag, then top up with the measured water to just cover the onions.

3 Leave the onions for at least 30 minutes before using.

4 For long-term storage, pour the liquid and the onion rings into a clean jar, seal with the lid and keep in the refrigerator for a week or so. If you use a sterilized jar (see tips below) they should keep for a few months.

TIPS & SWAPS

To sterilize a jar, wash the jar and lid thoroughly in hot, soapy water. Place on a baking tray and leave to dry in an oven preheated to 140°C fan, 160°C, Gas Mark 3 for 5–10 minutes. If your jar has a rubber seal, let this air-dry as the oven may damage it.

TRIO OF PESTOS

Here we have three different pesto recipes to show off how versatile pesto really is! I always like to make a big batch of pesto to freeze in ice-cube trays – once frozen I pop the cubes of frozen pesto out into a re-sealable sandwich bag to keep in the freezer. This is much easier to use than if you freeze all the pesto into one large container.

ROASTED AUBERGINE & TOMATO PESTO

Serves 3–4

1 large or 2 small aubergines (400–500g in total)
20g sunflower seeds, pumpkin seeds or cashews
150g sun-dried tomatoes packed in oil
juice of ½ lemon
1 garlic clove, crushed or very finely chopped
1 tablespoon olive oil
salt

1. Preheat the oven to 180°C fan, 200°C, Gas Mark 6.

2. Pierce the aubergines all over with a knife, then place on a baking tray and roast in the oven for 1 hour, or until soft. Cut the aubergine in half, scoop out the flesh and discard the skin.

3. If using a hand-held blender, finely chop the seeds or nuts and add to a jug or deep bowl with the aubergine flesh and blend together. Add the remaining ingredients and blend again, then season with salt to taste.

4. If using a blender or food processor, briefly pulse the seeds or nuts to break them down until coarse. Add the remaining ingredients and blend again, then season with salt to taste.

5. Store in a lidded container in the refrigerator for up to 3 days or see the introduction for a long-term storage option!

TIPS & SWAPS

Turn this pesto into a dip by blitzing in 120g (½ can) cooked cannellini beans plus 2 tablespoons tahini instead of olive oil.

Use 250g fresh cherry tomatoes instead of sun-dried tomatoes. Just roast them on the same tray as the aubergine for the final 30 minutes of roasting. If you already have roasted tomatoes to hand, use 120g instead of the sun-dried tomatoes.

LEFTOVERS: see pp228–233

- Sun-dried tomatoes, fresh tomatoes or roasted tomatoes
- Aubergine
- Lemon juice

BROCCOLI PESTO

Serves 3–4

½ medium head of broccoli, cut into florets
small handful of basil, leaves and stems
2 garlic cloves, crushed or very finely chopped
juice of ½ lemon
4 tablespoons extra virgin olive oil
large pinch of salt

1 Place the broccoli in a pan and just cover with boiling water. Bring to the boil, then reduce the heat and simmer for 10 minutes. Drain, then return the broccoli to the pan and mash with a potato masher or back of a fork.

2 Finely chop the basil and add that to the pan together with the garlic, lemon juice, olive oil and salt, then stir together to combine. Alternatively, use a hand-held blender in the pan or a freestanding blender to blitz everything together.

3 Store in a lidded container in the refrigerator for up to 3 days or see the introduction for a long-term storage option!

LEFTOVERS: see pp228–233

- Basil
- Lemon juice

BASIL & ROCKET PESTO

Serves 2–3

20g pumpkin seeds,
   sunflower seeds or cashews
40g (a few big handfuls) basil,
   roughly chopped (stems and leaves)
40g rocket leaves (or use spinach instead)
4 tablespoons extra virgin olive oil or olive oil
1 garlic clove, crushed
4 tablespoons water
generous pinch of salt
juice of ½ lemon

1 If using a hand-held blender, finely chop the pumpkin seeds and add to a jug or deep bowl. Roughly chop the basil and rocket and add them too. Blend a little to start breaking the green stuff down then add the remaining ingredients and blitz until it as smooth as you can get it.

2 If using a blender or food processor, briefly pulse the seeds to break them down until coarse. Add the remaining ingredients and blend again until smooth.

3 Store in a lidded container in the refrigerator for up to 3 days or see the introduction for a long-term storage option!

LEFTOVERS: see pp228–233

- Basil
- Lemon juice

DRESSINGS

A good salad dressing is the key to turning a pile of drab leaves into a bowl of joy. These dressings appear throughout the book, but it's also useful to have them all in one place.

TAHINI DRESSING

Serves 1–2

2 tablespoons tahini
1 garlic clove, crushed or finely chopped
pinch of salt
juice of ½ lemon

1 Put all the ingredients together in a screw-top jar, cover with a lid and shake to emulsify. Store in the refrigerator for up to a week.

PEANUT-GINGER DRESSING

Serves 2

2 tablespoons peanut, almond or cashew butter or tahini
1 teaspoon granulated sugar or honey
   or 1 tablespoon Date Paste (see page 221)
juice of ½ lime
1 tablespoon soy sauce or tamari
1 teaspoon grated fresh root ginger

1 Stir all the dressing ingredients together in a bowl, then add enough water to make a thick, spoonable dressing. Store in the refrigerator for up to a week.

MISO DRESSING

Serves 2–3

2 tablespoons miso, any kind
4 tablespoons olive oil
1 garlic clove, crushed or very finely chopped
1 shallot or ¼ red onion, finely diced
2 teaspoons granulated sugar or honey
1 tablespoon lemon juice or apple cider vinegar or rice vinegar

1 Put all the ingredients together in a screw-top jar, cover with a lid and shake to emulsify. Store in the refrigerator for up to a week.

CORIANDER-COCONUT DRESSING

Serves 2–3

20g fresh coriander leaves
10g piece of fresh root ginger, peeled and very
   finely chopped or grated
juice of 1 lemon
2 tablespoons soy sauce or tamari
1 tablespoon granulated sugar or honey
   or 2 tablespoons Date Paste (see page 221)
1–2 pinches of chilli flakes
80ml coconut milk or 30g creamed coconut plus
   4 tablespoons hot water

1 Blend all the ingredients together until smooth using a hand-held blender and jug or a freestanding blender. Store in the refrigerator for up to a week.

HONEY-THYME DRESSING

Serves 2–3

2 teaspoons honey
3 tablespoons olive oil
juice of 1 lemon
pinch of salt
¼ red onion, finely chopped
4 sprigs of thyme, leaves picked

1 Put all the ingredients together in a screw-top jar, cover with a lid and shake to emulsify. Store in the refrigerator for up to a week.

BASIL-AVOCADO DRESSING

Serves 2–3

10g (a large handful) basil leaves
½ avocado, stoned and peeled
pinch of salt
3 tablespoons water
juice of ½ lime

1 Blend all the ingredients together until smooth, either with a hand-blender and jug OR a freestanding blender. Store in the refrigerator for up to a week.

LIME-SOY DRESSING

Serves 2–4

1 tablespoon soy sauce or tamari
2 teaspoons honey, maple syrup or golden syrup
juice of 1 lime
1 tablespoon toasted sesame oil

1 Put all the ingredients together in a screw-top jar, cover with a lid and shake to emulsify. Store in the refrigerator for up to a week.

GINGER-LIME DRESSING

Serves 3–4

2 teaspoons very finely chopped or grated fresh root ginger
juice of ½ lemon or lime
1 teaspoon honey or maple syrup
2 tablespoons soy sauce or tamari
1 spring onion, finely sliced
2 tablespoons olive oil or rapeseed oil

1 Put all the ingredients together in a screw-top jar, cover with a lid and shake to emulsify. Store in the refrigerator for up to a week.

APPLE YOGURT DRESSING

Serves 3–4

1 dessert apple, grated
1 tablespoon honey
generous pinch of salt
80ml olive oil
6 tablespoons natural yogurt or crème fraîche
2 tablespoons apple cider vinegar

1 Cook the apple and honey in a small frying pan over a low heat until softened. Leave to cool then pour into a jug together with the salt, olive oil and yogurt or crème fraîche and blend using a hand-held blender until smooth. Alternatively, chuck it all into a blender and blend until smooth.

2 Stir in the vinegar and thin with enough water to make a pourable dressing. Store in the refrigerator for up to a week.

Gluten Free Make sure that you are using certified gluten-free tamari or soy sauce, when using.

MAKEOVERS WITH LEFTOVERS

FRUIT & VEG

Apple
Any-fruit Galette (p188)
Apple Cinnamon Scuffins (p39)
Broccoli Apple Yogurt Slaw (p55)
Cannellini Bean & Apple Salad (p87)
Caramelized Apple & Pecan Bread Pudding (p197)
Chickpea 'Tuna' Salad (p69)
Olive Oil Any-fruit Crumble (p196)
Overnight Oats (p18)

Aubergine
Aubergine, Pomegranate & Chickpea Salad (p68)
Aubergine, Red Lentil & Coconut Curry (p95)
Chickpea, Date & Ginger Tagine (p94)
Easy Summer Pasta (p149)
Frittata (p162)
Pizza (p158)
Roasted Aubergine & Tomato Pesto (p224)
Stir Fry (p174)
Sweet Miso Aubergine & Walnut Salad (p62)

Avocado
Avocado Cream (p219)
Corn, Peach & Pearl Barley Salad (p81)
Crispy Tortilla Strips with Corn & Quinoa (p125)

Bananas
Banana Bread (p194)
Banana Bread Porridge (p28)
Banana Chocolate Chip Blondies (p195)
Banoffee Peanut Bites (p40)
Coconut-Banana Granola Bars (p45)
Smoothie Boxes (p38)

Beetroot
Beetroot, Hazelnut & Crispy Sage Salad (p72)
Beetroot Flatbread (p59)
Roasted Beetroot, Cumin & Crispy Chickpeas (p65)

Blackberries (fresh or frozen)
Any-fruit Galette (p188)
Olive Oil Any-fruit Crumble (p196)
Smoothie Boxes (p38)

Blueberries (fresh or frozen)
Any-fruit Galette (p188)
Lemon, Blueberry & Corn Cake (p211)
Microwave Blueberry 'Muffin' (p26)
Olive Oil Any-fruit Crumble (p196)
Smoothie Boxes (p38)

Butternut Squash (raw)
Orzo with Squash, Chilli, Lemon & Peas (p126)
Roasted Squash with Brown Rice & Halloumi (p92)
Squash, Cauliflower & Roasted Garlic Gratin (p109)
Squash & Cinnamon Dip (p47)
Squash, Potato & Chilli Cakes (px76)
Taco (p166)

Butternut Squash (roasted)
Frittata (p162)
Pizza (p158)
Taco (p166)

Cabbage (red or white)
Frittata (p162)
Miso Mango Slaw (p55)
One-pan Creamy Pasta with Asparagus, Lemon & Basil (p145)
Stir Fry (p174)
Taco (p166)

Cavolo Nero
Creamy Cavolo Nero, Leek & Pea Pasta (p147)
Lazy Potato Hash (p114)
Minestrone (p130)
Pizza (p158)
Roasted Potato 3 Ways (p98)
Rice Bowl with Greens & Coriander-coconut Dressing (p117)
Spanakopita Quesadilla (p78)
Stir Fry (p174)
Taco (p166)

Carrots (raw)
Cannellini Bean & Apple Salad (p87)
Carrot Breakfast Bread (p23)
Carrot Cake Overnight Oats (p18)
Carrot Ribbon, Cinnamon & Halloumi Salad (p83)
Cauliflower, Leek & Sage Pie (p133)
Chickpea Stew 3 Ways (p129)
Chickpea 'Tuna' Salad (p69)
Chocolate Peanut Fudge Cake Bars (p185)
Frittata (p162)
Paprika Bean Stew (p134)
Roasted Carrots with Couscous & Pickled Onion (p67)
Roasted Tomatoes & Carrots with Black Beans & Tahini (px80)
Smoothie Boxes (p38)
Stir Fry (p174)
Taco (p166)
Tahini Carrot Slaw (p54)
Zingy Carrot & Rice Noodle Salad (p155)

Carrots (roasted)
Frittata (p162)
Pizza (p158)
Stir Fry (p174)
Taco (p166)

Cauliflower
Frittata (p162)
Pizza (p158)
Squash, Cauliflower & Roasted Garlic Gratin (p109)
Warm Roasted Cauliflower & Chickpea Salad (p84)

Celery
Cauliflower, Leek & Sage Pie (p133)
Chickpea Stew 3 Ways (px129)
Chickpea 'Tuna' Salad (p69)
Frittata (p162)
Paprika Bean Stew (p134)

Courgette
Courgette & Garlic Quesadilla (p78)
Easy Summer Pasta (p149)
Frittata (p162)
One-bowl Chocolate Cake (p207)
Pesto Crumb Courgettes with Weeknight Focaccia (p110)
Pizza (p158)
Potato, Halloumi & Courgette Bake (p105)

Corn, Peach & Pearl Barley Salad (px81)
Olive Oil Any-fruit Crumble (p196)
Peach & Raspberry Overnight Oats (px18)
Scrambled Chickpea Tacos with Peach Salsa (p31)
Taco (p166)

Pear
Any-fruit Galette (p188)
Olive Oil Any-fruit Crumble (p196)
Pear, Ricotta & Chicory Salad (p88)

Pepper
Frittata (p162)
Lentil & Yogurt Pitta Dip (p106)
Orange, Fennel, Olive & Pearl Barley Stew (p154)
Paprika Bean Stew (p134)
Pizza (p158)
Potato, Halloumi & Courgette Bake (p105)
Shakshouka (p131)
Stir Fry (p174)
Taco (p166)

Pineapple
Taco (p166)

Plums
Any-fruit Galette (p188)
Olive Oil Any-fruit Crumble (p196)

Pomegranate
Aubergine, Pomegranate & Chickpea Salad (p68)
Fattoush Dip (p51)
Roasted Squash with Brown Rice & Halloumi (p92)

Raspberries (fresh or frozen)
Any-fruit Galette (p188)
Chocolate Chip, Raspberry & Almond Cake (p208)
Doughnut Porridge (p29)
Olive Oil Any-fruit Crumble (p196)
Peach & Raspberry Crunch Overnight Oats (p18)
Smoothie Boxes (p38)

Red Onion
Aubergine, Red Lentil & Coconut Curry (p95)
Carrot Ribbon, Cinnamon & Halloumi Salad (p83)
Chickpea 'Tuna' Salad (p69)
Corn, Peach & Pearl Barley Salad (p81)
Frittata (p162)
Lime-chilli Corn & Crispy Onions (p63)
Quick Pickled Red Onion (p223)
Pear, Ricotta & Chicory Salad (p88)
Potato, Caramelized Onino & Thyme Pizza (p160)
Warm Roasted Cauliflower & Chickpea Salad (p84)
Roasted Squash with Brown Rice & Halloumi (p92)
Stir Fry (p174)
Taco (p166)

Rhubarb (fresh or frozen)
Any-fruit Galette (p188)
Olive Oil Any-fruit Crumble (p196)

Spinach (baby, fresh)
Carrot Ribbon, Cinnamon & Halloumi Salad (p83)
Corn, Peach & Pearl Barley Salad (p81)
Egg, Spinach & Cherry Tomato Pizza (p161)
Frittata (p162)
Ginger-pickled Mushrooms with Date Rice (p66)
Minestrone (p130)
Miso-garlic-chilli Broccoli with Pasta & Tomato (p121)
Pesto, Spinach & Sweet Potato Galette (p101)
Roasted Potato 3 Ways (p99)
Roasted Squash with Brown Rice & Halloumi (p92)
Smoothie Boxes (p38)
Spanakopita Quesadillas (p78)
Spinach & Feta Balls with Spaghetti (p122)
Stir Fry (p174)
Sweet Miso Aubergine & Walnut Salad (p62)
Thai Green Curry Pea Soup (p143)

Strawberries (fresh or frozen)
Any-fruit Galette (p188)
Oat Squares with Stawberry Compote & Coconut (p21)

Olive Oil Any-fruit Crumble (p196)
Smoothie Boxes (p38)

Sweet Potato (raw)
Chilli Roasted Potatoes with Granola & Lime-soy Dressing (p60)
Frittata (p162)
One-bowl Chocolate Cake (p207)
Pesto, Spinach & Sweet Potato Galette (p101)
Roasted Potato 3 Ways (p96)
Smoothie Boxes (p38)
Spiced Sweet Potato Fries with Smoky Dip (p52)
Spiced Sweet Potatoes with Raw Beetroot & Miso Dressing (p53)
Taco (p166)

Sweet Potato (roasted)
Frittata (p162)
Pizza (p158)
Taco (p166)

Tomatoes (raw)
Cannellini Beans with Balsamic Onions (p71)
Chickpea Stew 3 Ways (p129)
Easy Summer Pasta (p149)
Fattoush Dip (p51)
Halloumi Tacos with Mango Salsa & Rice (p169)
Miso-garlic-chilli Broccoli with Pasta, Tomatoes & Spinach (p121)
Pizza (p158)
Roasted Potato 3 Ways (p99)
Scrambled Chickpea Tacos with Peach Salsa (p31)
Roasted Tomatoes & Carrots with Black Beans & Tahini (p80)
Taco (p166)

Tomatoes (sundried)
'Chorizo' Dip (p47)
Crispy Tortilla Strips with Corn & Quinoa (p125)
Pizza (p161)
Roasted Aubergine & Tomato Pesto (p224)

Tomatoes (canned, chopped)
Chickpea, Date & Ginger Tagine (p94)
Chickpea Stew 3 Ways (p129)
Curried Tomato-Coconut Soup (p144)
Lentil & Fennel Ragu (p150)

Tomatoes (roasted)
Taco (p166)

White Potato (raw)
Chilli Roasted Potatoes with Granola & Lime-soy Dressing (p60)
Frittata (p162)
Lazy Potato Hash (p114)
Potato, Caramelized Onion & Thyme Pizza (p160)
Potato, Halloumi & Courgette Bake (p105)
Roasted Potato 3 Ways (px96)
Squash, Potato & Chilli Cakes (p76)

DAIRY & NON-DAIRY ALTERNATIVES
Avocado Cream
Pizza (p161)
Scrambled Chickpea Tacos with Peach Salsa (p31)
Taco (p166)

Coconut Milk
Aubergine, Red Lentil & Coconut Curry (p95)
Oat Squares with Stawberry Compote & Coconut (p21)
Curried Tomato-coconut Soup (p144)
Halloumi & Mango Noodle Salad (p153)
Rice Bowl with Greens & Coriander-coconut Dressing (p117)
Stir Fry (p174)
Thai Green Curry Pea Soup (p143)

Creamed Coconut
Aubergine, Red Lentil & Coconut Curry (p95)
Oat Squares with Stawberry Compote & Coconut (p21)
Coconut-banana Granola Bars (p45)
Curried Tomato-coconut Soup (p144)
Smoothie Boxes (p38)
Spicy Coconut Rice with Brussel Sprouts Stir Fry (p179)
Thai Green Curry Pea Soup (p143)

Crème fraîche
Cannellini Bean & Apple Salad (px87)
Creamy Cavolo Nero, Leek & Pea Pasta (p147)
Easy Summer Pasta (p149)

Half-oat Pastry (p217)
Miso-garlic-chilli broccoli with Onion, Cumin & Beans (p121)
Pizza (p161)
Roasted Cauliflower & Garlic Soup (p142)
Spiced Sweet Potato Fries with Smoky Dip (p52)

Feta Cheese or Sun Feta
Beetroot Flatbread (p59)
Lime-chilli Corn & Crispy Onions (p63)
Pesto, Spinach & Sweet Potato Galette (p101)
Pizza (p161)
Shakshouka (p121)
Spanakopita Quesadillas (p78)
Spinach & Feta Balls with Spaghetti (p122)

Halloumi Cheese
Carrot Ribbon, Cinnamon & Halloumi Salad (p83)
Halloumi & Mango Noodle Salad (p153)
Halloumi Tacos with Mango Salsa & Rice (p169)
Potato, Halloumi & Courgette Bake (p105)
Roasted Squash with Brown Rice & Halloumi (p92)

Mozzarella Cheese
Easy Summer Pasta (p149)
Peas, Potato & Mozzarella Frittata (p164)
Pizza (p160–161)

Ricotta Cheese
Creamy Cavolo Nero, Leek & Pea Pasta (p147)
Easy Summer Pasta (p149)
Frittata (p162)
Half-oat Pastry (p217)
Pear, Ricotta & Chicory Salad (p88)
Pizza (pp160–161)
Ricotta Gnocchi with Pesto & Courgettes (p138)

Yogurt
Almond Cookie Baked Peaches (p202)
Broccoli Apple Yogurt Slaw (p55)
Cannellini Bean & Apple Salad (p87)
Carrot Cake Overnight Oats (p18)

Chickpea 'Tuna' Salad (p69)
Courgette & Garlic Quesadilla (p78)
Falafel Smash (p56)
Half-oat Pastry (p217)
Lentil & Yogurt Pitta Dip (p106)
Microwave Blueberry Oat 'Muffin' (p26)
Miso-garlic-chilli Broccoli with Onion, Cumin & Beans (p121)
Roasted Beetroot, Cumin & Crispy Chickpeas (p65)
Roasted Cauliflower & Garlic Soup (p142)
Roasted Tomatoes & Carrots with Black Beans & Tahini (p80)
Smoothie Boxes (p38)
Spiced Sweet Potato Fries with Smoky Dip (p52)
Taco (p166)

MISC
Firm Tofu
Charred Lettuce with Baked Tofu & Peanut Dressing (p75)
Noodles, Crispy Crumbled Tofu, Bean Sprouts Stir Fry (p178)
Taco (p166)

Miso
Cauliflower, Leek & Sage Pie (p133)
Cauliflower Miso Mac & Cheese (p102)
Chickpea, Date & Ginger Tagine (p94)
'Chorizo' Dip (p47)
Curried Tomato-coconut Soup (p144)
Easy Freezer Chocolate Chip Cookies (p204)
French Toast with Miso-date Butter (p34)
Lentil & Fennel Ragu (p150)
Miso-garlic-chilli Broccoli (118)
Miso Mango Slaw (p55)
Paprika Bean Stew (p134)
Warm Roasted Cauliflower & Chickpea Salad (p84)
Roasted Cauliflower & Garlic Soup (p142)
Roasted Potato 3 Ways (p98)
Scrambled Chickpea Tacos with Peach Salsa (p31)
Spiced Sweet Potatoes with Raw Beetroot & Miso Dressing (p53)
Stir Fry (p174)
Sweet Miso Aubergine & Walnut Salad (p62)

MAKEOVERS WITH LEFTOVERS

Nut Butter
Banana Bread Porridge (p28)
Banana Chocolate Chip Blondies (p195)
Banoffee Peanut Bites (p40)
Charred Lettuce with Baked Tofu & Peanut Dressing (p75)
Chocolate Peanut Fudge Cake Bars (p185)
Cookie Dough Balls (p182)
Double Chocolate Cookies (p192)
Microwave Blueberry Oat 'Muffin' (p26)
Single-serve Chocolate Chip Cookie (p183)
Smoothie Boxes (p38)

Pesto
Lazy Potato Hash (p114)
Pesto, Spinach & Sweet Potato Galette (p101)
Pizza (p158)
Ricotta Gnocchi with Pesto & Courgettes (p138)
Roasted Carrots with Couscous & Pickled Onion (p67)

Tahini
Aubergine, Pomegranate & Chickpea Salad (p68)
Charred Lettuce with Baked Tofu & Peanut Dressing (p75)
Crispy Broccoli & Barley Bowl with Tahini Dressing (p113)
Lentil & Yogurt Pitta Dip (p106)
Pea Hummus (p46)
Roasted Squash with Brown Rice & Halloumi (p92)
Roasted Tomatoes & Carrots with Black Beans & Tahini (p80)
Smoothie Boxes (p38)
Spiced Sweet Potato Fries with Smoky Dip (p52)
Tahini Carrot Slaw (p54)

Thai Green Curry Paste
Stir Fry (p174)
Thai Green Curry Pea Soup (p143)

HERBS & AROMATICS
Basil
Basil & Rocket Pesto (p225)

Cannellini Beans with Balsamic Onions (p71)
Corn, Peach & Pearl Barley Salad (p81)
Courgette & Garlic Quesadilla (p78)
Halloumi & Mango Noodle Salad (p153)
Miso-garlic-chilli Broccoli with Pasta, Tomatoes & Spinach (p121)
One-pan Creamy Pasta with Asparagus, Lemon & Basil (p145)
Orange, Fennel, Olive & Pearl Barley Stew (p154)
Peas, Potato & Mozzarella Frittata (p164)
Pesto Crumb Courgettes with Weeknight Focaccia (p110)
Pizza (p161)
Potato, Halloumi & Courgette Bake (p105)
Ricotta Gnocchi with Pesto & Courgettes (p138)
Roasted Potato 3 Ways (p99)
Scrambled Egg, Pea, Onion & Basil Tacos (p173)
Stir Fry (p174)

Chilli
Aubergine, Pomegranate & Chickpea Salad (p68)
Zingy Carrot & Rice Noodle Salad (p155)
Charred Lettuce with Firm Tofu & Peanut Dressing (p75)
Chilli Roasted Potatoes with Granola & Lime-soy Dressing (p60)
Lime-chilli Corn & Crispy Onions (p63)
Miso-garlic-chilli Broccoli (p118)
Paprika Bean Stew (p134)
Pizza (p161)
Squash, Potato & Chilli Cakes (p76)
Stir Fry (p174)

Coriander (fresh)
Aubergine, Red Lentil & Coconut Curry (p95)
Blitzed Corn, Coriander & Spring Onion Pizza (p160)
Carrot Ribbon, Cinnamon & Halloumi Salad (p83)
Zingy Carrot & Rice Noodle Salad (p155)
Chickpea 'Tuna' Salad (p69)
Crispy Broccoli & Barley Bowl with Tahini Dressing (p113)
Curried Tomato-coconut Soup (p144)
Falafel Smash (p56)

Fattoush Dip (p51)
Halloumi & Mango Noodle Salad (p153)
Miso-garic-chilli Broccoli with Onion, Cumin & Beans (p121)
Miso Mango Slaw (p55)
Rice Bowl with Greens & Coriander-coconut Dressing (p117)
Roasted Potato 3 Ways (p99)
Roasted Squash with Brown Rice & Halloumi (p92)
Roasted Tomatoes & Carrots with Black Beans & Tahini (p80)
Shakshouka (p131)
Stir Fry (p174)
Taco (p166)
Tahini Carrot Slaw (p54)
Thai Green Curry Paste (p221)
Thai Green Curry Pea Soup (p143)

Mint
Aubergine, Pomegranate & Chickpea Salad (p68)
Fattoush Dip (p51)
Lentil & Yogurt Pitta Dip (p106)
Roasted Beetroot, Cumin & Crispy Chickpeas (p65)
Roasted Tomatoes & Carrots with Black Beans & Tahini (p80)
Stir Fry (p174)
Taco (p166)

Sage
Beetroot, Hazelnut & Sage Salad (p72)
Cauliflower, Leek & Sage Pie (p133)
Pasta with Mushrooms, Crispy Sage & Garlic Breadcrumbs (p141)
Pizza (p161)

Spring Onions
Aubergine, Red Lentil & Coconut Curry (p95)
Cannellini Bean & Apple Salad (p87)
Zingy Carrot & Rice Noodle Salad (p155)
Charred Lettuce with Baked Tofu & Peanut Dressing (p75)
Chilli Roasted Potatoes with Granola & Lime-soy Dressing (p60)
'Chorizo' Dip & Red Pepper Frittata (p165)
Crispy Tortilla Strips with Corn & Quinoa (p125)

Fattoush Dip (p51)

Ginger-pickled Mushrooms with Date Rice (p66)

Halloumi & Mango Noodle Salad (p153)

Miso Mango Slaw (p55)

Pizza (pxxx)

Quinoa, Pea & Broccoli Stir Fry (p176)

Rice Bowl with Greens & Coriander-coconut Dressing (p117)

Roasted Potato 3 Ways (p99)

Squash, Potato & Chilli Cakes (p76)

Taco (p166)

Thai Green Curry Pea Soup (p143)

Thyme

Beetroot Flatbread (p59)

Cauliflower, Sweet Potato & Thyme Frittata (p164)

Creamy Cavolo Nero, Leek & Pea Pasta (p147)

Pear, Ricotta & Chicory Salad (p88)

Pizza (p161)

Roasted Cauliflower & Garlic Soup (p142)

Spanakopita Quesadillas (p78)

Squash, Cauliflower & Roasted Garlic Gratin (p109)

GRAINS, BEANS & OTHER STARCH

Black Beans

Miso-garlic-chilli Broccoli with Onion, Cumin & Beans (p121)

Roasted Tomatoes & Carrots with Black Beans & Tahini (p80)

Bread, stale

Caramelized Apple & Pecan Bread Pudding (p197)

Crispy Broccoli Tacos with 'Chorizo' Dip (p170)

French Toast with Miso-date Butter (p34)

Pasta with Mushrooms, Crispy Sage & Garlic Breadcrumbs (p141)

Spinach & Feta Balls with Spaghetti (p122)

Squash, Cauliflower & Roasted Garlic Gratin (p109)

Brown Rice, cooked

Chickpea, Date & Ginger Tagine (p94)

Frittata (p162)

Ginger-pickled Mushrooms with Date Rice (p66)

Miso-garlic-chilli Broccoli with Soy Sauce, Ginger & Rice (p120)

Rice Bowl with Greens & Coriander-coconut Dressing (p117)

Roasted Squash with Brown Rice & Halloumi (p92)

Stir Fry (p174)

Taco (p166)

Canellini Beans

Beetroot, Hazelnut & Sage Salad (p73)

Cannellini Bean & Apple Salad (p87)

Cannellini Beans with Balsamic Onions (p71)

Cauliflower, Leek & Sage Pie (p133)

Frittata (p162)

Lazy Potato Hash (p114)

Miso-chilli-garlic Broccoli with Onion, Cumin & Beans (p121)

Roasted Cauliflower & Garlic Soup (p142)

Roasted Chickpeas (p44)

Roasted Potato 3 Ways (p99)

Chickpeas

Aubergine, Pomegranate & Chickpea Salad (p68)

Chickpea, Date & Ginger Tagine (p94)

Chickpea Stew 3 Ways (p129)

Chickpea 'Tuna' Salad (p69)

Falafel Smash (p56)

Frittata (p162)

Oaty Snack Cake (p191)

Roasted Beetroot, Cumin & Crispy Chickpeas (p65)

Roasted Cauliflower & Chickpea Salad (p84)

Roasted Chickpeas (p44)

Scrambled Chickpea Tacos with Peach Salsa (p31)

Flatbread, Tortilla, Pitta Bread

Chickpea, Date & Ginger Tagine (p94)

Chickpea 'Tuna' Salad (p69)

Courgette & Garlic Quesadilla (p78)

Falafel Smash (p56)

Fattoush Dip (p51)

Lentil & Yogurt Pitta Dip (p106)

Scrambled Chickpea Tacos with Peach Salsa (p31)

Taco (p166)

Tortilla or Pitta Chips 3 Ways (p42)

Kidney Beans

'Chorizo' Dip (p47)

Fattoush Dip (p51)

Miso-chilli-garlic Broccoli with Onion, Cumin & Beans (p121)

Paprika Bean Stew (p134)

Pastry, Half-oat or Olive Oil

Any-fruit Galette (p188)

Cauliflower, Leek & Sage Pie (p133)

Pesto, Spinach & Sweet Potato Galette (p101)

Pearl Barley

Corn, Peach & Pearl Barley Salad (p81)

Crispy Broccoli & Barley Bowl (p113)

Orange, Fennel, Olive & Pearl Barley Stew (p154)

Stir Fry (p174)

Wholemeal Pasta (cooked)

Cauliflower Miso Mac & Cheese (p102)

Creamy Cavolo Nero, Leek & Pea Pasta (p147)

Easy Summer Pasta (p149)

Frittata (p162)

Lentil & Fennel Ragu (p150)

Minestrone (p130)

Miso-garlic-chilli Broccoli with Pasta, Tomato & Spinach (p121)

One-pan Creamy Pasta with Asparagus, Lemon & Basil (p145)

Orzo with Squash, Chilli, Lemon & Peas (p126)

Pasta with Mushrooms, Crispy Sage & Garlic Breadcrumbs (p141)

Spinach & Feta Balls with Spaghetti (p122)

MENU PLANS

For 2 people

Here is an example of a menu plan and shopping list based on recipes from this book. It shows how you can prepare ingredients at the weekend to use throughout the week. It also shows how to double up on ingredients when you cook them during the week so that you can use them in other meals (which is especially useful when it comes to prepping lunch boxes). If you have a well-stocked store cupboard, it shouldn't be too much hassle to buy the fresh ingredients needed for a weekly shop and use the same ingredient a few times without getting bored!

SHOPPING LIST

FRESH INGREDIENTS

large bag of carrots
1 head of celery
pot of natural yogurt
2 oranges
bag of lemons
small bag of pea shoots
10 dessert apples
2 large bunches fresh
    coriander
6 small sweet potatoes
200g block of feta
small bag of mixed salad
    leaves
2 heads of broccoli
8 eggs

small bag of frozen petits
    pois or peas
milk
unsalted butter
    (if making the miso-date
    butter for the French toast)
chilli (if not using chilli flakes)
bunch of spring onions
200g cherry tomatoes
small bunch of mint
1 pepper
Bunch of cavolo nero
small bunch of basil
small Parmesan wedge

STORECUPBOARD INGREDIENTS

SPICES
Ground cinnamon, ginger, cumin, coriander and turmeric, smoked paprika, chilli flakes, green cardamom, fennel seeds, mixed dried herbs, salt

GRAINS/LEGUMES/BEANS/STARCH
Dried chickpeas (or 3 x 400g cans chickpeas), dried Puy or green lentils, brown rice, strong wholemeal flour, plain white flour, oats, pasta (orzo or another small pasta shape)

AROMATICS
Red onions, garlic, ginger

NUTS & NUT BUTTERS
Tahini, nut butter, creamed coconut (or coconut milk), sesame seeds, desiccated coconut

'BAKING' INGREDIENTS
Fast-action dried yeast, raisins, dates, sugar, honey

OTHER
Soy sauce, Worcestershire sauce (optional), vegetable stock (cubes), apple cider vinegar, balsamic vinegar, 1 x 400g can chopped tomatoes

Weekend

Roast 6 small sweet peeled and cubed potatoes in 2 tablespoons olive oil and a pinch of salt, in an oven preheated to 180°C fan, 200°C, Gas Mark 6 for 30–40 minutes. Flip halfway through.

Soak 300g dried chickpeas, then drain and cook (see cooking table on page 11) – you need 720g chickpeas. Or buy 3 cans of chickpeas (drained weight of each can should be 240g).

Cook green or Puy lentils – use 375g dried lentils (you should get 900g cooked lentils). See cooking table on page 11.

Make a double batch of Quick Pickled Red Onion (see page 223)

Mix up a batch of wholemeal pitta or flatbread dough (see page 215) and bake. Store at room temperature in an airtight container or freeze to defrost in the toaster as needed. Alternatively, buy 6 wholemeal pitta breads.

Prep a double batch of Carrot Cake Overnight Oats (see page 18).

Prep lunch for tomorrow.

Monday

BREAKFAST Carrot Cake Overnight Oats (see page 18).
LUNCH 2 baked pittas (see page 215) + 1 recipe for Chickpea 'Tuna' Salad (see page 69).
DINNER Make Paprika Bean Stew (see page 134). Replace the beans with the pre-cooked chickpeas + 2 pitta breads. Prep lunch for tomorrow. Make extra Tahini Dressing (see page 226) so you have enough for lunch and dinner.

Tuesday

BREAKFAST Carrot Cake Overnight Oats (see page 18).
LUNCH 300g cooked lentils + 2 carrots, peeled into ribbons + 1 recipe for Tahini Dressing (see page 226) + 1 tablespoon sesame seeds + handful of chopped coriander + 1 diced apple.
DINNER Roasted Squash with Brown Rice, Halloumi & Tahini Dressing (see page 92). Replace the squash with the roasted sweet potato and use raisins instead of pomegranate. Use pea shoots and mixed salad leaves instead of spinach and use feta instead of halloumi. Bake Carrot Breakfast Bread (see page 23). Prep lunch for tomorrow.

Wednesday

BREAKFAST Carrot Breakfast Bread (see page 23) with nut butter + an apple each.
LUNCH 2 baked pitta breads (see page 215) + recipe for Falafel Smash (see page 56).
DINNER Rice bowl with Greens & Coriander-coconut Dressing (see page 117). Cook extra broccoli and peas and make extra dressing for lunch tomorrow. Prep lunch for tomorrow.

Thursday

BREAKFAST Carrot Breakfast Bread (see page 23) with nut butter + an apple each.
LUNCH 300g cooked lentils + 1 recipe for Coriander-coconut Dressing (see page 117) + some Quick Pickled Red Onion (see page 223) + handful of mixed salad leaves + the extra cooked peas and broccoli from dinner.
DINNER Orzo with Squash, Chilli, Lemon & Peas (see page 126). Replace the squash with roasted sweet potato.

Friday

BREAKFAST Carrot Breakfast Bread (see page 23) with nut butter + an apple each.
LUNCH 300g cooked lentils + 50g crumbled feta + handful of pea shoots + 2 small roasted, cubed sweet potatoes + 1 recipe for Tahini Dressing (see page 226) + handful of raisins.
DINNER Frittata template (see page 162) – use up leftover ingredients.

Saturday

BREAKFAST Use the remaining Carrot Breakfast Bread to make French toast with Miso-date Butter (see page 34).
LUNCH Roasted Tomatoes & Carrots with Black Beans & Tahini (see page 80). Use chickpeas instead of black beans.
DINNER Lentil & Fennel Ragu (see page 150). Use celery instead of fennel and omit the walnuts. Eat with the rest of the dried pasta (the orzo or small pasta shapes) instead of taglietelle.

INDEX

ACKNOWLEDGEMENTS

READERS! Over the years of following my food journey along on my blog and Instagram, you have been my biggest drive and source of creative ideas. It's an honour to have you reading and making my recipes and it makes me so happy to have your encouragement.

MUM, DAD, JASPER As per usual, thank you for providing me with endless inspiration, support and love. It's cliché to say but I know I wouldn't have been able to make this cookbook without you all there.

ROBERT I think you really are my number one fan and I honestly couldn't be more glad. You have always egged me on and kept me going throughout my whole career.

ANDY I couldn't have asked for a kinder, more supportive human being to know. Thank you for not getting sick of me forcing food upon you and thanks for all the help with the washing up!

MARTINE (AND MIMI) without you ladies to guide me through this, there wouldn't have been a book. Thank you for all the hard work you put in to helping me bring my initial ideas to a fully formed concept.

ALISON, ELLA, JULIETTE Your belief in my vision for the book made this whole process so lovely! I'm so pleased with how it all came together and, with your help, became an actual real life book.

CAS, SAM, HAMISH, ALEX, ANNA, JAKE, ISAAC You all know that in some way you inspired some of the recipes in this book! Especially you, Anna, I'm already missing our chef/sous-chef days.

BEA, RHIANNON, SARAH You're always there for me. You always make me laugh and fill my life with happiness. Oh, and you're always willing to be force-fed whatever food I've been testing!

MAX, ELLIE AND PORTIA You ladies kept me motivated to keep on cooking and photographing for a whole month, even on days when I was seriously lacking motivation. You were all awesome and I can't thank you enough for all the help!

RECIPE TESTERS My lovely, lovely recipe testers! I'm so pleased you were able to get involved with the book-writing process and give me honest recipe feedback. Thanks for your generosity in helping this gal out! Shout out to Clare Robinson, Sarah Duignan, Ela , Shirl, Myrsini, Maggie Kolasky, Susan Barrie, Maggie McKune, Christine Monaghan, Jessica Chan, Kelsey Blodgett, Shoshana Snider, Jasmine Delves, Melissa Golubski, Alexandra Inchenko, Sarah Lundqvist, Katja Haudenhuyse, Alyssa Vratsanos, Lisa Maxwell, Maureen Bilyeu, Winnie Reeves, Kate Loannou, Lauren O'Sullivan, Lizzie Henderson, Indira Shinn Rees, Rebecca Webber, Zara Britton-Purhonen, Samira Zippel, Sian Poulton, Caroline Hunt, Emilia Luis, Daisy Nutting, Sarah Cutter, Injy Rawlings, Jennifer Buggica, Martino Mandelli, Dana Gerard, Danielle Deskins, Katie Wesolek, Kelsey Tenney, Isa Ouwehand, Rachel Chen, Louise Hadley, Lucia Hua, Jaqui Tuthill, Sarah Nelson, Eva Donlon, Anne-Katherine Schirlitz, Elise Akin, Marie-Eve, Marie Nyberg, Ubavi Nesta, Brady Johnson, Tjitske Boersma, Lucie Costes, Katrin Erb, Laura Valli, Beth Kerr, Yvonne Barber, Emily Jelassi, Cori Moen, Aislinn Hyde, Linnea Sansqvist, Carina Mancione and Hanna Hoskins.

IZY HOSSACK is a 21-year-old blogger and Instagram sensation, and her hit blog izyhossack.com is the go-to place for delicious sweet and savoury recipes on both sides of the Atlantic. She has an impressive fan base, with more than 220,000 followers on Instagram.

Much of Izy's food is inspired by her Italian-American heritage. Many of her recipes are gluten free and/or vegan. Izy collaborates with many different publications and brands including JamieOliver.com, IKEA, Cuisinart UK, Green & Black's, Romeo Gelato, theKitchn.com, Food52.com, Miss Vogue and SORTED to name a few. Izy has appeared on Channel 4's 'Daily Brunch' and has made videos for Waitrose TV, Endemol Shine's new channel Wild Dish and for Tesco Real Food. *The Times Magazine* recently named Izy as one of the world's most followed foodies and she has been featured in British *Vogue*.

Her first cookbook *Top With Cinnamon* was published by Hardie Grant in the UK and Rizzoli in the US in Autumn 2014, and reissued in paperback in Spring 2016 as *Everyday Delicious*. As well as being a food writer, Izy is a photographer and food stylist, and styled and photographed all the food for her books herself. Izy is studying Food Science and Nutrition at Leeds University.